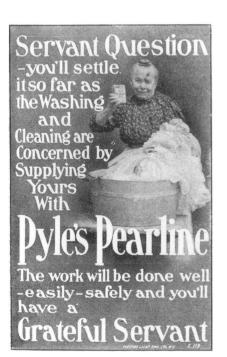
About Big Trees—

INSTEAD of planting the usual nursery stock you can save 20 to 50 years by planting full grown trees and shrubs with our patented tree moving equipment, which transplants shade trees up to 2 feet in diameter and 6 feet around, and evergreens up to 50 feet high, with but few laborers and a team or tractor. We will deliver all this equipment to your estate together with a skilled man to operate it at $50 per day for a minimum of 15 days, in which time a great many large trees can be transplanted.

If you have no large trees on your estate that you wish transplanted, our foreman can locate for you some suitable trees on farm properties in the vicinity or on other estates where they must be transplanted to permit the remaining trees to spread out.

We keep 30 of these machines with foremen busy on many estates that have used them for several months each year for the last 5 to 15 years.

If you have used this service we urge you to place your order now, because during the Spring rush we have heretofore always had to postpone some jobs till Fall. If you have never used this service we urge you to give it a 15-day trial; and you will be amazed at the results that can be obtained with a few laborers and use of this equipment with foreman.

If the trees on your estate are growing too closely together and are beginning to crowd, they should be transplanted to more suitable locations, thereby saving the trees moved and also spacing the remaining trees so that all your trees will then continue to develop into handsome specimens.

We can deliver to you by motor truck or ship you by freight large specimen trees of oaks, elms, lindens and maples 20 to 40 feet high, and Douglas blue spruce and white and Ausman pine 10 to 20 feet high. These trees are fully guaranteed.

Your gardener or architect is acquainted with our service.

You are urged to visit any of our nurseries which have a large selection and the finest collection of large trees and old boxwood in America.

We would take pleasure in mailing you our literature and pricelist, together with a booklet of letters from many of America's best-known estate owners and architects.

LEWIS AND VALENTINE COMPANY
Largest Organization for Planting Trees and Shrubs
47 West 34th Street, New York City

Long Island: Roslyn, Valley Stream   *Westchester:* Rye (on Post Road)   *Philadelphia:* Ardmore   *Florida:* Palm Beach

THE AMERICAN COUNTRY HOUSE

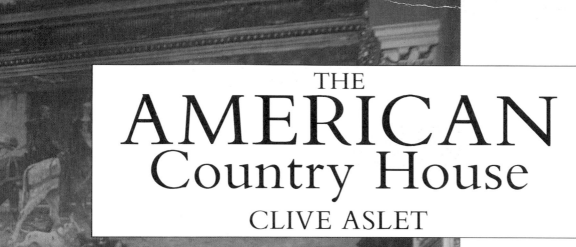

THE
AMERICAN
Country House
CLIVE ASLET

Yale University Press
New Haven & London
1990

To Emily and Sophie

Designed by Faith Brabenec Hart
Set in Linotron Bembo by Best-set Typesetter Ltd., Hong Kong
Printed in Yugoslavia by ČGP Delo by arrangement with Papirografika

Library of Congress Catalog Card Number: 90-70279

ISBN 0-300-04757-6

(*half-title page*)
Carved term from the garden loggia at Castle Hill, Massachusetts.
The house stands near the sea and this is reflected
in the shell imagery of this figure.

(*frontispiece*)
Costume dinner at George Gould's Georgian Court, New Jersey.
Note the servant observing from the balcony.

PREFACE

THIS BOOK about American country houses from 1865 to 1940 grew out of one on the same theme in Britain. While I was writing *The Last Country Houses*, published by Yale in 1982, I became convinced that there were rather more and sometimes rather better examples of my subject on the other side of the Atlantic. I was surprised to find that, when I first mentioned the idea to American friends, most of them held the belief that country houses in anything like the European sense did not exist in the United States. I felt sure that they were mistaken and I set out to discover what I could about the "Edwardian" country house there.

Turning the pages of the architectural magazines of the day quickly dispelled any hesitancy that this was a non-subject. Publications such as the *Architectural Record* in its early years seemed positively obsessed by the country house. This was even more true of general magazines like *Country Life in America*, *House and Garden*, and *Town and Country*. They presented the country house, not just as a piece of masonry set down in a wilderness, but as the focus for a host of sports and pursuits that formed part of a familiar, shared world for those lucky enough to afford it. In the 1920s a major preoccupation of *Vanity Fair*, for example, was the country house weekend. It was becoming obvious that the American country house was not only an architectural phenomenon. It existed to serve a way of life that was instantly recognizable to the large numbers of people who either enjoyed it, aspired to it, or were appalled by it. There was a currency of jokes and gossip as well as endless suggestions as to how its finer details could be improved.

So many country houses were built in the United States that it is impossible to regard them as isolated examples. They belonged to a self-conscious country house movement. They shared many characteristics, some of which were specifically American; indeed the common identity of these houses is so marked as to be, in some though certainly not all cases, frankly monotonous. For the scholar this tendency to repetition must be a cause of joy rather than dismay, for it helps resolve the central question: how is the American country house to be defined? Clearly, though the American country house has a kinship with the country house in England, it is not at all the same thing. I discuss the relationship in some detail in chapter 2. But it may be just as well to risk pre-empting myself and state, at the outset, that the primary sense in which the term "American country house" is used in this book is identical to one given by Barr Ferree in his *American Estates and Gardens* of 1904: "the great country house as it is now understood is a new type of dwelling, a sumptuous house, built at large expense, often palatial in its dimensions, furnished in the richest manner and placed on an estate, perhaps large enough to admit of independent farming operations, and in most cases with a garden which is an integral part of the architectural scheme.'' The reference here to the estate is important. The American country house stands on its own land, beyond the suburbs and other planned developments, out of sight of other houses, possessing at least the appearance of an independent, possibly self-sufficient, landed life, even though the money that supported it never came from the land. All this might be possible on as little as twenty acres.

The definition alone would be enough to suggest that the American country house has a personality quite distinct from that of country houses in other lands. It is the purpose of this book to analyze that individuality. In the first section I have taken three houses which in their different ways embody strongly American qualities. They illustrate an ambivalence on the part of the American people to any house of display, which haunted the discussion of the country house throughout this period. The second section both examines those features that the American country house borrowed from its English role model and highlights aspects that appear to me to be especially, sometimes uniquely, American. These themes are illustrated in general by that archetypal area of country house activity, the Main Line west of Philadelphia, and in particular by Winterthur, Henry Francis du Pont's home in Delaware. What, beyond the gratuitous display of wealth, were the motive forces behind the creation of so many costly houses? The answer lies largely in sport and the desire for a wholesome rural life, symbolized by the farm group. This is the subject of my third section. In the fourth section I discuss the country house response to two factors that are specific to the United States: the balmy climate of California and Florida and the tradition of the summer resort. In the final chapter I describe a house which not only epitomizes many of the traits adduced in the preceding pages, but in itself constitutes an original and moving work of art.

Had I begun my research now rather than then, fewer people would have told me that American country houses do not exist. The building of large houses has revived in recent years, and this has inspired the rediscovery of previous work. Within some architectural offices and university departments interest in the American country house has soared. A measure of the change is that the term itself is now widely used and accepted. This has not only given me reassurance that I am not artificially imposing European values on an American subject, but has made me hope that there is something significant to be gained by looking at the American country house through English eyes.

I have deliberately refrained from providing a gazetteer of country houses at the back of the book. The subject is simply too vast: a sample of only one or two hundred could never be adequate. A gazetteer that did anything like justice to the material would itself constitute a book, perhaps of several volumes. What I have sought to do is to visit as many centers of country house building as I could, looking wherever possible at original documents. This has been one of the great pleasures of my task, since it took me to many unfamiliar, often surpassingly beautiful, regions of the United States, leading me sometimes to explore places that rarely see visiting Englishmen. I cannot express enough gratitude to the many people whom I met on this quest: in memory I seem to have been received with courtesy, patience, friendship, and generosity at every turn. I must particularly thank the owners and staff of the houses that I visited, whether private or institutional, for opening their doors to me. Sometimes the doors were many. The idea of this book largely originated in Richard Cheek's bookroom in Belmont, Massachusetts, and I would like to thank Richard and his wife, Betsy, for their hospitality to me there, as well as for hours of discussion. Without the help of Susan Ward at Biltmore, James Ryan at Olana, Thomas Rosenbaum in the Rockefeller Archive, T. Mark Cole around Philadelphia, Craig Gilborn in the Adirondacks, John Cherol in Newport, Earle Shettleworth in Maine, Doris Littlefield at Vizcaya, and John Sweeney at Winterthur, my ideas about those places would have remained nugatory indeed. Enjoying their company greatly eased the burden of traveling, and in this I have been doubly fortunate in Mark Fiennes, who took the specially commissioned photographs. He not only proved one of the most rewarding and tolerant of traveling companions during our all too few days on the road together, but from his odyssey around what seemed like the whole of the United States he brought back some of the most stimulating interpretations of houses that one could hope to see. It was my further good fortune to work with the photographer Michael Boys around Philadelphia and at Nemours for articles in *Country Life*. And in this connection I must render the fullest of thanks to Jenny Greene, the editor of *Country Life*, for both her encouragement and her exemplary patience during the closing stages of the book.

Michael Adams shared with me his considerable knowledge of country house architecture and helped me delve through some of the obscurer periodicals, besides providing many insights into country houses in Ohio. Unfortunately I only got to know Alfred S. Branam, Jr., in the last days before the manuscript went to the printers, but he provided advice at a crucial stage. I would like to thank Michael Hall who read the proofs. Altogether I have stored up too many debts of gratitude to thank everyone by name. Those who cannot on any account be omitted include Mosette Broderick, Mary Cornyn, Jane Egan, Esmé Fink, David Gebhard, Thomas Gould, Robert McKay, Arthur A. Miller, Jr., John Franklin Miller, Christopher Monkhouse, George Moss, Roger Moss, James Pahlau, Ellen Rogers, Nancy Tinker, Margaret Tramontine, Carol Traynor, and the staffs of the Avery, Huntington, New York Public, and Yale University Libraries. Faith Hart, having consummately edited and designed *The Last Country Houses*, may well have been daunted to find that there seems to be no such word as "last" in this field. I am therefore all the more grateful to her for editing and designing this book with her customary meticulousness, sensitivity, and brio. My thanks, and more, go to my wife, Naomi, not only for understanding during inevitable absences abroad and at the word processor, but even more for accompanying me on some of the trips.

1. Library at Harbor Hill with the Mackay family at tea, about 1923, painted by Sir John Lavery. Private Collection

CONTENTS

TYPES

The one on my right was a colossal affair by any standard – it was a factual imitation of some Hotel de Ville in Normandy, with a tower on one side, spanking new under a thin beard of raw ivy, and a marble swimming pool, and more than forty acres of lawn and garden. It was Gatsby's mansion.

F. Scott Fitzgerald
The Great Gatsby

"Oh, *yes!*" she cried. "Oh, *yes!* that's it: a little gray house with sort of white around and a whole lot of swamp-maples just as brown and gold as an October picture in a gallery. Where can we find one?"

F. Scott Fitzgerald
The Beautiful and Damned

2. Entrance Hall at Harbor Hill, about 1903, painted by Sir John Lavery. Harbor Hill on Long Island was built for Clarence H. Mackay by McKim, Mead and White in 1899–1902. Private Collection

— 1 —

The Country House as Stately Home
BILTMORE

"ABOUT TEN MILES LONG and two and a half wide": if one were to overhear this remark from one of the half million or so tourists who annually visit George Washington Vanderbilt's Biltmore in North Carolina it would be no cause for surprise. Instead, however, it was made by Vanderbilt's architect, Richard Morris Hunt, then at the zenith of a career largely spent forming an architectural image for the American rich. Clearly Hunt was as thrilled as anyone by the Wagnerian scale of the place. "The château is beginning to hum," he wrote on another occasion. "The mountains are just the right size and scale for the château!"[1]

Everyone who went there was struck by the immensity of Biltmore, the achievement of getting it built, the novelty of such splendor in a land with little recent tradition of great houses. In the uncomplicated judgment of Asheville's local paper, the *Daily Citizen*, it was "no small shakes of a house.... Vive la Asheville!" Even Henry James, fastidiously shrinking from the impersonal character of the grand rooms, had to admit that he admired it "as mere masonry."[2]

For a point of comparison James's mind turned naturally to Europe, and with forgivable hyperbole he wrote to the English critic Edmund Gosse that this "extraordinary colossal" house could swallow up two or three of the Rothschild palaces in Britain. It was certainly not to his taste, and he remained resolutely unimpressed. But other visitors were inspired by the grandeur of the house, and to them the European analogy seemed very appropriate. The *Evening Telegraph* of New York must have shocked the republican instincts of some readers when it declared that Biltmore was set to become "the ancestral home of one line of the Vanderbilts."

Biltmore is the paradigm of one kind of American country house. Both the architecture and the way of life it was designed to shelter pay a debt to some aspects of European experience. This would have been no reason for apology on the part of Biltmore's creators, for by drawing freely on what they saw as being the finest examples of the Old World, synthesizing and updating them, they believed that they could achieve something new, *sui generis*, and essentially American.

Originally Vanderbilt did not envisage a house of this kind. His first thoughts seem to have been of a comparatively modest frame structure. When work began in 1889, he was still only in his middle twenties and a bachelor. Yet, by the time of his marriage to Edith Stuyvesant Dresser (Plate 14) in 1898, Biltmore was all but complete. No wonder, therefore, that his architect thought the scale of it all worthy of comment. What did the

3

3. George Washington Vanderbilt's Biltmore House, Asheville, North Carolina.

4. Construction workers at Biltmore, posed on a section of the railroad specially built to transport building materials to the house. In this remote location, building the house was a heroic undertaking.

place represent to Vanderbilt? What on earth possessed him to create it? In larger terms I hope this book will provide part of the answer by showing that the building of country houses was becoming a natural form of expression for those with the money and energy to afford it. But in such a personal activity as the building of a house it was inevitable that private considerations also came into play.

Rivalry among Vanderbilt brothers was probably one consideration. The Vanderbilts perfectly illustrate a phenomenon often observed in the Old World: the first generation of a family creates wealth, the second consolidates it, the third builds a country house. The Vanderbilts all had the building gene. Grandchildren of the "Commodore," railroad builder, and capitalist, several of George W. Vanderbilt's eight brothers and sisters (or their husbands) set themselves up in the country. Moreover, architecture had already played a special role in the Vanderbilt myth. It had helped to establish the family as a social force in New York. The Fifth Avenue house that Hunt had built for George's brother, William Kissam, and his powerful wife, Alva, was still the showiest dwelling in New York. It was, famously, the housewarming ball that finally vanquished Mrs. Astor's resolve to exclude the newcomers from society. The house symbolized Alva's social ambitions.

It was through building Biltmore that George W. Vanderbilt was able to express the obsessive determination to conquer Nature that was so characteristic of his family. For he had no interest in business and was in many ways unlike the other members of his clan. A Sargent portrait of him, surprisingly small and lacking the artist's usual flair, makes him seem a brooding, uncomfortable, melancholy figure – somewhat disdainful, thin-faced, full-lipped and with dark eyes sunk deep in their sockets. Religiously inclined, he was a gifted linguist, devoted to his mother, and – the youngest of the family – generally regarded as "too much and too long sheltered by female relatives." Some people thought him almost simple-minded when they first met him; certainly his sense of humor, as revealed in the Biltmore House Book of Nonsense, was juvenile even

4

5. The entrance façade of Biltmore. It was designed by Richard Morris Hunt and built between 1888 and 1895.

by the undemanding standards of his class and day. But he had little interest in chorus girls or racehorses. He was not easily parted from his money. He loved art; he loved the open air. Biltmore was his passion.

Hunt had done his best to fuel this passion. Having studied at the École des Beaux-Arts in Paris, he knew France well, and looked so much like a Frenchman that he was frequently mistaken for one – much to his fury. Not only did Hunt conduct his client on a visit to the chateaux of the Loire, but he took him to stay in one of their modern counterparts in England, a Rothschild country house. Once the fire caught, it proved unquenchable. Some of the fierce competitiveness of the Vanderbilts emerged in

George's attitude to building. When in Europe, he would pace out the grandest rooms of the palaces he visited and joyfully declare his own gallery to be a few feet longer or broader. He also sought to excel contemporary house builders in the United States, creating what Louis V. LeMoyne, author of *Country Residences in Europe and America* of 1908, would call "probably the largest and finest estate in America." The *Architectural Record* went further: it doubted whether a "nobler residential edifice" had ever been built on either side of the Atlantic.[3]

6. Detail of the central tower at Biltmore. The richness of the entrance front complements the formal setting which frames this side of the house; the rear elevation, overlooking open country, is relatively unadorned.

When Vanderbilt came to Asheville, over two thousand feet above sea level, it had already shown the first stirrings of becoming a reasonably successful health resort. The railroad had come in 1880; the first big hotel, the Battery Park, was built six years later. Doctors had recently found mountain air to be of benefit in the treatment of tuberculosis. This was Asheville's great attraction: its "ozoned atmosphere" would be celebrated in a local board of trade brochure of 1898 subtitled *A Million Invalids Couldn't Strain this Climate*. Perhaps it was the air that had first drawn Vanderbilt, not a strong

7. Detail of the staircase, derived from the Château de Blois.

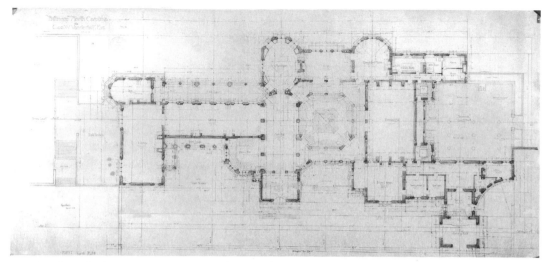

8. The plan of Biltmore, organized strictly according to Beaux-Arts principles. With a winter garden and "main hall" in the center, and a gallery along the spine, the circulation spaces are unusually generous.

man, to the region. He came with his mother and stayed at the Battery Park. Apart from the hotels, however, there was little other prosperity. Farming was particularly bad. It was conducted on a primitive scale, each farmer taking what he could from the land, including timber, and impoverishing it for himself and his successors.

In this remote region of North Carolina, tremendous obstacles had to be overcome in building the house. The brow of a mountain was sliced off like the top of an egg to form the terrace on which it stands. A reporter from the *Citizen* rode over the estate. "There burst upon us a scene of life and activity which was perfectly marvelous in this seemingly barren and deserted wilderness," he wrote in December 1889.

> Fifty teams were at work hauling away the earth, and men were industriously digging away the top soil from eight acres of land and loading it into the carts which carried it to a large dump on the hillside above. Here the rich ground that had been removed formed a mound two hundred feet long and from twenty to forty feet deep. Several acres of clay had been laid bare, which were as hard as a road from the constant passing and repassing of the teams. Trees were being cut down and the stumps were being taken out. All the clay will be removed to a depth of twenty feet.[4]

Freestone for the farm buildings and the foundations of the main house could be had from a quarry opened on the road to Hendersonville. A brickworks was also made, but the dressed limestone came to Asheville by rail from distant Indiana, a journey of six hundred miles. From there a private spur of track had to be specially laid so that it could be hauled to the site of the house (Plate 4). It was important to ensure a regular supply – not always forthcoming – since building delays were expensive.

The style of the house – French Renaissance – could almost have been chosen to flaunt Vanderbilt's victory over the mountains. It is closely similar to that which Hunt developed in the William K. Vanderbilt house in New York, and this hint of Fifth Avenue makes the work seem all the more urbanely confident. Great expanses of smooth ashlar, broken by little more than the moldings over the windows, emphasize the mighty scale of the edifice: three hundred and seventy-four feet long, excluding the stables. Pageantry comes in the silhouette. With its crestings and crockets, peaked roofs and pinnacles, turrets and chimneystacks, the roofline seems as brave and animated as the banner that beats from the tower (Plates 5 and 6).

For the details Hunt trawled the sourcebooks of François Premier chateaux; most conspicuously, the semi-octagonal staircase tower is a tribute to Blois (Plate 7). The planning, however, is virtually a textbook example of Beaux–Arts practice. It has a logic and a geometry and a beauty of its own – though this is better appreciated by studying the plan on paper than by visiting the building (Plate 8). One glance reveals the primary enfilade along the line of the gallery, and this is almost bisected by the secondary axis of the main hall. This is quite unlike the often haphazard, accretive planning of the French

9. The winter garden. The arcade gives a sense of openness that was characteristic of the American country house.

chateaux on which Biltmore is based, which often evolved piecemeal over a long period of time. Another difference is that one space opens into another largely without the interruption of doors; indeed the center of the whole building is a winter garden, confined only by an arcade (Plate 9). Except for the entrance vestibule, none of the rooms reached from the surrounding corridor and main hall had conventional doors to seal them off. The billiard room and breakfast room had doors of steel and plate glass, minimizing the visual division. Otherwise, heavy portière curtains would have been the sole protection against drafts. Perhaps in the age of central heating, drafts were considered extinct.

When the press described life at Biltmore, they mentioned coaching parties, hunting, fox chasing, quail shooting, and fishing. These were the conventional pursuits of the very rich, though Vanderbilt was equally happy in his library (Plate 10). Of themselves the pastimes do not explain why he felt that he needed such a large house. Unlike the chateaux of the Loire on which it was based, Biltmore was not intended to shelter a court. Nor were there house parties of power and influence, as might have been found in the great houses of Victorian England. The plan and the accommodation ("a vast succession of sleeping chambers and some twenty bathrooms")[5] suggest that the house was designed to receive them; but they were destined never to come. Though Vanderbilt later sometimes liked to entertain luminaries of the literary world – Edith Wharton and the novelist Winston Churchill as well as Henry James – the guestbooks show that, even after his marriage, he was for the most part visited only by family and a small circle of friends, none of them national figures. Vanderbilt, who built for the love of building, must have been conscious of excess capacity. There were so many rooms on the main

10–11. The library and the banquet hall at Biltmore. Perhaps because Vanderbilt was a bachelor when the house was designed, few of the rooms strike a feminine note. The frieze over the banquet hall fireplace is Karl Bitter's *The Return from the Chase*.

floor that at least one of the principal ones, the Music Room, remained unfurnished at his death.

For all Biltmore's size and splendor, it is not architecture alone that makes it such an outstanding example of the American country house. The house itself might have existed almost as comfortably at Newport, Rhode Island, where Hunt had already designed Marble House and The Breakers for Vanderbilt's brothers. What distinguishes it is the immense estate on which it stands, amounting eventually to a hundred and twenty-five thousand acres, and the full panoply of subsidiary buildings that go with it. These include church, village, lodges, and farm. Site as well as masonry make the Loire chateaux memorable – Blois dominates its town, Chenonceaux bestrides its river, Chambord stands amidst a noble park. In this respect Biltmore is their equal (Plate 3).

Vanderbilt had needed convincing about the architecture of the house. But from the time that he first began secretly buying land through his agent Charles McNamee (the husband of a cousin) it seems that the estate surrounding it formed part of a larger idea. He had a clear vision of what the estate should become: an enormous landscape park on the English model. To achieve this he employed the landscape architect Frederick Law Olmsted, then an old man, but active, with decades of experience behind him (Plate 12). In earlier days Olmsted had traveled widely, partly as a sailor, and his own naturalistic style, always seeking to draw out the particular character of the place, had been substantially inspired by the great landscape parks of England, which he viewed with rapture on his first visit in 1850. While Biltmore was rising he determined to make "a tour on wheels" of English nurseries and gardens to refresh his spirit and to order plants.

Nevertheless, Olmsted was forced to advise that not all the Biltmore estate was suitable to be turned into a park. The soil was poor, the trees were in bad condition from overcropping by small farmers, and the topography was inappropriate. "Such land in Europe would be made a forest; partly, if it belonged to a gentleman of large means, as a hunting preserve for game, mainly with a view to crops of timber." This, he emphasized, would be an appropriately "dignified" and aristocratic business for Vanderbilt to engage in: "My advice would be to make a small park into which to look from your house; make a small pleasure ground and garden, farm your river bottom chiefly to keep and fatten live stock with a view to manure; and make the rest a forest, improving the existing woods and planting the old fields."[6] Gardens, parkland, farming, and forest: Vanderbilt followed Olmsted's prescription to the letter, though the park and gardens could only be called "small" in relation to the estate as a whole. The gardens extend southward from the house and include the Italian Garden, Shrub Garden, four acre Walled Garden, and Spring Garden; the deer park occupies some two hundred and fifty acres to the west and south.

Whatever Olmsted's reservations, there were some ways in which Vanderbilt's ambition to create an English-style landscape was peculiarly well blessed. Few eighteenth-century gentlemen seeking to bring a little of the warmth of the Campagna to their rain-soaked English estates ever had Vanderbilt's opportunities of scale or natural landscape. The scope of the views along the broad valleys, over silver sheets of water, past noble oak trees in the fields, around hills whose contours have been softened by careful planting, exceeds that of any English park. A votary of the Picturesque would quicky have identified a likeness between the Blue Ridge Mountains that form the backdrop to these distant views and the romantic scenery of Claude Lorrain's paintings, the guiding spirit of so much landscape endeavor.

Like Humphry Repton, Olmsted sought to bring out the latent beauties of the estate by excising its least noble features and judiciously supplementing the rest. As a first step

12. Party surveying the estate. Vanderbilt is standing on the right, with Hunt to the left. In front of them, on the ground, is Frederick Law Olmsted, the landscape architect.

13. Vanderbilt's wife, Edith, driving a tractor. She was an enthusiastic supporter of agriculture in the state.

the drive to the house was moved from the ridge, along which it had run, to the bottom of the valley, where it passed through a wild but always fairly enclosed landscape, with no great views. Forest to either side of the drive was heavily thinned to a depth of a hundred feet, leaving only the best trees – be they pines, oaks, or wild plums; the valley bottoms were similarly cleared of all but the finest. Whether Olmsted knew it or not, his letters sound very like Repton's. The reasons that he gave for creating four islets near the north bank of a lake reveal something of his philosophy. First he argued, as Repton might well have done, that what the mind imagines is just as important as what actually exists. The effect of the islands "would be to enlarge the apparent extent of the water, because, in looking toward them from the opposite shore, the imagination would assume a larger recession of the main shore behind them than would actually exist, and there would at least be more effect of intricacy and mystery." The islands would have the further merit of helping to disguise a regrettably "rigid and unpicturesque" shoreline, thereby saving the money needed to alter it. What is more, they would encourage wildlife: "Swans, herons and all wild fowl disposed to nest on the south, would be disturbed by carriages passing. It is customary, where swans are kept in water with no islands, to make wooden platforms or rafts for them to breed upon which are not pretty objects."[7] This was the wisdom of long experience.

The moment of drama came when the visitor, having driven for miles through this relatively intimate landscape, suddenly "passed with an abrupt transition into the enclosure of the trim, level, open, airy, spacious, thoroughly artificial Court, and the Residence, with its orderly dependencies, breaks suddenly and fully upon him."[8] Beyond this, opened out the stupendous distant view of the mountains which was the justification for Vanderbilt's difficult mountaintop site.

For Olmsted, a man in his late sixties, the labor of constructing a park on such a scale, in such poor, uncultivated surroundings, was formidable. For both Hunt and Olmsted the accommodation was spartan, and to Olmsted in particular the fatiguing journey and change in climate were punishing. He found the servants "good, big, blundering, forgetful, thoughtless children." When he caught Hunt's grippe in 1890, a local doctor treated him with a combination of whiskey, quinine, and sleeping drugs until his ears roared. Exhausting days would be spent surveying and planning on horseback. At least

12

14. Edith Vanderbilt, about 1900, by Giovanni Boldini. Biltmore House, Asheville

the food would improve when Vanderbilt arrived in his private railroad car, complete with black cook. But obstacles remained legion, and it is understandable that the surviving correspondence of the clerk of works, Richard Sharp Smith, should sometimes lapse into bitterness. He waged a running battle with McNamee to have his letters sent out and delivered promptly, and had difficulty obtaining a horse.

There was some determination that the agricultural estate should prove capable of supporting the house. This was indeed the theory behind the English country house, though it had by now become outdated. People in England liked the pleasures and associations of landed life, but by the 1890s they did not expect it to pay. Most American country house builders would have shared exactly this attitude. Vanderbilt was more ambitious. His main crop was timber, and to get the most from it he virtually called into existence a science that had hitherto been little developed in the United States, commercial forestry.

On Olmsted's recommendation he was fortunate enough to hit upon the gifted young Gifford Pinchot to initiate a forest plan. Pinchot came from a rich Pennsylvania family for whom Hunt had designed a house called Grey Towers. Later, after Pinchot had headed the Division of Forestry in the Department of Agriculture, Theodore Roosevelt would hold that "among the many, many public officials who under my administration rendered literally invaluable service to the people of the United States, he, on the whole, stood first." When Pinchot came to Biltmore in 1892, however, he had had little other experience, though he had studied at the forestry school at Nancy, France. "Here was my chance," he wrote in his autobiography. "Biltmore could be made to prove what America did not yet understand, that trees could be cut and the forest preserved at one and the same time. I was eager, confident, and happy as a clam at high tide."[9] He practiced two systems. One was to cut selectively in those areas of the forest that were visually sensitive; a major innovation was to teach the loggers how to fell and remove timber without damaging other trees. Elsewhere larger areas were clear-felled and replanted year by year. By the end of the first year he was able to show a small profit. But even Biltmore – and the estate now included the whole of Pisgah Mountain – did not allow him enough scope for his talents. He left, and his place was taken by an autocratic Prussian with waxed moustaches named Schenck.

"It is Vanderbilt the farmer, not Vanderbilt of the Chateau, who has proven to be the great benefactor of Western North Carolina," wrote the *Asheville News and Hotel Reporter* in 1897. "He has shown the Carolinans the productive capacities of their virgin soil ... by the scientific drainage, the improved machinery, the importation of fine stock, the judicious and lavish use of fertilizers, and the most up-to-date and scientific methods of farming."[10] Edith Vanderbilt was as enthusiastic in the cause of agricultural reform as her husband, championing the setting up of a state agricultural fair (Plate 13). Such promotion of improved agriculture would have reinforced W.J. Ghent's view, expressed in *Our Benevolent Feudalism* that American millionaires were developing into a beneficent baronial class. Feudal ideals – reflected in the monograms and Vanderbilt acorns that encrust the architecture – touched the estate in other ways, too. Every Christmas the employees and their families – two thousand souls – would assemble at Biltmore where Edith personally gave each one a present. She kept a ledger to ensure that gifts were not repeated. For a tenant, slippers in 1909 might be followed by socks in 1910, gloves in 1911, pipe in 1912, and easel in 1913. Through the church, paid for by Vanderbilt, she established classes in weaving, carving, needlecraft, and domestic science. In 1901 the Vanderbilts started Biltmore Industries, making furniture based on models at the big house, to help provide local employment.

14

15. The new village of Biltmore, at the gates of the park. The old settlement called Best was swept away and rebuilt at Vanderbilt's expense, including the church.

The ramshackle settlement at the main gate, called Best, was transformed into the model village of Biltmore (Plate 15). Vanderbilt built the houses, which were apparently based on examples in Cheshire (perhaps he was thinking of the princely new cottages, lodges, and farmhouses on the Duke of Westminster's Eaton Estate); he also imposed strict rules, by which dogs, hen roosts, and live in servants were forbidden.

This may not have been unreasonable, but it was resented. Despite all that Vanderbilt had done to help the local community, this earnest, shy, aloof man was not able to make himself popular. Much of his work was misunderstood. Local people could not fathom why land that had been arduously won from forest and from Indians was being put back to forest again. It was a region of fierce individualists. The mountain folk, living in one-room cabins, were poor, but independent and highly sensitive to their rights. Schenck, known by his students as "the man that looks like the Kaiser," did not help matters; his authoritarian manner might have been calculated to inspire hostility. The nadir in Vanderbilt's relations with the locality came in 1912 when arsonists systematically put torch to the forests, destroying timber worth hundreds of thousands of dollars. Though it was widely believed, in the words of an Irish workman on his Mount Desert estate, that "Vanderbilt don't feel the cost of a thousand dollars more'n you or I would a penny,"[11] these were losses that he could ill afford.

It is not surprising that Vanderbilt had anxieties over Biltmore, given the difficulties of building and running it. As early as 1897 the *New York Times* repeated the story that he had gone off to hunt tigers in India to escape the problems of the place. Supposedly, the last straw had come when Vanderbilt asked for a drink of water, only to be told that the pump had stopped.

The sunken foundation, the cracked marbles, the idle sawmill, the unproductive dairy farm, the expensive forestry school, the unprofitable truck farm, and all the failures that had been pointed out came rushing in on him. He could have stood all these, but he could not stand this climax. He had spent $10,000,000 on Biltmore, and he could not get a drink of water.[12]

15

16. The 1905 carriage parade in Biltmore village. Edith Vanderbilt can be seen seated with her daughter Cornelia.

All this was denied by a Vanderbilt relative whose comment was quoted briefly at the end of the piece; but no one who read the article was likely to believe in smoke without fire.

However much truth there was in the story, things only got worse. It was not that Biltmore did not work. It did, but expensively. Legend has it that Vanderbilt had poured untold sums into the estate; his *New York Times* obituary put the figure at $87 million. That was certainly an exaggeration. On his father's death in 1885 he had inherited a far smaller sum than his brothers: only $10 million, and half of that in trust. Tales of the George Washington Vanderbilts' closeness with money were legion. Whistler could not believe that Edith noticed the price of one restaurant over another. ("It costs a little more, but what of that?")[13] Traveling in Germany the couple stayed in such spartan accommodation that the *Washington Post*, eager to maintain the dignity of American millionaires abroad, was moved to comment. "Their Economy Shocking," ran the subheading of the article. "Apartments Reached by Passing Through the Kitchen of the Owner of the Little Berlin Establishment."[14] Parsimony may or may not have been at the bottom of it, but the fact was that they had less money than was expected of them. Hamilton Twombly berated Frederick Olmsted for letting Vanderbilt spend more on landscaping than he could afford. The arboretum that Vanderbilt had long been planning was abandoned.

As a quasi-feudal structure the Biltmore estate survived until Vanderbilt's early death in 1914; by 1920, however, Edith began to sell land. One of the first things to go was the village (though she retained the church and the hospital): it fetched $1 million, suggesting that Vanderbilt's investment may not have been as rash as it had appeared to his friends. Other land went to the making of a residential park; the Southern Railroad Company bought a third swathe for a new station. Biltmore Industries had already been sold in 1917. After Edith's marriage to Senator Peter G. Gerry in 1925 Washington became the center of her interests. She became well known as a political hostess and she had less and less reason to visit Biltmore. By the time a disgruntled butler made his report on the state of the house, which he ran with only three housemaids, in 1936, the place had begun to fall into decay. "It is only fair to myself to state here," he wrote, dismayed that six years of hard work had not done more, "that I found the draperies, rugs and furniture in a terribly run down and deplorable condition." That year Biltmore House opened to the public for the first time; it was the saving of it.

What are we to make of Biltmore, this ne plus ultra of the American country house? Contemporary opinion was divided. The cheeky reporter from the *Sun* said that it looked like a hotel, and in a way it did, for that is how many great houses of this date functioned. Biltmore was designed to receive frequent invasions of house guests, even if the parties rarely materialized. Some thoughtful visitors could not be happy with Biltmore's all too obvious display of concentrated wealth, making so vast a contrast with the lives of the mountain people who were Vanderbilt's neighbors. On the other hand some guests were simply dazzled by the splendor of it all: the architecture, the works of art, the furniture, the tapestries, the upholstery, the craftsmanship, the gardens, the landscape. Whatever one may sometimes think of its appropriateness, Biltmore achieves a universal standard of excellence. "Not even all that has been said prepared me for this place, its beauty, its splendor, its amazing possessions!" gushed one young lady guest. "I go and sit in the library for hours, just making myself aware of it all; and the proportions and scale, combined with the details, fills one with the kind of peace which comes from artistic perfection, and which is like touching a fountain of perfection."[15]

For the present age perhaps the most important thing is that it has survived; in this, Biltmore is unlike a large number of its contemporaries, which have been demolished. To the generation told that a house was a Machine for Living In it must have seemed a domestic horror, virtually impossible to heat and keep clean. For the visiting public, however, this has only added to the delight. If, as the writer in the *Evening Telegraph* believed, it was intended as an ancestral home, it can be called a partial success. The house is still in the hands of the family who built it. It has literally repaid its investment, being more of a business success as a tourist attraction than Vanderbilt's own forestry ever was. In a changed world it occupies a happier position than some of the stately homes in Europe on which it was based. Relatively few of these are still lived in fully, if at all, and many have passed out of family ownership or been demolished. Biltmore is no longer lived in, but it is owned by Vanderbilt's grandson and beautifully maintained.

Ancestral home, possibly. But that was not the meaning of the word Henry James had in mind when he told Edith Wharton that, "for a tasteful Southern *home*, it merely makes me weep!" James was joined in his censure by some of the very men who created it, including Pinchot and Olmsted's son Frederick Law, Jr., known as Rick. However, even the doubters were forced to recognize, in Rick Olmsted's words, "the beginning of an era of great American country places and country houses."[16]

— 2 —

"The registers of our very latest days"
WITHDRAWAL FROM THE CITY

BILTMORE is "the most conspicuous example" of a type of house that was becoming
increasingly common – a type that "approximates in many respects to the family seat of
an English country gentleman, and is the product not merely of wealth, but of leisure."
That comment was made by Harry Desmond and Herbert Croly in a book of 1903
significantly entitled *Stately Homes in America*. Literature of this kind – and it was
plentiful – sought to identify a tradition of domestic architecture in the United States
equivalent to that of the country house in Europe, in other words the American country
house. At the turn of the century this seemed a vivid and fresh idea, quite specific and of
recent origin. Again to quote Croly, editor of the *Architectural Record* and future editor of
the *New Republic*, this time writing under the pseudonym of William Herbert in 1907:
"With a few exceptions 'great American estates' are the creation of the past twelve years.
The majority of them are probably not more than five or six years old."[1] Barr Ferree,
editor of *Scientific American Building Monthly*, shared his opinion. In 1904 he wrote that
the "very brief space of ten years has been sufficient to develop an entirely new type
of American country house, the house to which the words 'stately' and 'sumptuous'
may be indifferently applied, with, at times, a quite realizing sense of their utter
inadequacy."[2]

Large and costly dwellings had been known before in the United States. Before the
Civil War the greatest concentration was seen by those travelers who risked taking a
steamboat down the Mississippi; they often expressed admiration for the white-pillared
mansions that rose behind alleys of live oaks and azalias. Some of these plantation houses
were built by men of leisure, open to foreign ideas and rich enough to afford the best
foreign building materials and furniture. But, as the symmetrically disposed slave cabins
proclaimed, such houses were still conceived to be the working center of the estate. This
put them into an entirely different category from the American country houses that
developed in their fullest form after 1885. Though the latter were, by definition,
surrounded by their own land, this merely served to put a further barrier between them
and the true sources of their owners' wealth. Biltmore showed this to perfection.
Though New York was the ultimate source of the fortune that financed it, it was, as
Desmond and Croly observed,

> not situated near New York, so that its owner can go quickly to and fro; it is not
> designed merely as the occasional residence of a man who only sojourns from
> Saturday to Monday in his own house, and who is satisfied with a big veranda and a

19

17. Aerial view of Nemours, Delaware. Carrère and Hastings's mansion of 1909 stands behind the formal gardens completed to
the designs of Alfred Victor du Pont and Gabriel Massena in the 1930s.

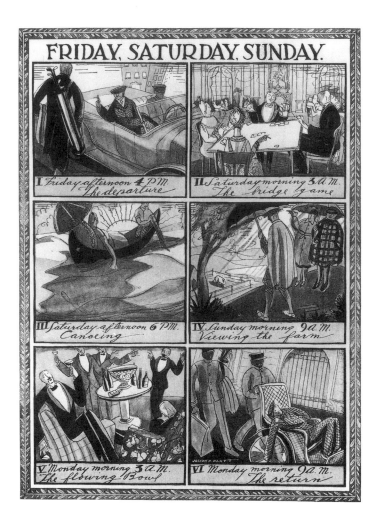

18. Many country houses were within easy striking distance of large cities and could be visited for weekends. The practice caused frequent comment in society papers such as *Vanity Fair*. This illustration appeared in July 1923.

view. It has been laid out as the country home of a cultivated gentleman who has the use of his own time, who wants to build up an all-round country place, and who has all the time and money he needs in which to do it.[3]

Biltmore was unusual in its isolation. Most owners wanted either to be within striking distance of a major city or to establish themselves in an area already known for its country houses, where there would be no shortage of congenial company. But that they were striving to create "an all-round country place" is indicated, not just in the size of their houses, but in the variety of other structures that went with them. In some cases the complete kit included lodges, stables, garages, gazebos, terraces and other garden architecture (Plate 17), glass houses (Plates 19 and 20), sports buildings, workers' cottages, model farm, and church. These, as one critic commented of Biltmore, were the "dependencies and surroundings that are necessary to make a true chateau."[4] Sometimes, as we have seen, these buildings indicated that the country house builder was willing to shoulder the traditional burden of the landowner, in assuming a fatherly responsibility for the community; more often, however, one suspects that they were decorative – part of the scenery in a stage set version of country life which had little purpose beyond pleasure, relaxation, and sometimes showing off. Nevertheless, they were an essential element of the country house phenomenon at the turn of the century, which, along with regal size, expensive materials, and elaborate decoration, served to distinguish the houses built then from those of any previous period in American history. The type was well defined by Ferree:

> Country houses we have always had, and large ones too; but the great country house as it is now understood is a new type of dwelling, a sumptuous house, built at large expense, often palatial in its dimensions, furnished in the richest manner and placed on an estate, perhaps large enough to admit of independent farming operations, and in most cases with a garden which is an integral part of the architectural scheme.[5]

Standing some miles outside the city, beyond the suburbs and out of easy reach of other houses, in a community that was not laid out by a developer, every American country house was, by definition, surrounded by enough land to be called an estate. Not everyone owned mountains and valleys as did George W. Vanderbilt; an estate of only a thousand acres was considered large. Yet many estates very much smaller than this still managed to convey the illusion of self-sufficient landed life – providing their own produce for the table and every form of outdoor amusement for family and guests. Even where the landholding was reduced to miniature proportions, there needed to be no weakening of country flavor. When *Country Life in America* cast its eye over Mrs. Arthur V. Meigs's place at Radnor, Pennsylvania – a mere twenty-three acres – in the 1920s, it discovered amazing completeness and variety. The plan alone was enough to show its character (Plate 21).

> "Pastures" imply cows, "Chicken Yards" imply chickens, "Paddocks" imply horses, "Vegetables" imply something good to eat in the summer, "Poikiles," "Sunset Towers," "Potagers," "Dipping Tanks," "Paduan Gardens," and so forth imply another state of mind, and the sum total implies a world of what a great many people have definitely settled in their minds to be an unutterable amount of trouble.[6]

But this unnecessary trouble was thought to be well worth taking by the builders of the American country house, just as it had been by, for example, the Bostonian elite, keenly supporting the Massachusetts Society for Promoting Agriculture, a century before. The difference between the early twentieth century and the early nineteenth was the greater pretentiousness of the architecture, expressed perhaps by Mrs. Meigs's Poikile, which *Country Life in America* revealed to be an outside porch inspired by Hadrian's Villa. Independence from the outside world – or the appearance of it – was even more easily achieved in California, where, if allowed, dense and luxuriant vegetation soon blotted out all evidence of life beyond the boundary. Estate buildings tended to be placed near

19–20. The architecture of the estate was often as elaborate as that of the main house. These glasshouses at Lyndhurst, New York, date from about 1865 and 1891.

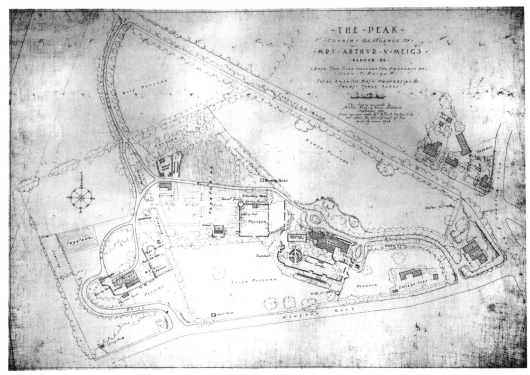

21. Plan of the Peak, Mrs. Arthur V. Meigs's "country residence" at Radnor, Pennsylvania, 1921. Into this estate of only twenty-three acres have been fitted a chicken yard, paddock, pasture, potager or formal vegetable garden, nursery, orchard, and various garden buildings.

the entrance, where the visitor would not miss them, and then the drive wound by a tortuous route to the main house, heightening the apparent extent.

Probably the city that spawned the greatest number of country houses was the most urban of all, New York. They were to be found by the hundred on Long Island, by the score on the banks of the Hudson, by the dozen in the northern half of New Jersey. But New York was far from alone: nearly every great city inspired some of its citizens – often the ones who had most profited by it – with the urge to withdraw into the country. Boston's North Shore, Philadelphia's Main Line, Pittsburg's Sewickley Heights, Cleveland's Chagrin Valley, and Chicago's Lake Forest and Lake Geneva bear witness to the phenomenon. Fords and Dodges built country houses outside Detroit; Firestones and Seiberlings outside Akron. Such activity was not confined to the East Coast and the Midwest. Writing in *Sunset Magazine* in 1906, Croly observed that near the larger cities of California "the rich are making country places which are intended to afford an opportunity for the most elaborate and expensive pleasures of country life."[7] For a moment – the moment lasted about thirty years – it seemed that the building of Biltmores and other houses of that class would become an unalterable fact of American life.

Though no one could doubt that the American country house was inspired by European example, many people also considered it to be, in the way that it developed, a peculiarly American achievement. Indeed, one of the most perceptive commentators on American social life, Marianna van Rensselaer, found that the nation's architecture was nowhere so original or characteristically American as in the country house. This, she

22

maintained, was not to be wondered at, since climate, social conditions, and landscape all generated needs that were quite specific to the United States. Until 1890 the cheapness and adaptability of wood made it the main building material, and this also caused an obvious difference with country houses of other lands. Although wood was superseded in popularity by more costly and permanent materials, many of the assumptions reflected in the country house – assumptions about privacy, about luxury, about servants, about the countryside itself – remained distinct from those in Europe. As the magisterial Mrs. van Rensselaer summed up: "In no other architectural branch have we been thrown so largely upon our own resources; therefore in none was the development of some kind of originality so probable."[8]

The *Architectural Record* was even more certain of the American country house being an essentially national product. "Nothing comparable to it exists elsewhere in the world," it trumpeted in May 1903. It was unlike both the European country houses on which it was based and the houses built at other periods in American history.

The buildings it has produced (and in the future will demand) are very decidedly differenced from the English country house, their nearest contemporary analogue. They differ even more from the American country homes that arose after the war and when prosperity had returned to the country. Neither are they at all kindred to those old Colonial houses which added the chief charm to our early social life, the remaining examples of which still retain an indestructible atmosphere of delight.[9]

The reason for the difference lay in the nature of the clients. They were glowingly described as Merchant Princes who seemed closer to the Medici of Renaissance Italy than to the Southern planters and New England traders of eighteenth and nineteenth-century America. Consequently the magazine believed that the American country house would in the future acquire immense importance as, if nothing else, a sociological document. "These buildings are the registers and, let us hope, enduring chronicles of our very latest days, of our rapidly accumulating wealth, of the prodigious rewards of high finance, and the extraordinary degree of luxury that has become compatible with American life."

Naturally the people who created these country houses were not always conscious of this historic role. Sometimes they were frankly puzzled by the impulses that drove them to build. "Why is it that a man, just as soon as he gets enough money, builds a house much bigger than he needs?" reflected Harvey S. Firestone, surprised at finding himself, by conventional standards, considerably over-housed:

I built a house at Akron many times larger than I have the least use for; I have another house at Miami Beach, which is also much larger than I need. I suppose that before I die I shall buy or build other houses which also will be larger than I need. I do not know why I do it – the houses are only a burden. But I have done it, and all my friends who have acquired wealth have big houses. Even so unostentatious a man as Henry Ford has a much bigger house at Dearborn than he really cares about. I wonder why it is.[10]

There might, he considered, be something atavistic in it, harking back to feudal days when a big house was needed for protection; entertaining guests was the purpose of some houses; a few were built simply to show off the owner's wealth. But most of the great houses built by self-made men were started without any very clear motive; and when finished no one knew why they had been begun. Their owners, he concluded, would have been better off living in a hotel than running a country house that much resembled one.

23

22. Harvey S. Firestone's Harbel Manor outside Akron, Ohio. The owner was uncertain why he had built so big a house, though rivalry with Franklin A. Seiberling of the Goodyear Tire and Rubber Company, who built Stan Hywet, may have had something to do with it.

Oddly enough, despite these protestations, Firestone's motive in enlarging the already sizeable Harbel Manor (Plate 22) seems to have been all too palpable, if undeclared: he was locked in fierce competition with his friend, neighbor, and rubber rival, Frank A. Seiberling, founder of the Goodyear Tire and Rubber Company, who built the even bigger Stan Hywet Hall. One can easily imagine that, honor satisfied, a man of his relatively simple tastes could find little use for the domestic monster he had created. It is difficult to know how many country house builders shared his unease about their motives – more, perhaps, than one would think. But others certainly had a very precise idea of how they intended to use their houses, not to mention what they expected them to express. This can be seen from both the letters and the telegrams with which they pursued their increasingly distraught architects. Even clients who were little interested in architecture had views about the particular rooms they needed in the main house and the subsidiary buildings they required on the estate. In this way, as the *Architectural Record* had predicted, the American country house became the accurate mirror of a way of life; and just as the life was in some respects unlike that of other nations, so too were the country houses.

How did the American country house stand in relation to its cousins in Europe? European and particularly English houses formed the model, in terms of scale, way of life, and sometimes form. Yet a superficial comparison would suggest that the differences outnumbered the similarities. There was no monarch to impress in the United States; there were no lawless, land-hungry upstarts or rioting tenantry to subdue. The American country house was not somewhere from which a large stretch of country could be physically dominated. Being part of a landed class did not of itself secure political influence or ensure that the owner would have some role, however modest, in running the country. Nor was the American country house on the whole a place where political stratagems were hatched. But this is to compare the American country house at the turn of the century with country houses of other epochs in England. By 1890 the English country house had itself largely outgrown earlier roles. Its meaning had both narrowed and spread. It had narrowed because the country house no longer occupied the position of real power it had held in previous generations; the motive forces were now prestige, tradition, gardening, and sport. It had spread because the people who built new houses tended to prefer the illusion to the substance of country life. Land, ownership of

24

which was the traditional basis of the country house, had become considerably less attractive as an investment. To many people it was important to be near a major city. Houses were getting smaller; the suburbs were getting closer. The kinship is closer than it first appears.

The changes in the English country house were shrewdly recognized by Fiske Kimball, that highly urbane art historian, when he set out to define "The Country House in America" in 1919:

> By the "country house" in America we understand no such single well-established form as the traditional country house of England, fixed by centuries of almost unalterable custom, with a life of its own which has been described as "the perfection of human society." Even in England today the great house yields in importance to the new and smaller types which the rise of the middle classes has strewn over the country and on the fringes of the city, and with [which] the variety is infinite, from the dwellings of the further suburbs to the distant, self-sustaining estate. Yet the common characteristic of all is clear enough – a site free of the arid blocks and circumscribed "lots" of the city, where one may enjoy the informality of nature out-of-doors.[11]

There may be no Chatsworths or Blenheims in the United States, but there are many country houses that are close equivalents to those built by Ernest George and Edwin Lutyens from the 1880s to the 1920s.

Perhaps it is not surprising that a strong body of opinion disagreed with Mrs. van Rensselaer and the *Architectural Record*, and maintained that these new, luxurious houses, with their European affinities, were neither essentially American in character nor appropriate to a modern democracy. The display of wealth through architecture had for long aroused conflicting emotions in the United States. On the one hand there were those who believed that a fine dwelling filled with valuable art treasures symbolized the rapid advance of civilization and helped enhance the nation's standing in the eyes of the world. Rich men were leaders of society, and it was expected that they should have rich tastes. On the other were those who felt that this aristocratic taste for magnificence had no place in a republic nurtured on the Pilgrim tradition. The whole idea of the country house – or any house of display – not only seemed foreign but epitomized the excessive concentration of wealth that appeared one of the great social evils of the age. As the newspaper editor E.L. Godkin, discussing "The Expenditure of Rich Men," declared: "To erect 'palatial abodes' is to flaunt, in the faces of the poor and the unsuccessful and greedy, the most conspicuous possible evidence that the owner not only has enormous amounts of money, but does not know what to do with it."[12] It was a sentiment that Harvey S. Firestone might have understood. It also had a long pedigree. Though Godkin himself observed that most of the larger houses built before the Civil War were "simply moderate sized mansions which, on most estates in England or France, would be considered small," they had, in their own day, engendered suspicion. It is "in a stile which would be esteemed splendid even in the most luxurious part of Europe," wrote the architect Charles Bullfinch of William Bingham's seeming palace near Philadelphia: "far *too* rich for *any* man in this country."[13]

There was one respect, at least, in which critics were right to question the expenditure on great houses: they were not a lasting investment. But was it ever expected that they would be? "An attachment to locality is not a conspicuous trait of American character," observed Lewis F. Allen in the mid-nineteenth century.[14] He was one of many writers who commented on the readiness with which Americans uprooted and moved round the country "in the hope of bettering their condition." This was one explanation advanced by Charles Elliot Norton to account for the "lack of old homes in America," which he made the subject of an article in 1889. "The allurements of hope . . . and the love of adventure" overpowered the tenderer instincts that inspired "affection for the home of one's youth."[15] Consequently there was little obstacle, in terms of sentiment, to prevent houses changing hands. In the 1870s Martha J. Lamb observed the frequency with which mansions on the Hudson were bought and sold. "Houses are built, destroyed, and rebuilt with a celerity for which there has been no parallel in Europe," commented Desmond and Croly. This could all too evidently be seen at Newport, Rhode Island, where on the most fashionable street – Bellevue Avenue – some houses were torn down and rebuilt, or obliterated through remodeling, at least once every generation. The domestic monuments that we see today must have seemed much less permanent to their owners than they do to us. This was equally true of the American country house.

For all their size and elaboration, few if any of these houses were intended as dynastic seats – a question mark even hangs over Biltmore, for we do not know Vanderbilt's own thoughts on the matter. Owners rarely expected them to be lived in by even their sons and daughters. The massive sense of continuity that inspired eighteenth-century English gentlemen to plant parks that could benefit only their grandchildren was not present in the minds of turn-of-the-century American industrialists. So when they turned their hand to planting, they were likely to have some of the trees transported fully grown, for an effect that they themselves could enjoy (Plate 23). They were wise. Taste moved on so quickly in America that within a generation whole areas went out of vogue and their

23. The moving of mature trees enabled the creation of instant landscape parks. Hicks Nurseries move a mature tree onto the grounds of Killenworth, Long Island.

26

A CASTLE IN THE AIR
THESE YOUNG GIRLS WHO MARRY OLD MILLIONAIRES SHOULD STOP DREAMING

24. "That was what I wanted, a home," wrote Henry Flagler of Whitehall in Palm Beach, Florida. This shows the *bal poudré* with which it was opened in 1903.

25. The tension between the house of display and the simple place in the country is the subject of Charles Dana Gibson's "A Castle in the Air – These Young Girls who Marry Old Millionaires Should Stop Dreaming." From *Collier's Weekly*, June 1903.

country houses were abandoned. When the owners died or moved on, the houses were sold, as the realtors delighted to explain, at a mere fraction of what they had cost to build.

The very mobility of American society caused particular value to be placed on the home. The word became so encrusted with special meaning that it was, and still is, commonly used in preference to house. It was thought that home-like qualities were far more likely to thrive in the country than in the city. "We are going to have a home where the squirrels chatter, and the birds sing, and the beechnuts fall like hail," wrote Edward Powell Payson in a book actually called *The Country Home* in 1905. "Spell that word HOME in big capitals; for it is only in the country that one can find the best home."[16] Home virtues were so highly prized that even large and chillingly formal houses were routinely praised for the homeliness – or homeyness – with which they were supposedly embued. Henry M. Flagler, the developer of Florida, felt that he had achieved this quality at Whitehall in Palm Beach (Plate 24). "They wanted it higher to secure the right proportions," he said of Carrère and Hastings's first design for the hall. "But I wanted to feel at home and so I made them put it eight feet lower. I can come here and feel that it is my home." He saw no ambiguity in the Italian ambassador's comment that Whitehall was something unknown in the Old World, a palace to be lived in. "That was what I wanted, a home."[17]

There were many reasons for this emphasis on the home. One may have been the desire of the newly rich not to cut themselves off from the old ways with which they were comfortable. Another was the growing fear that, as a nation, America was losing its taste for domesticity. The willingness of young couples to start married life in a hotel or boarding house, to help the wife shed the burdens of housework, was widely cited as a symptom of the malaise. American women were accused of "orientalism," presumably in reference to the idleness and luxury of the harem. It was said that they preferred shopping in department stores to keeping house. Contrasted with this was the myth of home encouraged by popular literature, in which American heroes were shown as having risen to greatness from, and thanks to, the simplicity of their beginnings.[18]

This idea of the home as a focus of moral and spiritual values found its echo in the American country house. The connection between the two had been forcefully made in

27

26. Naumkeag at Stockbridge, Massachusetts, built by Stanford White in 1885–86. "What a luxury it will be to escape from the city, and to roll on the grass, ride over the hills and float in the Stockbridge Bowl," wrote the owner, Joseph Hodges Choate, from New York.

the mid-nineteenth century by Andrew Jackson Downing. Though Downing was only thirty-six when he died in a steamboat accident in 1852, his writings were exceptionally influential. His books on architecture and gardening "are to be found everywhere, and nobody, whether he be rich or poor, builds a house or lays out a garden without consulting Downing's works," wrote Frederika Bremer, a Swedish traveler powerfully affected by his idealism and handsome brown eyes.[19] In 1850 Downing published *The Architecture of Country Houses*. This appeared to be a pattern book in the accepted tradition, offering readers a choice of many different designs of country house. But, unlike all previous American works of this kind, it did not confine itself to practical advice, but emphasized the moral nature of the choices confronting the prospective house builder. For Downing believed passionately in the civilizing, social, and moral character of the home, and particularly the country home. The latter he described as "the most refined home in America – the home of its most leisurely and educated class of citizens."[20] Miss Bremer wrote of Downing's own home at Newburgh-on-Hudson, "A soul has here felt, thought, arranged."

Downing's idea of a country house, however, was very different from the large, fully equipped mansions described in turn-of-the-century literature. The most expensive of his designs was estimated to cost only $14,000 – hardly an excessive sum even in 1850. Indeed, he goes out of his way to inveigh against the extravagance that he can already detect in the building of some country houses. "Fortunes are rapidly accumulated in the United States, and the indulgence of one's taste and pride in the erection of a country-seat of great size and cost is becoming a favorite mode of expending wealth. And yet these attempts at great establishments are always and inevitably failures in America." They were not appropriate in a country in which inheritance played so little part. In fact pretentiousness of all forms was to be avoided. Though Downing's designs displayed a wide variety of idioms – Normandy, Italian, Romanesque, Rural Gothic, Pointed, and Plain Timber – the main object, he believed, was to find a style that suited the personality of the inhabitants.

Once Downing had tied the knot between morality and house building, no man could put them asunder. When John Calvin Stevens and Albert Winslow Cobb published their *Examples of American Domestic Architecture* they took it for granted that the virtues of restraint and simplicity would be approved by their readers. Working principally in Maine, they were able to condemn the "evidently demoralizing luxury" developing in "other sections of our country."[21] By the first years of the next century, such sentiments had become commonplace in the swelling body of journalism on houses and decoration. "Avoid pretentious things. . . . Avoid the unusual," counselled Isabel Bevier in 1907.[22] A book tellingly called *The Honest House*, written by Ruby Ross Goodnow and published in 1914, was typical in its condemnation of showiness and vulgarity as the besetting sins of the age. If Downing's morality survived into the twentieth century, so did the sense in which he used the term "country house" – signifying a place removed from the evils of the city, straining towards a more complete and more spiritual life, but comparatively modest in size, style, and expenditure. This meaning was very different from that being forced on it, some would say unnaturally, by Ferree, LeMoyne, and Desmond and Croly.

In the early years the two kinds of country house were not easy to tell apart. The informal, largely wooden architecture of the 1870s and early 1880s, with its multiplicity of verandas and porches and dormers, its studied quaintness and asymmetry, its cozy corners and curious joinery, did not lend itself to great pomp. When the revival styles – first Colonial and French Renaissance, then Louis Seize, English Georgian, and Tudor – were ushered in after 1885, Downing's idea of the country house rapidly started to diverge from that which owed more to Europe. The two decades following 1890 were a time of big houses built by big firms with big names (McKim, Mead and White, Carrère and Hastings, Peabody and Stearns), who yet remained nimble enough to move from one style to another with each new commission; when it came to the interior many different styles were incorporated within the same building. Having edged towards monumentality through a series of increasingly symmetrical houses from the early 1880s, McKim, Mead and White led the dance. Their long experience of handling intricate volumes throughout the Shingle Style years, combined with Stanford White's genius for ornament, gave their later houses a richness that no other architect could match.

The slightly younger firm of Carrère and Hastings, natural successors to McKim, Mead and White's country house work on the death of Stanford White in 1906, never quite shed a tendency to flatness perhaps acquired at the École des Beaux-Arts; but they were the acknowledged nonpareils of planning. Their work was largely French in character, inspired equally by the Loire chateaux of the seventeenth century and the neo-Classicism of the eighteenth. Thomas Hastings's own house on Long Island was called Bagatelle. An even suppler master of stylistic footwork was the Philadelphia architect Horace Trumbauer. Trumbauer began his career, at the age of only twenty-four, designing an immense house, Grey Towers, for the heir to a sugar fortune; it was familiarly known as The Castle from the suggestion that it gave from some angles of Windsor Castle, and the cost, as Moses King observed with grand vagueness in his *Notable Philadelphians* of 1902, was "in the millions." Over the next thirty years he roamed up, down, and around the Main Line building in all the fashionable styles: Tudor for George W. Elkins, Italian Renaissance for William Luken Elkins, Georgian for Peter A.B. Widener, Palladian for Edward Stotesbury ("so thrilling in its loveliness," wrote Mrs. Stotesbury in a note of thanks), French for a number of clients (particularly after the first black graduate from the University of Pennsylvania, Julian Abele, became his chief designer in 1906), and even neo-Georgian for Colonel Robert Montgomery's Ardrossan, which was closely based on the admired English architect Ernest Newton's Ardenrun in Kent. To the *Architectural Record* Trumbauer's work exhibited "the eclectic facility which is one of the characteristics of the modern American architects."[23] It was "never crude," but it puzzled them because it was impossible to guess the architect's own taste. But he had one certain preference, and that was for size. Looking at Trumbauer's houses one detects such a definite pattern that it amounts almost to an unalterable rule: the bigger the commission, the better the result.

Downing, of course, would have been appalled. But the building of smaller, home-like country houses continued throughout this period of grandeur. Charles Edward Hooper's book called, simply, *The Country House* of 1913 is about nothing else. When *Country Life in America* published practical articles about beekeeping or raising hens, it was generally this kind of country house that it had in mind. They were likely to call it, at its most modest, the Twenty Acre Place or the House that Will Keep Servants. It was in great demand from middle-class people who were just as disenchanted with city life as the richest millionaires. The architect Frank Miles Day saw it as one of the principal building types of the first years of the century. "It is safe to say," he wrote in 1911, "that in no other country and at no other time has the suburban or country house of moderate size been so rapidly multiplied as within the last decade, in the United States."[24]

When the European-style country house itself began to get smaller, the two traditions once more came near to joining hands. Confidence among builders of great houses was dampened by the introduction of income tax after 1913, then largely sunk by the 1930s depression. "Generally speaking, Americans of to-day like simple homes," commented *Town and Country* in 1931.[25] But, with the exception of the automobile cities, the boom town of Chicago, and William Randolph Hearst's San Simeon, a reduction in scale had been visible long before either date. Of the new generation of architects who found their feet after 1900, only John Russell Pope and David Adler regularly built very large country houses. Charles A. Platt, a painter and gardener before he turned architect, developed a successful practice designing country houses of more moderate size in which the key element was harmony between the house and its grounds. Quiet in style, invariably symmetrical in plan, these houses never made a show of dramatic or novel effects, their greatest originality being sometimes to evoke Italian villas. Yet what could he not have done? He was said to have an "almost hypnotic" power over his clients.[26] Delano and Aldrich worked on a similar scale, being less drawn to the mighty chateaux of the Loire than to the exquisite Petit Trianon at Versailles. Though Harry T.

27. William L. Bottomley's Reedsdale, Virginia, home of Leslie H. Reed of the Imperial Tobacco Company, 1925. This is a reinterpretation of Carter's Grove, perhaps influenced by the work of the British architect Sir Edwin Lutyens.

28. An example of the Cotswold style of the 1920s in Connecticut: Charles Wesley Dunn's house at South Norwalk, designed by Frank J. Forster.

Lindeberg built a large estate for James Stillman at Pocantico Hills in New York in 1907 – all the buildings covered with shingle thatch – it was for "beautiful simplicity," "intimacy and friendliness," and an "almost austere renunciation of applied ornamnent" that his work was later praised by Royal Cortissoz.[27] Again, Ernest Flagg, a rather older architect, landed two monster commissions from Frederick G. Bourne, president of the Singer Manufacturing Company, around 1900 (Plate 95), but in 1922 turned his thoughts to *Small Houses: Their Economic Design and Construction* ("small houses" that were likely to have a chauffeur's flat over the garage). As Matlack Price commented apropos the work of Dwight James Baum: "It is a sociological fact, quite as much as an architectural fact that this country's greatest need is for the well-designed house of moderate and small size."[28] Baum, born in 1886, was one of a generation of architects for whom moderation was not merely a virtue but a passion.

One theme emerged to dominate the 1920s country house, regionalism. Architects such as Baum, Robert R. McGoodwin, and Frank J. Forster could still glide easily from style to style, but now their styles were derived, not from the great works of architectural history, but more from anonymous buildings of medium size. Colonial architecture became, if possible, even more avidly admired because the new, more modest scale of country house was now exactly that of the original (Plate 27). Next in popularity came the Cotswold manor house (Plate 28), a style particularly well suited to the Philadelphia area with its plentiful building stone; the Normandy *manoir*, which allowed some fantasy in the play of steep pitched roofs, dormers, towers, and irregular roof levels and window openings; and the English cottage, all leaded lights and wobbly beams. Such rustic fare had a charm for jaded palates.

Regionalism, however, was more than just a ramble through the byways of Europe. Many centers outside the Northeast had become rich enough to support their own architects with their own ideas. The outstanding talent was Philip Trammell Shutze in the renascent city of Atlanta. Shutze had trained at the Georgia Institute of Technology, at one of an increasing number of architectural schools in the United States to offer an education on Beaux-Arts lines. In his masterpiece, Swan House, he used all the alchemical skill of a Stanford White to distill, blend or, in some cases, frankly copy elements of English Palladianism and Italian Baroque. The cascade of the garden front

31

(Plate 29) was inspired by the Palazzo Corsini in Rome; plasterwork in the staircase hall was cribbed from 30 Old Burlington Street, at Mayfair in London, which happened to be the showrooms of the celebrated decorators Lenygon and Morant.[29] Other firms took regionalism yet one stage further, by developing an idiom based on the architecture of their own area. In the case of William Lawrence Bottomley, particularly associated with Richmond, Virginia (Plate 27), or R. Brognard Okie, based in Philadelphia (Plate 112), this is hardly noticeable: they were studying the Colonial buildings of their areas at a time when architects all over America were doing the same. But with John Gaw Meem in New Mexico, David R. Williams in Texas, and Wallace Neff and George Washington Smith in California – even more with the irrepressible Addison Mizner in Florida – the local influence can hardly be overlooked. "It has been said that there are no houses in Spain so Spanish as those that are built in America," observed a contemporary enthusiast. It was almost as marked a departure as the International Style which dazzled some imaginations in the next decade.

29. The strongly Italianate garden façade of Swan House, Atlanta, 1926–28, with a cascade inspired by the Palazzo Corsini in Rome. By contrast the entrance front of this skillfully eclectic house is derived from neo-Palladian buildings in Britain.

30. Windshield on Fishers Island, New York: a luxurious country house though in a modern idiom. It was built by Richard J. Neutra in 1936–38. Museum of Art, Rhode Island School of Design

When we reach Richard Neutra's Windshield (Plate 30), the native Downing tradition of the country house would seem to have reasserted itself over Desmond and Croly's less indigenous vision. "In spite of having almost unlimited means," observed Neutra, he strove to give the house "a simple dignity . . . expressing the spirit of our time and the puritanic character of New England."[30] But Desmond and Croly are not quite lost from view. Large, expensively made and so difficult to clean (every speck of dust showed) that several of the servants quit the first summer, this thirty-seven room mansion seemed as shocking, as foreign, to the Browns' neighbors as any beetling chateau might have done three decades before. Equally, it had its stylistic affectations. The exterior, though made of wood, was painted silver-gray to suggest more machine age materials. In Frank Lloyd Wright's Fallingwater, sufficiently a country house to have its own dairy barns, closeness to nature could hardly be more complete: the house with its famous cantilevered terraces is built over a waterfall, the noise of which is literally inescapable. But for all the Japanese aesthetic it was the clients rather than the architect who insisted that it should remain a simple, informal place "for city people to renew themselves in nature."[31] They declined Wright's suggestion of putting gold leaf on the concrete or using paint laced with shiny particles of mica.

The tussle between the two conceptions of the American country house continued throughout the period of this book, but not much longer. Soon the tradition of the Desmond and Croly country house would be forgotten – so thoroughly forgotten that today most Americans use the term "country house" to mean either a holiday place out of town or, more technically, a simple vernacular country building, not an imposing mansion with estate and dependencies. What of the buildings themselves? We are left, all too often, with the husks of houses from which family life has long since fled, but whose interest, as the *Architectural Record* foresaw, lies in what they reveal of that vanished life – and rather more than that. There was idealism in the heroic construction of Biltmore, conspicuous symbol of all that Desmond and Croly wished to promote. Olana, described in the next chapter, became a work of art. Though the scale was somewhat greater than he had prescribed, Downing would have saluted it.

The Country House as Rural Retreat

OLANA

OLANA, home of the painter Frederick Edwin Church, stands at the opposite remove of the American country house from Biltmore. Whereas Biltmore and similar houses could be justifiably likened to hotels or clubs, Olana is an entirely personal building, its design and arrangement largely determined by the owner rather than the architect. It was in every sense a house of art. In heroically constructing Biltmore, George W. Vanderbilt had also shown devotion to an ideal of culture and beauty; but his ideal was perceived in terms of marble and mahogany, ormolu and Aubusson, while the life of the house remained very similar to that of any other rich man's abode. Olana, by contrast, was built for a family who self-consciously lived beauty in every way they could. This meant that the tone of life was undoubtedly high-flown, perhaps at times a little self-conscious; the basis of it, however, was as home-like as even Downing could have wished.

Olana also possesses something of the moral quality that Downing advocated. But this is hardly surprising, for to Church not only architecture but the entire created world could be a mighty symbol shot through with moral significance. While revealing the wonders of the continent to his fellow Americans, Church's great landscape paintings also hint at the divine meaning which seemed immanent within these tremendous phenomena of Nature. Such sublime compositions fulfilled a need in a people aching to discover their destiny. They were highly priced and exceedingly popular: thousands would troop to see works such as *The Heart of the Andes* when they were exhibited in one-painting shows, for which admission was charged.

On top of this, Church was a remarkably handsome man and had a beautiful, if diminutive, wife. Consequently the admiration of his contemporaries reached fever pitch. When the Churches walked into the opera house the audience would break into applause. But fame had its drawbacks. Too many would-be purchasers paid social calls to Church's studio; too many hostesses wanted to lionize him. It was time to move to the country. The American Rhine, as the Hudson was often called, offered scenery of a splendor to suit even Church. Long travels in search of mighty subjects for his landscapes did not dull his appreciation of its excellence.

In making his way to the Hudson, Church went down a well-beaten literary and artistic path. Most famously, that genial bachelor Washington Irving had bought a little Dutch house at Tarrytown in 1835. "I am living most cozily and delightfully in this dear, bright little home, which I have fitted up to my own humour," he wrote to his brother Pierre the next year. "Everything goes on cheerily in my little household, and I

35

31. Distant view of Olana, New York, built for the painter Frederick Edwin Church in 1870–74. It was designed by Church in collaboration with the architect Calvert Vaux.

32. Olana in the Clouds, a sketch by the owner, Frederick Edwin Church, dated 1872. Olana, New York

would not exchange the cottage for any chateau in Christendom." With the help of his friend the painter George Harvey, who lived nearby at Hastings-on-Hudson, but no architect, Irving remodelled the house, which he called Sunnyside. It became one of the most frequently sketched houses in America and caused an avalanche of New Yorkers to descend upon the vicinity.[1] Among the many artists who came to settle in the region was Albert Bierstadt, who painted *The Home of Irving* looking northwest from his studio.

Church knew the area around Hudson-on-Hudson of old. His teacher Thomas Cole had a house on the opposite bank, in the Catskills, and Church had lived there from 1844 to 1846. In 1845 he is known to have gone painting on the property that he would later own, since there is a dated sketch now at Olana. The place was then known as Wynson Breezy's Farm. Church bought it in 1860 and immediately put up a new cottage designed by Church's friend Hunt, later architect of Biltmore. To begin with, this building was simply called "the farm," then Cozy Cottage. The farm was kept as a working unit, with the former owner retained as manager, and over the next few years Church was at work putting up farmbuildings: ten by 1867, according to a letter of that year, "and they haven't cost much either."[2] Church's infant son fed the chickens out of his own hand and was delighted when one of the pigeons walked into the parlor. The old farmhouse, built in 1794, was kept for the use of guests and, later, for hired help.

The fields of Wynson Breezy's Farm went up nearly, but not quite, to the summit on which Olana was later built (Plate 32). From the beginning it seems that Church planned to buy the summit. This is hardly to be wondered at. According to the *Art Journal* of October 1876 it was perhaps the crowning glory of the Hudson:

36

Here is the grandest and most impressive view of the Catskill Mountains. In the deep valley flows the Hudson River between high and wooded banks. To the south it suddenly broadens to a width of two miles, forming a beautiful lake with picturesque shores. In the distance rise various mountain chains, including the Highlands at West Point, sixty miles away. Easterly is a long meadow-like valley forming the base of Blue Hill ... beyond is the Taghanic Range.... A glimpse of the river is seen near Albany, and beyond lie the more southern mountains of Vermont.[3]

For a few years the summit eluded him. He had to wait until 1867 to acquire it and, when he did, he paid a big price – two or three times per acre what he had given for the lower land. "I have just purchased the wood lot on the top of the hill," he wrote. "I want to secure if possible before I leave, every rood of ground that I shall ever require to make my farm perfect."[4]

Having captured the summit, Church next attacked the question of building a new house. He approached Hunt and the latter proposed a fairly conventional villa. But in November 1867 Church unaccountably put aside thoughts of house building and set off, with his wife, infant son, and mother-in-law, for over a year's travel in the Middle East. Once he had seen Islamic architecture at first hand, he would have no other style. It was a bold choice, though perhaps less extraordinary in the Hudson River Valley than it might have been elsewhere. For the banks of the Hudson were already well stocked with country houses in many styles. Downing himself, whose own house was at Newburgh-on-Hudson, had done much to encourage the idea that the river's majestic but rugged scenery required architecture of equal force and character. To Mrs. Lamb this could even justify a house in mixed Elizabethan-Gothic-Swiss taste. For Church the style of Olana was above all a personal decision. "I have got plenty of capital ideas and new ones about house building," he wrote from Berchtesgaden in Germany to his friend, the painter William H. Osborn.[5]

Hunt had to go. While George Vanderbilt would succumb to being molded by Hunt, Hunt found Church's personality too strong, and he was replaced by Calvert Vaux. Vaux, an Englishman, had first been Downing's draftsman, then his partner. He had worked with Olmsted on New York's newly opened Central Park; moreover he was the brother-in-law of another Hudson River school artist, Church's pupil Jervis McEntee. Like Downing he published a book, *Villas and Cottages*, which came out in 1864. It was similar to *The Architecture of Country Houses*, but different in some points of emphasis. For one thing he recommended more costly designs – the most expensive is for a $60,000 house; he also, somewhat impudently, thought it was about time that rich Americans learned how to spend money. At Olana he was employed for his structural skills, little more. Of the three hundred or so architectural drawings preserved at Olana (Plate 33), all but a fraction are in Church's own hand (Plates 34 and 35). "Yes," Church said, discussing the design of Olana at the end of his life, "I can say, as the good woman did about her mock turtle soup, 'I made it out of my head.'"[6]

It was frustrating for Church to be reliant on Vaux for the execution of his ideas. For his part, poor Vaux must have been driven close to despair. Like many amateurs, Church became absorbed to the point of obsession with his building, and nothing less than twenty-four hour attendance would have satisfied him. "I have been much delayed by being separated from my Architect although he has been up several times to see me," Church complained to the sculptor Erastus Dow Palmer in July 1870.[7] Priorities domestic and otherwise were set out in a letter to A.C. Goodman the next year:

1st I am building a house and am principally my own Architect. I give directions all

37

33–35. Three studies for Olana. The top one by Calvert Vaux is stamped 28 May 1870. The lower two, for the south and east façades, are by Church himself, who took an increasing, even obsessive, role in the design.

36. Samuel Colt's Armsmear at Hartford, Connecticut, built in 1856–62. It suffered "a severe touch of the Oriental," according to Martha J. Lamb in *The Homes of America*, 1879. Since Church's family came from Hartford, it is possible that the style influenced Olana.

day and draw plans and working drawings all night, 2nd I have my studio affairs outside and inside to attend to, 3rd I have a large farm to keep an eye on, 4th I have my family to take care of, 5th I have been away on business three or four times since you wrote, and 6th An infant daughter aged four days has engrossed a good deal of my time.[8]

Church spent his evenings poring over books on the architecture of Persia, though, as he happily admitted to friends, his travels had not actually taken him there. It was in Beirut and Damascus that the idea of a richly decorated Moorish courtyard house had been formed. However, the name of the house appears to derive from *olane*, meaning a fortified treasure house of ancient Persia; to an imagination as versed in symbolism as Church's, it was natural that the treasure his house protected should be his new young family.

In size the house was quite modest; Cozy Cottage was kept in commission and used as an overflow when there were guests. The broad shape of Olana was oddly conventional, being massed much like one of the Italianate villas in Vaux's book. What was not conventional was the style. However, it had a distinguished pedigree. Since the early nineteenth century, architects such as Owen Jones from England and Gottfried Semper from Germany had been traveling in the East, initially in quest of the lustrous color harmonies known to have disappeared from the Classical buildings in Greece. A Moorish house had been built in the United States in 1848, P.T. Barnum's Iranastan. Downing considered that "The Saracenic, or Moorish style, rich in fanciful decoration, is striking and picturesque in its detail, and is worthy of the attention of the wealthy amateur." Vaux also gave it qualified approval in *Villas and Cottages*. The style offered "isolated features" of interest and provided some "good suggestions" for verandas, but was so expensive as to be really appropriate only to countries where workmen were hired for a bowl of rice a day.

The most exotic house of the 1860s incorporating some Eastern features had been the revolver-maker Samuel Colt's Armsmear (Plate 36) at Hartford, Connecticut. Hartford was Church's home town and he knew the Colts. There is also a comparison to be made with the painter Frederic Leighton's 12 Holland Park Road in London. Church visited London twice in the 1860s, so it is possible that he met his fellow artist. Though Leighton's Arab Hall, containing his collection of Persian tiles, was not added until 1877–79, he had been traveling in the East since 1849 and it is likely that he conceived the idea for the room several years before it was built. Could he have discussed it with Church?

For some details the source can be found in Church's own library. On 1 September 1870 he wrote a check for a book on Persian architecture. This might have been *Monuments de la Perse*, by Pascal Coste (Paris, 1867). Church based his water tower on

37. Detail of the polychrome brickwork. This is not a characteristic of Persian architecture but suggests the influence of Ruskin.

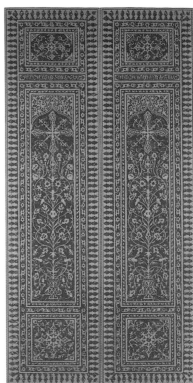

38–39. View from the library into the Court Hall (the Adirondacks chair is from Church's studio in New York), and a plate from *Les Arts arabes* that inspired the stencil decoration on the doors.

the plate *Vue de la cour de la Mosque Mesdjid-i-Chan*, while a simplified version of the columns in the Pavillon des Miroirs at Isfahan was used for the columns in the piazza. *Les Arts arabes* by Jules Bourgoin (Paris, 1868) was the source for the cast window with its wooden screen and the stenciling of the doors inside (Plates 38 and 39). On the other hand the polychrome brickwork of the upper stories does not seem particularly Persian, and another detail certainly is not. Church had the whimsical idea of finishing the top of each of the corner towers, barely visible from the ground, with a curiously shaped finial that, on closer inspection, turns out to be nothing other than a teapot.

The turning point of the plan was always the spectacular views. Church painted the landscape constantly and believed that the windows of the house should act as frames to the beauties of the world outside (Plate 40). The cross axis of the house is aligned on the valley. "We are having splendid Meteoric displays – Magnificent sunsets and Auroras – red, green, yellow and blue – and such – in profusion," wrote Church of another revelation of nature. "I have actually been drawn away from my usual devotion to the new house to sketch some of the fine things hung in the sky."[9] Shortly after building Cozy Cottage, Church began to improve the landscape around the house. "My young trees absolutely laugh to find their toes in the water," he wrote to Palmer in 1867.[10] Around Olana hemlocks and spruces were planted to complement its picturesque silhouette. "Thousands and thousands" of trees were used to form clumps or woods on the lower slopes. In 1884 Church again wrote to Palmer: "I have made about $1\frac{3}{4}$ miles of

41

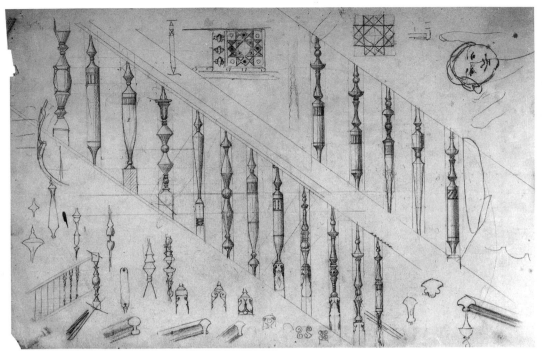

41. Church's study for the staircase balusters. Thought was poured into every detail of Olana's design.

road this season, opening entirely new and beautiful views. I can make more and better landscapes in this way than by tampering with canvas and paint in the studio."[11]

Work began in May 1870, with Church elaborating some of the details of the design to the builders as things progressed (Plate 41). He was pleased with his team. The carpenter had already been tried and tested by Palmer, who built a house in Albany. On 31 October 1870 Church wrote to Osborn: "My men are as good a set as can be found in this world and people come from far and near to see the bomb proof edifice going up – and wonder what it all means."[12] "Bomb proof" referred to Church's principal idea in building, that the walls should be thick and of stone, not wood. The foundations were so solid that, on his hilltop, he did not feel an earthquake "which startled the lower world."[13] His strong preference for stone may well have been influenced by seeing the ruins of Petra and elsewhere while he was abroad; they represented evidence of human continuity – a theme also suggested by the references to ancient civilizations in Olana's style and decoration.

The men, temporarily put up in the carriage house and stables, toiled like a thousand beavers. Yet it still took all of two years to build the shell of Olana, thanks to the evolutionary nature of design (it would be changed as work went on). There was also the problem of explaining the principles of Persian architecture, somewhat hazy even to Church, to workmen who were more familiar with brick schools, meeting-houses, and jails. But at last the Church children could write to Santa Claus asking for sailboats to launch in the bathtub of the new house. However, moving in was far from the end of the story: when McEntee visited in June 1873 he found the Churches "living in the upper part of their new house while the carpenters are at work down below."[14]

Inside, the ground floor is organized in the Persian manner around a central Court

43

40. Looking from the loggia, called the Ombra, towards the Hudson. As a painter, Church not only found a majestic landscape, but framed it like a painting. Hilltop sites commanding spectacular views are a feature of the American country house.

42. The Court Hall. All the main colours used throughout the house are brought together in this central room.

43. The sitting room. The colour scheme is taken from Church's painting of the ruins of Petra over the fireplace.

Hall (Plate 42); on plan it is a Greek cross and all the other rooms (except those in the later studio wing) open into it. Often the dominant wall color is taken from a painting that hangs in the room (Plate 43), and sometimes the colors of one room are picked up in the next, to create in the visitor a subtle sense of being drawn on through the house. The more fanciful contents give the impression of having been brought back from travels, but generally this is not the case: the majority came from New York dealers. Nevertheless, every detail of the house was artistically considered. "Exquisite flowers arranged only by Mrs. Church are always on the table, and every plate and pitcher and napkin is chosen for its beauty or prettiness," wrote Susan Hale during a visit in 1884. "Coffee is served after dinner in little cups with exquisite little spoons, each one different, in the shape of some flower or leaf; all these are Mr. Church's taste."[15]

Before Olana was built Church had begun collecting Old Masters. "I have already purchased – 30 – Are you astonished?" he wrote to Osborn in 1868. "The highest price I have paid for one is $30, the lowest one dollar."[16] He continued to buy in America, and was not above improving his purchases. His "hand is in," he wrote to his old friend Samuel L. Clemens (Mark Twain) in 1887; he had been amusing himself "lately in retouching some dilapidated 'Old Masters.'"[17] (Church's overpaintings were preserved when the paintings were recently restored.) Already in 1868 Church had an idea of the room in which he wished his collection to be housed: he wrote that he intended to have "one *old* room – with old furniture and old pictures – everything toned down to 400 years back."[18] This became the double-height dining room, lit austerely by four windows on the north wall which left plenty of hanging space on the other three.

Church admitted he would never finish Olana; he would always be altering it. In the 1880s he began another major building campaign to add a studio that would double as a guest suite when required (Plate 44). Despite advancing years, he set about the challenge as vigorously as ever, and this time was completely his own architect. He was busy "night and day" with plans.

The studio house for the successful artist was a significant development of nineteenth-century architecture. Generally they were in town, and often the studio itself had a separate entrance to spare the artist's wife the embarrassment of encountering socially doubtful models on the stairs. It was not a provision required by landscape painters. Church formerly used a studio half way up the hillside, though he also retained one in the fashionable Tenth Street Studio Building, designed by Hunt, in New York.

44. The studio, built in the late 1880s. The easel is set up for a left-handed painter, as Church suffered badly from rheumatism at the end of his life.

45. Sombreros form a typically flamboyant article of studio decoration. These were acquired by Church in Mexico, where he spent several winters.

Country studios were unusual but not unknown: George Inness, one of the landscape painters who was now beginning to succeed Church in popularity, built a "zoological glasshouse" at Montclair, New Jersey, so that he could paint winter scenes in comfort from behind securely closed windows. Typical studio furnishings were flamboyant and eclectic. According to Horace J. Rollin's handbook *Studio, Field and Gallery* of 1878, they might include "beautifully colored fabrics, the rich plumage of birds, autumn leaves . . . rare pieces of furniture, richly-colored rugs, elegant vases, and small pieces of statuary" – anything, in fact, that would "cultivate and refine the taste."

The Olana studio was filled with exactly this kind of rich eclectic jumble. The most striking feature was a collection of Mexican sombreros (Plate 45). Church had been visiting Mexico for several winters with his friend Charles Dudley Warner; indeed it was to Church that Sylvester Baxter dedicated *Spanish Colonial Architecture in Mexico* in 1901. Consequently, the style of the studio wing, with its squat tower and partly sheltered flat roof (or *azotea*), is Mexican rather than Persian. Upstairs the bathroom was provided in a kind of box tacked onto the outside. Church's carpenter did not know the Mexican style, so Church personally cut out full-size templates for the ornament. Probably because he had no architect, directing the workforce was more difficult than it had been before. "All summer I was anticipating a trip to Hartford," he wrote to Warner in September 1889, "but my old carpenter makes so many mistakes that I dared not leave home for a single day."[19]

Olana was finished just as Biltmore was begun, but they are worlds apart. Olana, though it had an estate of two hundred and fifty acres and a working farm, was never very large. The rooms are of human proportions; the furniture, though sometimes sumptuous in effect, was of little worth. There were only four or five servants, but plenty of animals. For all its gorgeous colors, fabulous roofline, unexpected excrescences, and Eastern arcades, it was built for a simple country existence. Country houses are the most personal of all types of building, but Olana was more personal than most. Not only was it designed by its owner, but Church himself mixed the colors for each room on his palette, dabbing them onto cardboard and scratching on the name of the room with the end of his brush. Whereas one morning in Paris was enough for George Vanderbilt to choose three hundred rugs, Church lovingly nursed Olana towards completion over four decades.

Yet were Biltmore and Olana as unreconcilable as they first seem? Neither was calculated to blend into its surroundings, as far as choice of architectural style was concerned. Both looked to foreign countries for inspiration, and took freely where they found it. Both were, in their different ways, houses of art, which aimed at perfection. Both owners actively set about planting trees and enhancing the natural features of their estates. In a typically American way both chose hilltop sites that commanded panoramic views over landscapes of extraordinary power and beauty. Neither could have been built in any country other than the United States.

What is more, both houses reflect their owners' sense of themselves, their family, and their place in the world. The struggle towards deciding which kind of American country house to build was, for some owners, the struggle to find the identity the family wished to project. It was not a choice on which all families found it easy to agree.

— 4 —

The Country House as Compromise
KYKUIT

BUILT on a generous site and on a generous scale, perhaps on a generous budget, less constricted than a house in town, clearly not a product of necessity, the country house reveals more about its owner than any other kind of dwelling. Not everyone gave much attention to the signals that they were unconsciously transmitting by this means. But some of the more thoughtful owners were very conscious of the image that their country houses were likely to convey. Prominent among them was the ever-thoughtful and cautious John D. Rockefeller, who built Kykuit at Pocantico Hills, New York. Kykuit was quite literally a product of the debate about the two characters that we have already seen implicit in the American country house – those of stately home and unostentatious rural retreat.

Rockefeller began acquiring his estate in 1893 as secretly as he could, to prevent the sudden rise in prices that would follow his name being known. At that date he was already a rich man, with a fortune of $50 million. By the time he finished building the house in 1910 this figure had increased by more than five times. But he saw that as no reason to indulge in the extravagance of a large and costly house. Having been brought up in the wilds of upstate New York he had strong feelings for landscape but almost none for architectural grandeur. He was studiously indifferent to public opinion. Not so his son, John D. Rockefeller, Jr., who believed that his father should have a house equal to his position in American life and, always with scrupulous deference, set about building it for him. The tussle of wills in the design and building of Kykuit makes vivid the different conceptions of the American country house that each man was determined to support.

When Rockefeller's first land purchases were announced in the *Tarrytown Argus*, the editor confidently described to his readers the "regal castle" that he would build at an anticipated cost of $1 million.

> The materials will be marble, stone and granite. Towers and porticoes will ornament various sides. It is safe to say that the structure will be in keeping with all of its grand surroundings and no expense will be spared in its erection, which will be undertaken as soon as the plans of the architect are completed.[1]

Judging from the priorities of other rich men in Tarrytown, many of whom built large houses, he might have been right. But he was not; the account is pure fiction. What it does accurately reflect is the public's expectations of how a millionaire should behave.

In the case of Rockefeller's brother, William, expectations had been adequately

49

46. Gates to Kykuit, the John D. Rockefeller house in Pocantico Hills, New York. Through them can be seen the Oceanus fountain, copied from a work by Giovanni da Bologna in the Boboli Gardens in Florence.

47. Rockwood Hall at Tarrytown, New York, the home of John D. Rockefeller's brother William. From *Harper's Weekly*, 6 September 1890.

48. John D. Rockefeller's home Forest Hill, outside Cleveland, Ohio. From a postcard.

fulfilled. He had come east as Standard Oil's New York representative while Rockefeller remained in Cleveland. In 1886 he bought a country house, with the apt name of Rockwood, at Tarrytown overlooking the Hudson (Plate 47). Originally built by Gervase Wheeler for Edwin Bartlett of the Pacific Mail Steamship Company, it had been one of the most splendid houses of its day. "It is a noble villa-estate," wrote Martha J. Lamb in 1879, "and would be esteemed worthy of a distinguished place even in England among those of the opulent gentry which have been ripening for centuries." She found that the "somber, rich beauty" of the library was "beyond reach of the pen." When William Rockefeller tore it down and reused the materials in his new stables, *Harper's Weekly* noted admiringly that all the old stones "sufficed for but a portion of the foundation." Rockefeller's architect was Ebenezer L. Roberts, known for his churches and business buildings in New York and Brooklyn; when he died in 1890 Carrère and Hastings assumed responsibility for the interior. It was rich with marble, onyx, and carved oak, and on a large scale: the circular hearthstone of one fireplace measured twenty feet across. Powdered footmen greeted arrivals at the porte-cochère while, in correct feudal style, more liveried servants waited on a bench in the great hall. Altogether Rockwood could be described as "the grandest country residence in America."[2] What it could not be called was "homelike," according to Louisine Havemeyer who visited it. "As we arrived, my husband and I, I looked through the hall and saw Mr. and Mrs. Rockefeller rise and come forward to greet us. The distance was so great that they appeared to lose size and seemed smaller than they should be."[3]

In Cleveland, John D. Rockefeller already possessed a country house on an estate of four hundred acres, Forest Hill (Plate 48), but he had acquired it more or less by default. In 1874 a syndicate of which he was part had built it as a hydropathic sanitarium serviced by its own railroad line. Neither sanitarium nor railroad could be made to pay, so Rockefeller acquired the building for his own use, for a time continuing to run it as a hotel as well as a country house. This was too much of a strain for Rockefeller's wife, Laura, and the building was converted to a summer home in which, finally, they lived all through the year. It was large and roomy, with the multiplicity of porches expected of hotels even more than houses; but it was of little architectural distinction. Rockefeller's interest lay entirely in the estate, where he loved hauling logs and planting trees and watching horses work. He laid out a racetrack and made a lake (Plate 49). Home life, if not house architecture, was intensely important to him. "I feel more than ever . . . the

49. John D. Rockefeller and his wife Laura bathing in the lake on their Forest Hill estate.

50. The old Parson-Wentworth house, bought with the property at Kykuit. John D. Rockefeller had no thought of replacing it until it burned down.

world is full of Sham, Flattery and Deception," he wrote once from New York; "our home is a haven of rest and freedom."[4]

Tarrytown was first thrust upon his consciousness by a persistent local realtor called Hoyt. Pocantico (an Algonquin name meaning stream between hills) appealed to him because of a resemblance to the scenery of Richford, New York, amidst which he had grown up. This bank of the Hudson, with its convenient rail service to the city, had already been colonized by rich New Yorkers: as one local writer put it, "You cannot throw a stone without hitting a millionaire." But Pocantico, inland from the river, was still being farmed when Rockefeller bought it. Initially prices were cheap, though they rose as soon as it was realized who was bidding. With no river frontage, the glory of the place was its superb views from the hilltop: a sixty mile sweep from the bluffs of West Point to the tips of the tallest buildings of New York. John D., Jr., known to his family as Junior and to his father's associates as Mr. Junior, later claimed that his father had always intended to build a house on this hilltop, though this is not borne out by the correspondence. What did immediately engage Rockefeller's attention was the landscaping. A tall observation tower was erected, much to the fascination of the local press; yet again the Olmsted firm, now Olmsted, Olmsted and Eliot, was retained; work went ahead amidst anxieties from Rockefeller that the professionals were fleecing him and that the workforce went home early. Landscaping ultimately extended to removing the houses and rebuilding the village at the gates of the park – an unconscious imitation of the controversial English eighteenth-century practice. Two hotels and a general store – the nucleus of the original scruffy village – were bought up and razed.

There was no hurry to build a house, because Rockefeller had bought several buildings with the land. He was perfectly happy to make one of these his home (Plate 50). Even in his beloved landscaping work he liked to proceed with circumspection. As he wrote to Olmsted's draftsman, Warren Manning, he wished them to feel their "way along, as to what the future will unfold for us."[5] His patience had served him well in his business life. Warmer-blooded associates must sometimes have been disappointed, as they were at Kykuit. But at Kykuit he had the additional restraint of a genuine attachment to his Cleveland home. "After the summer at Forest Hill, I find myself less inclined than when you wrote to enter upon any extensive work at Pocantico Hills," he wrote to Manning in 1896.[6] The cancellation of Manning's retainer at the end of 1897 suggests that his commitment had weakened further.

Then, in 1902, the house that Rockefeller had been using burned. It was a slow-moving fire, started by bad wiring, so that most of the contents were rescued and Junior was able to supervise moving them into another house on the estate. But this lacked the views for which Kykuit had been bought in the first place. It was Junior's trump card. Two months later came the first sign that he had embarked on the long campaign to persuade his father to build a house. In October he approached Chester Aldrich, only thirty-one years old, of Delano and Aldrich, the firm that would inherit the mantle of McKim, Mead and White and Carrère and Hastings as the leading country house practice but was then only just beginning to show promise. Aldrich and Junior remained firmly in league, even if Aldrich's ideas sometimes ran further ahead than Junior knew his father was likely to bear.

It took Junior ten months to summon up courage to present the first sketches to his father. It is understandable that he should have hesitated, given the character of their relationship. Junior was in his late twenties. Brought up among sisters, he had an almost feminine sensitivity to beautiful things. His education was wider than that of his father; but he was painfully shy. He had yet to show any aptitude for business life, his early years in the firm having been blighted by a $1 million swindle perpetrated upon him by the "Wolf of Wall Street," David Lamar. His father, now a dry and aging figure, hiding the baldness caused by alopecia beneath a variety of caps and wigs, had given him little reason to believe that he would rely on his advice. In December Junior wrote sadly to Aldrich saying that Rockefeller had in mind "a very much smaller house than we had contemplated." The horse had been brought to water but who could say if he would drink? "He talks from time to time of building and enjoys studying over his mental picture of a house, but as to whether he will ever take any active steps toward construction I do not know."[7]

Junior was shortly awarded his own chance to build, when Rockefeller gave him the old Kent house on the estate for himself and his wife Abby. Sentimentally renaming it Abeyton Lodge, Junior employed not Aldrich but the less glamorous figure of Duncan Candler, who would later also build the Playhouse and remodel Junior's house in Seal Harbor, Maine. It was not an undertaking that would bode well for Kykuit. At the age of eighteen Rockefeller himself had been told to build a house by his father, as a lesson in self-reliance. The unspoken test was to keep it within the estimates. He succeeded; Junior woefully failed. The estimate approved by Rockefeller had been $21,750. It came in at $33,621.81, with an additional extra of $2,707.70 on the furnishing. Junior's offer to pay the difference was declined, but the experience was not calculated to inspire Rockefeller with confidence in Junior's building ideas. When he did make up his mind to build Kykuit, he initially intended that the Standard Oil executive LaMont Montgomery Bowers, who had previously looked after the construction of the Rockefeller headquarters in Cleveland as well as the running of ore boats, would take charge of all business arrangements.

Junior's resolve may have been hardened in 1905 by the appearance of Ida Tarbell's "character study" of his father which appeared in *McClure's*. This scornful piece of writing specifically called attention to his failure to build a house of taste:

It is fair to judge something of a man's character from his homes – particularly when the man is one who is freed from the necessity of considering cost in building. Mr. Rockefeller's homes force several reflections on one. Certainly they show his cult of the unpretentious. No one of the three houses he occupies has any claim to rank among the notable homes of the country. They are all unpretending even to the point

51. Perspective of the first Kykuit, from the southwest, by the New York architects Delano and Aldrich.

52. The first Kykuit as it appeared in 1909, before the alterations required by Mrs. Rockefeller.

of being conspicuous. Not only that, they show him to have no pleasure in noble architecture, to appreciate nothing of the beauty of fine lines and decorations. Mr. Rockefeller's favorite home, the house at Forest Hill, is a monument of cheap ugliness – a great modern structure built in the first place as a sanitarium; it is amazing that anyone not compelled to do so should live in its shadow. His city house is without distinction, and there has never been an appropriate mansion at Pocantico Hills.[8]

In the current mood of anti-trust fervor one may be sure that, had Rockefeller owned a palace, he would have been savaged for excessive luxury. Nevertheless, the view expressed here to some extent coincided with Junior's own. Nor was it the last time that the theme was voiced. The *Country Calendar*, which visited Pocantico that November, put it more kindly than Miss Tarbell, but made the same point:

> Mr. Rockefeller's house by no means suggests unlimited wealth. He has some eighty tenants at Tarrytown, several of whom live in better dwellings than his own. Up to date, he has built no castellated "mansion," no "Rockefeller Court," no "Pocantico Lodge." . . . "Anything is good enough for me," he replied to a remonstrative friend.[9]

Junior sought only to serve his father well, and one aspect of his burden may have been to protect Rockefeller's reputation.

Rockefeller's own instincts showed themselves when he asked Dunham Wheeler to submit alternative plans for Kykuit. Wheeler, an undistinguished architect, had remodeled Golf House in Lakewood, New Jersey, which Rockefeller had bought in 1901. (While Forest Hill had begun life as a sanitarium, Golf House was originally a club house.) This had been intended to introduce a spirit of competition and thereby save money, but, as so often happens, it in fact caused extra expense. Rockefeller had naïvely imagined that Wheeler would prepare the drawings for nothing, in the hope of getting the commission, but Wheeler presented a bill for $1,600 after failing to win, and Rockefeller had to pay. However, the Golf House did in the end, at Rockefeller's insistence, exert some influence on Kykuit: in the orientation. It had to be "precisely the same, . . . as the sun exposure is satisfactory."[10]

Because Aldrich's original drawings have been lost it is not possible to follow the development of the design in detail. But it is clear from the letters that Rockefeller insisted on major reductions. He also tried to introduce a relaxed note, with a room for lady golfers. Where possible the cost of finishes was pared down. In this, the difference between Rockefeller and his son was partly generational. The spartan Rockefeller, often prepared to make do with what he had at hand, always seeking the most economical solution, carefully regulating how much gas was burned, eliminating waste, stayed true to the priorities of the pioneer. Junior, firm in the belief that the best would also be the cheapest in the long run (and if it was not, he would take it anyway), was a product of the Golden Age, an era in which people could afford quality and expected it.

This can be seen in Junior's ambitious plans for a new laundry. Junior proposed a complex in which every washing eventuality that could occur in either his father's household or his own would be foreseen. It was to be built of stone, like the main house, with a three-bedroom apartment for the laundry manager and his family, five bedrooms for the laundry maids, and an additional four bedrooms in the attic. The working area contained two completely separate laundries, one for each establishment. Six hundred square feet had been allowed for a laundry in the basement of the main house, but the decision to build a separate laundry was sensible, because of the noise. Nevertheless, even though the Kykuit operation serviced washing from the New York house as well, Rockefeller was alarmed at the potential cost and wrote in terms that he might have applied to a shaky business deal:

> I do not feel that we are justified in investing such a large sum of money for a laundry. We have different houses, which bring in only a small or nominal rent, which could be used for this purpose, if need be, including the one occupied by the painter, quite near the proposed laundry site. . . . I confess I am scared, and think we better call a halt. We are not cornered or shut up to this scheme.[11]

Junior got his detached laundry, but it was built of stucco and concrete block rather than stone. There were also fewer bedrooms, though Junior had been right to ask for them: with two hundred people permanently employed on the estate, excluding the contractor's team, accommodation was at a premium.

Work on the main house, excavating the cellar that would also provide the building stone, began in May 1906. Mercifully for Junior, his parents left almost immediately for Europe to visit their daughter, who was dying. They did not return until the house was finished, though the correspondence by letter continued. Bowers became distracted by

53. Aerial view of Kykuit after its second completion, with the addition of an extra story. The Japanese garden is in the foreground, below the formal terraces surrounding the house. The park forms a golf course.

other work and was ousted, leaving Junior in command. It was, oddly, his first major responsibility; it was also the making of him. It helped sharpen that gimlet eye for detail so highly developed in his father, and fostered a deeper understanding of human nature in a well-intentioned but naïve young man. Every faucet and baseboard, it seemed, required a decision; moreover, every change of mind was likely to incur a cost.

The house as finished was certainly a strange enough dwelling for a millionaire, though a work of some ingenuity on the part of the architect. A low, spreading, almost farmhouse-like roof helped the entrance front to seem broader than it really was, and at the back the width was further extended by projecting corner pavilions. These, however, looked extremely awkward on the flank (Plate 52). Tall chimneys seemed to peg the billowing tablecloth of roof to the walls. A wooden veranda ran around two sides of the building. The rear elevation, overlooking the terraces, had a pediment (Plate 51). Dressings were of Indiana limestone; there were attractive shutters to the windows and two rows of dormers in the roof. Otherwise the architecture struggles to rise above the relatively limited dimensions of the house. The entrance front, its roof like a low-browed, felt hat, was particularly underplayed. "For those who expected the palace of a Croesus the house will be a failure," commented *House Beautiful* approvingly (the magazine held no brief for palaces); "there are no columns of porphyry, no elaborate French decorations. In fact the house is not a palace at all. It is just the kind of country place that you or I or any other sane person would have built provided we had the necessary taste and money. The house was designed for comfort rather than show."[12]

Underplayed except in one respect: the hilltop site was magnificent and the most had been made of it, thanks to terracing (Plate 53). With the garden a new star appears in the Kykuit firmament, namely William Welles Bosworth. He was five years older than Junior, had trained first with the architects Shepley, Rutan and Coolidge, then with Frederick Law Olmsted, before traveling in Europe with the editor of the *American Architect*, William R. Ware. Junior believed Bosworth to have "more real genius" than anyone else involved with Kykuit. His garden was designed as a succession of enclosed spaces alternating with stunning open views; progress through it was punctuated by small pieces of architecture and statuary, as well as natural effects like cascades. In other words it was a combination of the Italian and English principles of gardening then in vogue. The eclecticism did not stop there. One of the most successful passages was the Japanese garden. It was formed partly as a means of coping with a boggy stretch of ground, partly to serve as a water hazard for the golf course that surrounded the house. The Rockefellers went so far as to bring over a Japanese carpenter, Uyeda, to build the teahouse in 1909 (though even the cost of this modest structure managed to reach double the estimate). Typically Rockefeller had a different assessment of Bosworth's genius from Junior. "His manner is pleasant," he commented drily; "his method is luxurious."[13]

Inside the house Junior had yet another luminary to deal with, and in many ways he was the most difficult of all. Ogden Codman, co-author with Edith Wharton of *The Decoration of Houses*, was that contradictory mixture, a gentleman decorator. He made his living by decorating; but he felt on terms of equality with his clients and invited Junior to dinner to see his silver ("only, of course," he added tactfully, "yours will be much handsomer").[14] His appointment was bitterly opposed by Delano and Aldrich, who wanted to keep hold of the interior. His careless business methods and endless absences on buying trips in France made the control of costs more tiresome than ever. How far Junior was prepared to lean on his advice can be seen in the freedom that he

54. The entrance front of Kykuit. Though narrow, it is enriched by a sculptural pediment and ribbon-like panels of carved stone.

gave him to purchase country house clutter in the form of "clocks, ornaments, tidies and inkwells and other things" for the bedroom chimneypieces. One might have expected that these little bits and pieces would most show the personality of the family, as opposed to that of the decorator. Paradoxically, though, it was in the larger things that Junior was his own master. Unlike his father, he enjoyed beautiful objects: he once accomplished the incredible feat of persuading Rockefeller to buy him some Chinese porcelain for $1 million. Shopping with Abby for antiques, mostly Georgian carved wood, was a pleasure. But it was to bring with it the painful lesson that furniture may not always be what it appears. The letter that he was compelled to write to Messrs. Koopman and Company of Boston is one of many to similar firms:

> I have [had] all of the furniture which I have been collecting for the past two years examined by the two best furniture experts in New York, both of whom you know well. They find among the collection of things which I have purchased from you some eight or ten lots which are either entirely new or else largely new. I am returning herewith the bill that you may have an opportunity of correcting the prices accordingly.[15]

It would have been sensible to have taken more professional advice. But the younger Rockefeller's own strong preferences explain why the Kykuit rooms – light, fresh, chintz-draped, Georgian, with soberly elegant Chinese porcelains on every surface – are different from the colder, more studiously formal look of Codman's other work, often in the French taste. When the work was over there was a suggestion that Codman may have thought that Junior and Abby were getting on with the job a little too easily. "Yours of the 14th reached me yesterday," he wrote from Paris on 26 September 1908,

55. Conversion of the horsebarn at Kykuit to house motorcars. With some regret, the Rockefellers accepted the inevitability of the automobile in 1907.

and I am delighted that you find the house so satisfactory. I wish I were there to help you arrange the furniture, pictures, etc. I should enjoy doing so very much, as in that way I am often able to give the rooms I decorate the air of livableness I like my own rooms to have; but there will be plenty of time to see just what the rooms lack, and I shall have many suggestions to make.[16]

Ultimately, however, it was not Codman who had to be pleased with Kykuit, but Rockefeller. And not just he – also a figure whom both he and all the other participants in the drama seem to have overlooked, his wife. Between them Rockefeller and Junior could hardly have taken greater care to ensure that the Kykuit project was carried through as successfully as any of their business undertakings. Every detail had been considered, weighed, discussed. To some extent it is understandable that Laura had no part in these conferences: she had been ill and Rockefeller had wished to spare her any involvement with the exhausting detail of the plans. Consequently her first intimation of what her new house would be came when she visited it. Her reaction was one of instant dislike. Whereas Rockefeller had been at pains to reduce all unnecessary expenditure and keep down the scale, to Laura's wifely eye it was simply too cramped. Because the Rockefellers did not entertain lavishly, the main rooms were adequate; but Laura expected something better for her guests than the meager bedrooms allowed them in the attic. The second floor hall was not, she believed, a proper place to have closets; and her own boudoir and sitting room were too small. She won her point. It was decided to take off the old, low-sweeping roof, raise the walls a story, and construct a new mansard roof. At the same time the entrance front (Plate 54) was built up, destroying the balance of the proportions. The old veranda of wood, a material specifically requested by Rockefeller, as he liked the lightness, was replaced by a loggia of stone. It all made nonsense of Rockefeller's economies.

It also had the effect of turning Kykuit into a much more imposing house. Aldrich had the indignity of having to work with Bosworth in executing the changes, and to increase his embarrassment, the original idea for the alteration came from Codman. The entrance front, now tall and cliff-like, was given a handsome sculptured pediment by Tonetti. Long thin panels of carving were hung like streamers either side of the central window. The porte-cochère was replaced with a glass canopy held up by opulent wrought-iron brackets. It was even decided to hide the service court by burying it underground. (This was the one part of the rebuilding that caught Rockefeller's imagination: he set to with a

58

will, supervising the operations personally, without an architect.) Such an aesthetic battleground as Kykuit could not be a complete success. The entrance front is too tall for the forecourt. With no sweep of roof or soaring chimneys to give balance, the side elevations seem long and awkward. Despite the years of careful thought, not all details had been considered: for instance there was no ready way to deliver coal to the furnaces, which meant much back-breaking labor for the employees of the estate carrying it in sacks. But today these defects seem lost in the splendor of the larger conception, in which site, landscape, garden, statuary, and architecture form a rare whole.

The cost? Ironically it came very near the $1 million that the *Tarrytown Argus* had predicted. When Junior mentioned this in a letter of 1908, his father was incredulous. "Is there not some mistake about the possible cost of the new house and the grounds!" he replied.[17] There was no error. In the course of time he became reconciled to an extravagance that contradicted the ingrained habits of a lifetime. But his point of view remained, at bottom, significantly at odds with that of Junior. Far from being concerned that people might think of him as living too frugally for a man in his position, he feared that extravagance at Kykuit would further provoke his critics. He wrote in 1910: "I would not want the public to know what our expenditure has been."

Junior's final judgment of the house was more complex. Just as the architecture of Kykuit was a compromise between divergent forces, so the spirit of it reconciled the two conceptions of the American country house. Many years later he summed up what he felt had been his achievement at the house:

> I frequently said to the architects and decorator that my ideal for the house was to have it so apparently simple that any friends visiting Father, coming from however humble houses, would be impressed with the homeliness and simplicity of the house; while those who were familiar with beautiful things and appreciated fine design would say, "how exquisitely beautiful!" That was the result obtained.[18]

If Kykuit was a compromise, it still had its influence on American culture. It has been argued that it was Junior's training ground, enabling him to assume responsibilities within his father's empire for which he would previously not have been equipped or trusted. No sooner had building work finished than the Colorado coal strike broke like a storm around his head. More specifically, Kykuit fired him with that passion for building which ultimately fathered The Cloisters, the Jackson Hole National Monument, Colonial Williamsburg, and Rockefeller Center. At another level Kykuit has acted as a nucleus for the Rockefeller family, or some of it, preserving a vital dynastic spirit. It was a phenomenon unique to the American country house that sometimes several full-blown houses were grouped together on a single estate (see chapter 6). In Pocantico Hills three of Junior's four sons – John D. Rockefeller III, Nelson, and Laurence – continued to live in the Rockefeller compound or close by. John D. III and Laurence built houses, while Nelson, in Kykuit, brought to the grounds a Marcel Breuer guest house and a startling collection of modern sculpture. Whether Junior's sensitivity to public image paid dividends is less certain. The public has always been permitted to explore the majority of the estate, with its woods and its wildlife. But it was not long before the park itself, where the houses are located, had to be fenced and patrolled. No magazine article was published to celebrate the second completion of Kykuit. Nor has any been since. Only now that it has passed to the National Trust for Historic Preservation can one look forward to the time, however far away, when the public will see the fruits of so much agony expended for its sake.

INSPIRATIONS

We are gaining ground in our domestic architecture when we follow our English cousins, just as we make our country life more rational when we plan it on English lines.

Horace Allison
in *Country Life in America*
1 October 1911

"One American thing we do stick to – real central heating! Maybe won't be as swell as some of these castles, but lot more comfy all right!"

Sinclair Lewis
Dodsworth

56. Meet of the Radnor Hunt at Ardrossan, Pennsylvania, painted by Charles Morris Young in 1925. Private Collection

Country Life

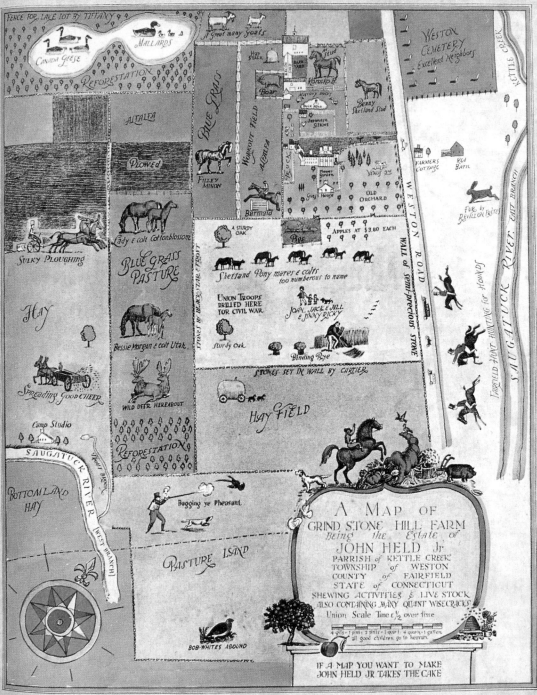

A MAP OF
GRIND STONE HILL FARM
Being the Estate of
JOHN HELD Jr
PARRISH of KETTLE CREEK
TOWNSHIP of WESTON
COUNTY of FAIRFIELD
STATE of CONNECTICUT
SHEWING ACTIVITIES & LIVE STOCK
ALSO CONTAINING MANY QUAINT WISECRACKS
Union Scale Time & ½ over time

4 gills = 1 pint; 2 pints = 1 quart; 4 quarts = 1 gallon,
all good children go to heaven

IF A MAP YOU WANT TO MAKE
JOHN HELD JR TAKES THE CAKE

June 1929 ~ Price 50 Cents

Doubleday, Doran & Co. Inc.

"As nearly as such a thing is possible in the Republic"

THE ENGLISH COUNTRY GENTLEMAN STYLE

BY THE TIME Kykuit was built the architect had come to experience, in classic form, the dilemma of the twentieth century, multiplicity of choice. It would not be long before *Town and Country* could write blithely about a Virginia House in New Jersey, a Cape Dutch House in Santa Barbara, a French Farmhouse in Connecticut, a Tudor House on Lake St. Clair, an Anglo-French House in Texas, and a version of Groombridge Place, Kent, on Long Island. "Our house was supposed to be a Norman villa," wrote Arthur Meeker, son of the owner of Arcady Farm in Lake Forest. "At least Mr. Heun, who built it, said so; we trustfully believed him. (On my first trip to France I searched with rising dismay for anything like it.)"[1] It was easy enough for architects to miss the spirit of the houses they were imitating. But that did nothing to dampen the enthusiasm with which they sought out foreign sources of inspiration, transplanting individual motifs with an ever growing accuracy, even pedantry.

For now virtually the whole world lay, if not at the architect's feet, at least on his library shelves. The reason for this was the boom in architectural publishing that took place from the late nineteenth century, inspired by the development of new techniques for printing photographs. Traditionally, an architect's education included some period of travel, during which he sketched copiously. In his subsequent career his sketchbooks would serve as a primary source of reference. This practice continued, but now his first-hand observations were supplemented by splendid folio volumes in which it seemed that every style and period was represented. These generously proportioned books with their full-page photographic plates did not entirely displace the older volumes of engravings beside which they often found themselves. However, they offered a considerably wider geographical and historical scope. Forward-looking architects paid equal attention to the magazines that, also printing photographs, showed recent work in America and overseas.

The library of the architect David Adler, whose Georgian mansions Meeker regarded (unlike Arcady Farm) as "austerely perfect," was typical of many:

> [It] included the vast "White Pine Series" of early American houses in its entirety, as well as the Asher Benjamins, Abraham Swans, William Pains, and Batty Langleys, to which the early American houses owed virtually everything. It had, of course, the major works on the English Georgian, Regency, and Adam styles, a collection on

57. Cover from *Country Life in America*, June 1929, showing some of the activities that took place on an American estate.

58. Hood of a Queen Anne doorcase illustrated in *The Smaller English House of the Later Renaissance, 1660–1830* by A.E. Richardson and H. Donaldson Eberlein, 1925, and the doorcase at Castle Hill, Massachusetts, which is based on it. The house as a whole is a cross between Belton House in Lincolnshire and Ham House in Surrey.

French châteaus and *manoirs* from Henri II to Louis XVI, and many volumes on Italian villas and gardens.[2]

That these books were well used can be seen from Castle Hill, the Crane house outside Boston. While the roofline is closely modeled on Honington Hall in Warwickshire, and the garden front on Ham House in Surrey, the doorcase (Plate 58) is quoted from a less familiar building illustrated in *The Smaller English House of the Later Renaissance, 1660–1830*. Not that books provided every morsel that a precedent-hungry architect needed to devour. In addition to the library, Adler amassed a huge collection of postcards of the buildings he had visited.

What was sauce for the architect-goose was also sauce for the client-gander. On two occasions Adler successfully fled the office when Cyrus H. McCormick appeared with a copy of Banister Fletcher's *A History of Architecture* in his hand. Thus equipped, McCormick felt himself just as able to quarry the architecture of the past as Adler. Occasionally, however, an architect was happy to enter into his client's enthusiams. "I have, as you know, a number of books about gardens, or showing gardens; at least I had," wrote James Deering of Vizcaya to Paul Chalfin. "It only at this moment occurs to me that you may have taken some of them."[3] Sometimes the architect had no choice. Though Henry E. Huntington was content to leave the detail of the San Marino Ranch, his new house in Pasadena and the future Huntington Art Gallery, to the professionals ("the style of architecture proposed when your Mr. Hunt was here, I think will be satisfactory," he wrote in February 1908), he had strong ideas of his own about the general form. He sent Myron Hunt and Elmer Grey a rough sketch that he had drawn himself, adding that he did not "want any material changes made in the plans."[4]

With so much to choose from, what made client or architect settle on any one style? Of course many never did, since they mixed several styles together within the same building. "Take, for instance, that minaret business on the west," the newly rich builder of a country seat exclaims in Winston Churchill's novel *The Celebrity*; "I picked it up from a mosque in Algiers. The oriel just this side is whole cloth from Haddon Hall, and the galleried porch next it from a Florentine villa." And so on. This satire would have had more point in the 1870s than in 1898 when *The Celebrity* was published. While owners, such as this one, sometimes got out of hand, architects had come to frown upon such uninhibited eclecticism. They not only had strict ideas about history but about which historical style could be used where. In this, landscape was held to be a major determinant. Conventional wisdom had it that certain styles suited particular types of countryside better than others, and some of the rules were perfectly straightforward and sensible. "Generally speaking, the formal Colonial and English styles harmonise best with the comparatively level site and the drooping fluffiness of deciduous trees," wrote Charles Hooper. "Rough, rugged sites . . . demand an irregular design of considerable force and strength – the rough stone wall would do very well."[5] But it was possible to make too much of the landscape influence. It could be used to justify almost anything, even, according to Porter Garnett, the building of an Elizabethan manor house in California because of the "more or less English character of the landscape due to the presence of so many stately oaks."[6]

In some cases a particular style had a special resonance for the client. In Delaware, family history turned Alfred I. du Pont to Louis Seize at Nemours: the du Ponts had gained honors at the French court before emigrating to America in 1799. The house Chelsea, at Muttontown on Long Island, was built shortly after the owners had returned from a long trip to the Orient. "We saw a house on the Upper Yangtze River," remembered Alexandra McKay many years later. "It was white with a black roof and had cattle in the courtyard and water around the corner. We decided right then and there that we wanted to try to reproduce that."[7] But not all stylistic tastes can be explained so simply. It is not known, for instance, why another Mrs. Mackay, the wife of Clarence H. Mackay, had such decided views about the style of Harbor Hill, but she did. In July 1899 she got down to work on the plans and asked Stanford White to send her express "some books about, and drawings of, Louis XIV chateaux. Very severe styles preferred."[8]

Perhaps the commonest course was for the owner to model his idea on what he took to be the English conception of the country house. This would have caused no surprise to those who, like W. J. Ghent, believed that it was "well known that our seignorial class founds its practices and canons (excepting only the canon regarding persons engaged in trade) upon English precedents."[9] One such seigneur was Hamilton Twombly, who married a Vanderbilt and had a very large house, Florham, built in New Jersey (Plate 59). "Twombly wants a house on the order of an English Country gentleman," wrote William R. Mead, of McKim, Mead and White, to his friend Frank Millet. "I don't think he knows exactly what he means, and I am sure I don't."[10] However, since Twombly was "the sort of man, who, if he gets what he wants, is willing to pay liberally for it," an English country gentleman house must have been what he thought he had. In its details Florham is strongly influenced by Wren, though in shape and proportion it is unlike any seventeenth-century English country house. When Frederick W. Vanderbilt's house in the Hudson River Valley was pulled down, Mead found that Mrs. Vanderbilt, who was

Twombly's sister-in-law, had similar leanings. As he wrote to his partner McKim, then in Egypt, she "kicked over the traces, and was disposed to build an English house, as she called it."[11]

In outward appearance the Vanderbilt house, Hyde Park, turned out to be much less English than French, but that hardly mattered. Style as such was not the dominant consideration in these so-called English houses. Much more important was the flavor of the place – how it felt, the kind of life that it seemed meant to serve. This life was, for many owners, bound up with a host of recreational activities that were still relatively unfamiliar in the United States. They included shooting driven game, breeding pedigree herds, playing polo, racing, yachting, and pursuing the "grand old sport of cross-country riding to hounds."[12] To this list could be added gardening and, for some, buying English pictures from Duveen. There was thought to be something worth imitating in the largely outdoor life of the English upper classes, whose habits and occupations had evolved over several centuries of settled affluence. "The people in England live more nearly the kind of life we lead, having made the most thorough study, and having the greater knowledge of comfort and beauty, combined in country living," wrote the Philadelphian country house architect Wilson Eyre.[13]

Sometimes the English ways were imported wholesale, in a manner very different from the sensitive romanticism of Wilson Eyre. "I have come to help Mr. Barber make

60. The drawing room at Ardrossan: a needlepoint picture by Mrs. Robert L. Montgomery executed in the 1920s.

59. Hamilton McK. Twombly's Florham, New Jersey, built by McKim, Mead and White in 1890–1900. William R. Mead wrote to the artist Frank Millet: "Twombly wants a house on the order of an English Country gentleman."

61. English planting in the Walled Garden at Old Westbury, the Phipps house on Long Island built for Jay S. Phipps and his English wife, Margarita Grace, in 1904–07.

62. Thatched garden building at Old Westbury. The family visited England every year and chose an English connoisseur and architect, George Crawley, to design the house.

this new home of his as English as it can be made," announced Herbert Morgan, Ohio Columbus Barber's house manager at Anna Dean Farm (named after Barber's daughter, Anna Laura, and his son-in-law, Arthur Dean Bevan). Morgan had been discovered in a hotel lobby by the *Beacon Journal*, reading an English paper and smoking "vile American tobacco." "I and my boys arrived here a short time ago at the instance of Mr. Barber. He has succeeded admirably in erecting a mansion that has considerable of the English in its architecture, even though it is not as pretentious as many English homes."[14] With their common language and often common heritage, Americans were likely to feel more comfortable with influences from England than from other European nations. They felt rather too comfortable at times, as when Matlack Price expressed the belief, apropos the work of Dwight James Baum, that English architecture seems "a thing that racially belongs to us more than any of the Latin styles." Like some aspects of the Colonial Revival this symbolized a closing of Anglo-Saxon ranks against the great numbers of immigrants from other countries who had arrived in the late nineteenth century.[15]

Owners were even more likely to be familiar with England and English ways than were their architects. Some traveled to Europe every year, and it was quite possible that they had daughters or friends who had married into English families. By 1915 no fewer than four hundred and fifty-four American women had married European aristocrats, according to the New York publication *Titled Americans*; and of course there were many unions with families not ennobled. Americans traveling in England were a common sight. Seated at Eaton Hall near Liverpool, where the transatlantic liners docked, the Duke of Westminster had a large equestrian statue by Watts erected in the forecourt of his house partly, as he wrote, to give these visitors an uplifting first impression of the country.

To most observers social conditions in the two countries seemed widely different, largely because, it was generally said, the United States had no leisure class. Not everyone shared this view, however, and W.J. Ghent elaborated the theory, described in his book *Our Benevolent Feudalism* of 1902, that American millionaires were developing into a baronial caste. Implicit to the argument of Thorstein Veblen's *The Theory of the Leisure Class*, first published in 1899, was the existence of a class of people "that has been consistently exempt from work and from pecuniary cares for a generation or more" and which was "now large enough to form and sustain an opinion in matters of taste."[16] Veblen never defined the exact character or extent of the leisure class: presumably it was one of the things that "direct observation or common notoriety" would have made

63. Leadwork bust and old roses at Old Westbury.

obvious to contemporaries. Certainly this view is supported by some of the gossip-writing of the hour which suggests that a growing number of people had the time and money to cultivate a style of life self-consciously based on that of the English gentleman. By virtue of its leisure this world had little direct influence on the destiny of the nation, so it has not been much studied by historians. But an insight into both its members and its values is given by *Fads and Fancies of Representative Americans at the Beginning of the Twentieth Century*, published by Colonel William Mann's scandal sheet *Town Topics* in 1905. Since *Fads and Fancies* was sold at $1,500 a copy and presumably bought only by the society figures who appeared in it, the text is hardly probing; rather, the men whom it features are shown in what they must have felt to be their most favorable light. Pride of place went to Colonel Astor of Ferncliff at Rhinebeck, in New York.

"Of the typical American gentleman of the first years of the Twentieth Century," announced the text,

> the " Master of Ferncliff" affords as admirable example as a wide knowledge of men and the times can choose. . . . What with the breeding stables established by his father, his droves of rare cattle, flocks of sheep, acres of fertile meadow and woodland, his gardens and his orchard, he approaches the English squire as nearly as such a thing is possible in the Republic that he loves.

Though the Colonel was described as personally overseeing every detail of the Astor empire, he had got this down to a fine art, for apparently it did not occupy more than a few hours a day for a few days a year. For the rest he was able to devote himself to a migratory pattern of life, rotating between the various houses that he owned or had access to. It was a pattern typical of many country house owners, who often possessed several places which they visited according to the seasons. William C. Whitney, for instance, owned no fewer than five country houses, his property including a house and five thousand acre estate in the Wheatley Hills of Long Island; a house, race track, and three hundred acres at Sheepshead Bay; a mansion at Lenox, Massachusetts, with seven hundred acres; nearby, the whole of October Mountain, used as a game farm; an Adirondack camp and game preserve; a large horse farm in Kentucky; and a two thousand acre estate at Aiken, South Carolina.[17]

Astor's year opened in New York City, where he had been since the Horse Show in November. Around Ash Wednesday he set off for a month's shooting at Aiken, South Carolina, or visited Florida, returning to Rhinebeck-on-Hudson in early spring. "It was on the Astor estate there, Ferncliff, that he was born, and there he always puts in a few weeks before running over to Europe in the Summer." By August he was at Newport, where he either leased somewhere for the season or stayed with his mother or his mother-in-law, both of whom had cottages. But his heart, it was emphasized, remained at Ferncliff – though even when he was there he was easily able to visit the city once a week.

Several dozen American gentlemen are described in *Fads and Fancies*, and nearly every one was presented – or had himself presented, since this was a subscription book – as a figure of the Colonel Astor breed, at home in his country house and his rural pursuits. For James Montaudert Waterbury, who inherited an estate at Westchester on the death of his merchant father, "country life and sports" had always been a hobby. The Westchester house had been made into "an ideal rural place" and the Waterburys entertained generously, on one notable occasion organizing an amateur circus in the covered riding school (for several weeks "men and women of New York's smart set rehearsed and practiced daily for the performances"). Howard Willets lived for the greater part of the year on his beautifully wooded, hundred and sixty acre estate of Gedney Farm at White Plains, outside New York City. "The tendency to desert the town for the pleasures of a country life, which has been a marked feature of American social development in recent years, finds abundant justification [in him]. . . . Inheriting a name that gave him an assured social position, and also a fortune more than ample to maintain it fittingly, all careers were open to him." None of them was sufficiently tempting, however, and Willets preferred instead "to be an American country gentleman, whose life is active and wholesome and whose home is a social center for the countryside."

The attractions of such a life were championed in other literature of the time. Doubleday, Page and Company were the first to seize on the commercial possibilities of country subjects, and they brought forth a steady stream of titles on gardening, amateur farming, crafts, and architecture from the 1890s on. So successful did they become that in 1910 they built a large printing plant called the Country Life Press in eighteen acres of landscaped grounds, complete with a collection of rare irises, in the significantly named Garden City suburb on Long Island. One of the Doubleday enterprises had been to bring out *Country Life in America* from 1901 (Plate 57). There can be little doubt that this was closely copied from the successful British publication *Country Life*, which had begun four years earlier. Whereas the British magazine was, and is, a weekly, *Country Life in America* (which ceased publication during the Second World War) appeared every month. Perhaps because it was more difficult to attract national real estate advertising in so big a country as the United States, there was somewhat less emphasis on country houses and rather more on what the city dweller could do to set himself up in the country. In its early years it seems to have been a success. It "began its career at a fortunate time when a widespread interest in country living was growing up, an interest which has constantly increased as the automobile has made the country accessible as a place in which to live," remembered a company history, *The Country Life Press*, published in 1919. "The magazine has tried to be an interpreter of the taste and beauty that is more and more an attribute of American country homes. It has been at the same time a recorder of the awakening interest in Nature."[18] Some of the early photographs of hummingbirds and caribou were regarded as pioneering examples of their art. Doubleday also published *Garden Magazine*, which "came into being coincident with a widespread gardening movement."

The country gentleman ideal lasted into the 1930s. It was encapsulated in a series that *Country Life in America* started in 1934 entitled "Full-length Portrait of a Country Gentleman." This featured, among others, Gerald M. Livingston of Long Island and Thomasville, Georgia, master of one of the few basset packs in America; the owner, rider, trainer, and breeder of bloodstock, Frederick "Brose" Clark of Long Island and Cooperstown, New York; Richard King Mellon of Rolling Rock, banker and "votary of out-of-door pursuits"; and the amateur jockey, polo international, and Master of Fox Hounds, James Watson Webb of Shelburne, Vermont. First in the series was Marshall Field III who was photographed in tweeds, in polo gear, and clambering onto an airplane (Plate 65). There was no doubt about the origin of the influences that formed his taste. As the first caption announced: "The Marshall Field conception of a country gentleman is English, and the Marshall Field accent is English. He has made a business out of being a country gentleman. His interest in horses is such that he often gets up and watches them exercise before breakfast."[19] His Long Island estate of Caumsett, comprising two thousand acres of Lloyd's Point near Oyster Bay (Plate 64), personified what might be called the English Country Gentleman style.

65. Marshall Field III, sportsman and the owner of the 2,000 acre Caumsett estate on Long Island.

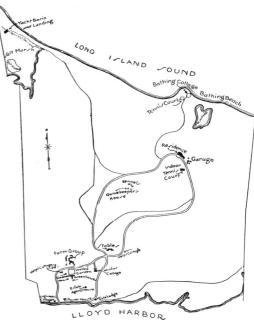

66. Plan of the Caumsett estate. The house and the sports buildings are grouped to the north; the working buildings can be seen clustered around the gatelodge to the south.

Field was the grandson of the founder of the famous Chicago store – an indomitable, self-made figure whose pitiless standards of achievement probably had much to do with the suicide of Marshall Field, Jr., when Field was a boy of twelve. This death was followed two months later by that of Marshall Field himself. Though his fortune was tied up in trusts, Field was now, as the newspapers widely called him, the Richest Boy in the World. Predictably, given the early years spent under his grandfather's austere shadow, he gave himself over to pleasure-seeking at the earliest opportunity: to some degree "country gentleman" can be read as a euphemism for "playboy."

But Field was not merely imitating the trappings of a foreign way of life. He knew England thoroughly, part of his education having been at Eton and Cambridge; and when he created Caumsett from 1921 to 1926, his wife of the time was an English-woman, the former Mrs. Dudley Coats. The intention at Caumsett was "to create an estate similar to those found in England, where, being without benefit of country club, the landed gentry are in the habit of developing their own places so as to make them practically self sufficient."[20] With his grandfather's blood in his veins, it was Field's nature to throw himself into everything that he did, to the limits of his capacity. Consequently, though he eventually tired of agriculture and turned instead to the publication of a surprisingly radical newspaper that tormented those of his friends who had not yet broken free of the country gentleman mold, Caumsett was a remarkable ensemble, more complete than many of its English inspirations and, unlike some of them, assembled within one generation.

It was intended that, as the visitor approached, his sensations should be those of one drawing near an English stately home. Pheasants scattered as he followed the drive to the house, the first hint of which was a slate roof seen above a bank of uncut grass. Up a rise, and then the whole house appeared, behind an expanse of lawn dotted with great trees (Plate 67). John Russell Pope, who designed the house, had clearly spent some time studying his books of Caroline architecture, since the obvious model is Belton (see Plate

64. From the roof of Caumsett, looking out over Long Island Sound. Yachting and bathing were important activities.

159). Great trouble was taken to find the right brick. The one chosen was a buff color mottled with pink, but it has to be said that this careful attention to materials was not enough to give vitality to a rather lifeless academic design. It may reflect Field's priorities that the main house is perhaps the least endearing of Caumsett's buildings. There are, however, many others.

In the immediate vicinity of the house stand the tennis house, to enable play during bad weather and at night, and the garage. The latter is a deceptive building. With three double doors it looks not much bigger than average when first seen, but it is in fact constructed on two levels and can accommodate twenty cars. Behind is a house for the chauffeurs of Field's guests – one of twenty-odd staff houses on the estate. The drive to the north of the main house leads to the bathing beach. The "bathing cottage," a charming Cape Cod structure, contained sitting room and dressing rooms, and had a shady veranda looking out over the water. Since he employed a staff of eighty-five, Field felt it necessary to designate two more beaches, each with bathing hut, one for indoor and one for outdoor help.

Going south from the main house the drive loops around the kennels and game-

67. The house as it first comes into view on the entrance drive. The setting was made as much like an English park as possible.

keeper's house. One of the gamekeeper's responsibilities was rearing birds for the driven pheasant shoots that were Field's greatest sporting pleasure. The woods were cut with "shooting rides" – long vistas that served both for shooting and for horseback riding, being laid out with hedges of brush to form jumps.

With the stables, for polo ponies and hunters, began the working end of the estate. They are planned around a courtyard, which is entered by an arch. The style is early Georgian, with inevitable stable cupola, though two gable ends project somewhat discordantly in the Dutch-influenced manner of half a century before. The farm group included barns for cattle, horses, farm equipment, and hay, not to mention manager's office, silo, and fire station. It was provided with spick and span functional architecture, clapboarded, and with a minimum of Georgian detailing (Plate 68). For this, Pope joined forces with the farm specialist Alfred Hopkins, and the result is perhaps the most attractive architecture on the estate. On the other side of the drive are the walled garden and greenhouses. Field himself was not particularly interested in gardening, but such was his drive to excel at everything that he even expected his crysanthemums to win prizes.

68. The farmbuildings at Caumsett, designed by the leading architect of the "barn group," Alfred Hopkins.

When the main house was shut up for the winter the Fields used a "cottage" for weekends (Plate 69). Being of comparatively modest size, it is in the Philadelphia Colonial style – more intimate than the English manner of the main house. Walls of rough gray fieldstone were soon ivy-clad, and the whole house nestled back among the trees and rhododendrons of a woodland garden. The engineer's cottage was also Colonial: the doorway was reproduced from an old house near Port Jefferson. This, the power house, and the gatelodge stand on the south edge of the estate, overlooking Lloyd Harbor.

As guests left Caumsett it may have struck them that they had been offered every sport except golf. Indeed, as *Country Life in America* graphically put it, were the ultimate horror to have befallen Long Island and every sports club been closed, Field's weekend guests would have survived with scarcely an inkling of deprivation:

69. The Marshall Fields' "winter cottage," used for family visits when the main house was shut up.

CONDUCTED BY LINDSAY GLEN

FOLLOWING IN THE SPORTSMAN'S FOOTSTEPS

IF "IT takes nine tailors to make a man" as has been averred, it takes only one to make a smart sportswoman, if she is wise enough to choose the right one.

Any one who can hang a bit of chiffon effectively can build an evening gown, but the turning out of a properly appointed sportswoman needs

OUTFITTING A SOCIAL TRAMP

THE lure of even a civilized camp in the Adirondacks is supreme, if only as a base of supplies for the rough tent life away off in the deep of the forest," a weary man was overheard to remark.

"It is all a fallacy" he went on, "the idea that we were freer and less hampered because we came equipped with only a new gun or the best

70. Heading from *Country Life in America*, September 1915. "The turning out of a properly appointed sportswoman needs careful selection," ran the text.

[They] would still have their choice of indoor and outdoor tennis, riding, pheasant shooting, skeet shooting, polo, trout fishing, a spin in a Loening amphibian, and playing with three Abyssinian jackasses – the latter being the gift of a grateful friend to whom Mr. Field (a licensed pilot) once gave an airplane lift in the Belgian Congo. They would still have a private beach to bathe on, the steam cruiser, *Corisande*, to cruise on; and twenty-five miles to drive over – with a choice of seven or eight automobiles. If all the flowers in every florist shop in town should curl up and die, and if all the milk in all the dairy shops should curdle, the Field house would still be bright with Orchids, and there would still be cream in the Field coffee, thanks to a fine herd of one hundred reliable Guernseys.[21]

It was all thoroughly English – or was it? The American note, shrewdly observed by the magazine, was the frantic determination with which Field set about even leisure activities. "An excellent all-round athlete, he may sandwich in half a dozen sports in one day, going from riding to golf to skeet shooting as if he were attending so many directors' meetings." Speed and success were equal passions. Also American, commented *Country Life in America*, was his continuing personal involvement in the $300 million Marshall Field business, which ultimately kept Caumsett going.

Given the importance of England as a model for the American country house, it is not surprising that houses of an English type should have been popular. In this, as we have seen, Englishness did not depend only on architecture. On the face of it there could have been nothing less English than the style of Samuel Colt's flamboyant Armsmear, but, as the *Art Journal* explained in 1876, one should not be deceived by superficial appearances:

There is no doubt it is [a] little Turkish, among other things on one side, for it has domes, pinnacles, and light lavish ornamentation, such as oriental taste delights in. . . . Yet, although the villa is Italian and cosmopolitan, the feeling is English. It is an English home in its substantiality, its home-like and comfortable aspect.[22]

This was before architects had begun to take their eclecticism seriously. But when, from 1890 onwards, they did start to place greater value on historical correctness, it was precisely for these "home-like and comfortable" qualities that the English styles were repeatedly praised.

"It is right that we should turn to England for our precedence, for England is a country of homes, and in England more than in any other country we recognize the fulfilment of our ideals of what home life means," wrote R. Clipston Sturgis, in defence of the Tudor style.[23] Where an American would attempt to build a palace, with giant Corinthian columns and plenty of carving, the Englishman, it was claimed by one author, would spend the same amount to achieve "a simple, quiet, modest cottage."[24] This preference for the cottage over the palace accorded well with the generation after Richard Morris Hunt who felt increasingly that the essence of good breeding lay in quietness and reserve.

This aspect of the country gentleman style had been defined by Barr Ferree as early as 1905: "it is not assertive, it demands no attention, it does not seek comment, but it has the distinguished air of the *grande seigneur*, the thorough gentleman who knows how to dress and behave himself, and who conducts his affairs in a thoroughly gentlemanly fashion." Reticence came to be even more highly valued after the First World War when the Cotswold manor, Normandy farmhouse, and Italian villa styles – all adapted from models that were much smaller than Elizabethan prodigy houses or Loire chateaux – became popular. Not, of course, that every country house owner sacrificed the comforts of scale. Those who did not, faced the challenge of how to build generously without appearing to do so. In 1923 *House Beautiful* wrote enthusiastically about a New Jersey country house under the title "A Large House that Looks Small."[25] Two years later the same journal described a house on Cape Cod whose owners were so anxious to look as though they were not there at all that they had made it out of a series of old cottages joined together.[26] One of the attractions of the Elizabethan style employed at Applegarth on Oyster Bay, Long Island, was that "no other form so lends itself to the achievement of size without conspicuousness."[27]

The details of Elizabethan and Tudor houses were just as carefully researched as those of David Adler's classical buildings. Before embarking on Stan Hywet outside Akron, Frank A. Seiberling, the busy co-founder of the Goodyear Tire and Rubber Company, still found time to go to England with his wife, daughter, and the architect Charles Schneider, head of the Cleveland office of George B. Post and Son. From Compton Wynyates, the most widely imitated of all Tudor houses, they derived the entrance composition of tower and porch. Later Schneider felt compelled to make a distinction between his work and the Duncan house at Newport, also based on Compton Wynyates. "Mr. Pope, the architect, has taken the main entrance straight, whereas I was only willing to be impressed by it when designing your house," he wrote when sending Seiberling some architectural magazines. "Perhaps you will think that Mr. Pope is more successful and got more out of it than I did, but I prefer not to take things too straight."[28] The interior, including the Great Hall (Plate 71), was largely inspired by Ockwells Manor, where the Seiberlings also bought furniture; they acknowledged their debt to this and other houses by hanging the romantic nineteenth-century prints from Joseph Nash's *Mansions of England in the Olden Time*, peopled with figures in costume, around the walls. Straight or not, Schneider continued to study the best examples of English work for every detail of the house long after his return to America. "I think the effect [achieved] by the use of brick piers instead of wooden posts will be very beautiful and is somewhat after the work done in English gardening," he wrote in 1916. "I have looked over the books in my library and find many examples of pergolas and arbors." Indeed an impression of Englishness was achieved as much in the setting as in the house itself. The rural quality of the estate was emphasized by the landscape gardener Warren Manning by bringing in the entrance drive through an orchard of apple trees, then

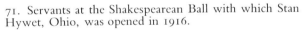
71. Servants at the Shakespearean Ball with which Stan Hywet, Ohio, was opened in 1916.

72. A dirigible over Stan Hywet, the home of Franklin A. Seiberling, founder of the Goodyear Tire and Rubber Company.

opening the principal axis of the house to a spacious view of the gentle, wooded Cuyahoga Hills.

Equally exact precedents were found for the design of Applegarth on Long Island. A balustrade was copied from St. Fagin's Castle in Wales, the porch was based on the "baptistry" of Canterbury Cathedral, the dining room reproduced the robing room at Chartres Cathedral (except for the ceiling, which imitated the Queen's Bedchamber at Knole), and even the brackets to some of the windows were copied from ones at Hampton Court. But sometimes, as here, devotion to period went further than strictly architectural form, for "it was useless to expect any impatient American to wait placidly through the long years required to give the gray-golden bloom of 'weathered' wood."[29] However carefully based on old sources, work that looked new inevitably failed to capture the charm of the originals on which it was based, because it lacked the "soft tints" of age.

Various expedients were used to overcome this unfortunate attribute of the Elizabethan style in America (Plate 74). The builders of Applegarth tried soaking English walnut shells (why English?) in alcohol to create a wash that could then be painted onto the oak. At the Lehman house at Tarrytown, designed by John Russell Pope – a structure pre-eminent for its "good breeding" – materials were carefully chosen "to impart to its surface the suggestion of long usage and the elimination of everything that would proclaim the recent origin of the building."[30] Augusta Patterson thought

73. Some of the doorhandles at Stan Hywet made by Samuel Yellin.

80

antiquing "always a silly and meretricious procedure" but was forced to record many examples in the pages of *Town and Country*.[31] The *House Beautiful* wrote approvingly of the "well-simulated texture of long weathering" that had been achieved. Carll Tucker's house at Mount Kisco, New York, "a splendid example of the more elaborate country houses being built in America today," was constructed, like others, from the stone from old walls dismantled around the estate.[32] The grounds were laid out informally, in the English landscape style, and large trees were moved in from elsewhere to give an effect of instant maturity. Tree moving – a difficult and risk-prone operation – was so common that *Country Life in America* frequently carried advertisements for specialist firms.

It was not practicable to reproduce every attribute of Tudor architecture. Thatch was a particular problem because of the absence of skilled thatchers. An appealing alternative, seen in the 1910s and 1920s, was therefore evolved out of shingle, laid in irregular courses and bent over at the eaves.

To overcome the difficulties of simulating age, another option existed for those with the time and patience to pursue it. This was to acquire parts of genuine old buildings in Europe and ship them across the Atlantic. "Practically everything in this stately house came from other centuries and other lands," ran a comment on Salisbury House, Carl Weeks's home at Des Moines, Iowa.[33] Certain decorating firms specialized in acquiring complete paneled rooms from France, Italy, and England, either chopping them down or extending them to make them fit their new locations. The practice seemed considerably less shocking than it would today, partly because of the poor state of repair in which the paneling was often found. "Today the collectors of this country display a keener appreciation of these emblems of the historic past than do their former owners," commented *International Studio*.[34] East Anglia yielded quantities of Jacobean paneling, much of it discovered in old pubs hidden beneath layers of paint. It was not unknown for whole buildings to be carefully dismantled, numbered, and reassembled in the United States, though the scale of such activity was probably exceeded by the anxiety among European conservationists that it caused. Half-timbered houses, which take apart like a kit, were best suited to the process, and some proved extraordinarily mobile. In 1923 the John Wannamaker department store of Philadelphia had a buyer acquire three Tudor houses, perhaps for the principal's own use. One of them, originally from Ashford in Kent, was subsequently bought and reassembled near Cleveland by Edmund S. Burke, later chairman of the Fourth Federal Reserve Bank. Burke, however, found little use for the place after he was transferred to New York, and just after the Second World War it was purchased and moved once again, this time to the Leonard C. Hanna estate outside Cleveland. Hanna, nephew of the industrialist and philanthropist Marcus A. Hanna, had been slowly nurturing a clutch of buildings in the half-timbered style since 1924. To be able to introduce a genuine Tudor structure as the centerpiece must have seemed providential. It was, however, too small for use, and new wings in a sympathetic style but canted at a very un-Tudor angle had to be added. Agecroft Hall in Virginia, now shown to the public as "an authentic fifteenth century English manor house," is perhaps the best known of these peripatetic buildings. In this case what strikes one is how much newer it looks than some early-twentieth-century houses in the Tudor style, built of carefully selected materials and treated with artificial weathering techniques. Age itself is not the key, but the poetic spirit in which the process of building is carried out, leaving plenty of bumpy surfaces and eschewing straight lines.

It would be wrong to suggest that the romance of age was uniquely associated with England. Far from it. The wizard of the rusty nail and wormeaten chair leg, Addison

Mizner, cast a spell over the houses of Palm Beach, wondrously whisking them back to Old Spain. Equally, the greatest collector of architectural "motifs," William Randolph Hearst, was just as likely to buy a Spanish monastery or an Italian wellhead as a medieval English barn, transporting them by his own kind of magic (money) to California. "You will find a lot of motifs at the Hacienda [de Pozo da Verona] in the stuff belonging to me," Hearst wrote to his architect, Julia Morgan, who was invited to hunt for things that she could make use of.[35] American castles, of which perhaps twenty were built, express another form of enchantment with the mysterious past, and these are generally not English in style. More potent images were offered by Spain and the Rhine (Plate 81). While the worlds of Philadelphia and New England often looked back to their English roots, there were many other cultural references that they were anxious to assert, many of them specifically American. Just to confuse matters further, an Abraham Swan room might well be found in an otherwise impeccably English Georgian building, studiously based on the best precedents, such as in David Dows's house on Long Island.[36] Or a French reception room, lined with old panels, can be seen in Edward Stotesbury's no less Georgian Whitemarsh Hall (here the gardens, though assertively Versailles-like in their general composition, possess English herbaceous borders and distinctly Italian steps) (Plate 195). Indeed, such was the eclecticism of the period that, when it comes to the interior, inspirations are sometimes exceedingly difficult to disentangle. The pages of *Town and Country* frequently give chapter and verse for the origins of particular rooms, which often enough would offer a buffet of different tastes that could be sampled according to mood. In Mrs. Edward Hutton's Mar-a-Lago at Palm Beach the visitor risked severe cultural indigestion. While the Spanish detail of

74. The Edward F. Hutton residence on Long Island. Hutton and his wife Marjorie Merriweather Post, who had inherited the Post Cereal Corporation fortune on the death of her father in 1914, also built Camp Topridge and Mar-a-Lago, illustrated in Plates 200 and 223.

75–76. Junior half-timbering. The hut at Meadow Brook Hall, Detroit, was for the security guard watching over the Dodge children. The children's playhouse on the right is from the Edsel Ford estate in Grosse Pointe, outside Detroit.

the exterior (Plate 223) had been carefully researched by a Viennese professor, the styles inside ranged kaleidoscopically from Roman in the dining room (based on Mussolini's palace) to Venetian Gothic in the living room, Florentine Renaissance and Louis Seize in Mrs. Hutton's apartment, to Dutch, American, and "very modern" (though with a "rather exciting iron bed" from Spain) in the bedrooms.[37]

But to see the impact that the English country house ideal made on the American imagination, and the sometimes alarming consequences of the collision, it is only necessary to travel to the big industrial cities of the Midwest, where in the ring of country houses that generally surrounds them, often dating from the 1920s, English styles outnumber any other. That is to say, the vast houses of the Dodges (Plate 75) and the Firestones imitate aspects of fifteenth and sixteenth-century English architecture. This does not mean that their owners modified their lives or requirements to suit their architecture: naturally the houses were planned to accommodate early-twentieth-century American living. As a result, buildings that outwardly based themselves on those of other nations incorporated elements that could be found nowhere other than in the United States.

— 6 —

The American-ness of the American Country House
PRACTICAL, CONVENIENT, COMFORTABLE, EFFICIENT

WHILE THERE WAS no denying that the American country house owed a great deal to the English example, most people believed that it was also to some degree a specifically national product. "If the architect of the Parthenon deserves consideration because he was the true son of his era, giving to the world a noble expression of himself under the conditions of his environment," declared George William Sheldon in the 1880s, " . . . in like manner the architect of the representative American country-seat, in the last quarter of the nineteenth century, may be styled a true son of his epoch."[1] Even at this relatively early date Sheldon was convinced that America's Artistic Country-Seats, as he called his book, had "won the admiration of Europe." This view only became more entrenched as the century turned. "Our country houses have a distinction of their own which arouses the respectful admiration of all who are competent to judge of their merits," wrote Donn Barber in the introduction to John Cordis Baker's *American Country Homes and their Gardens* of 1906. "They faithfully express our modern American civilization and show a certain sensible comfort to be found in no other land."[2]

Author after author shared this sentiment. Many were anxious to place the American country house in the context of contemporary domestic architecture in Europe, some of which was highly regarded. They felt that the native work stood the test well. "He may not altogether like it; he probably misunderstands its significance, but he cannot ignore it," was how Desmond and Croly summed up the probable response of a European observer.[3] Like many people, Frank Miles Day felt that English house design still led the world, but "perhaps if he were candid and had traveled here," he added diffidently, an informed Englishman "might admit that we were doing nearly as well in this difficult art of house design as his own countrymen. Surely that would be high praise."[4] Writing in the late 1920s, Matlack Price was more confident. While modern English architecture had "served most successfully here as a point of departure," any unprejudiced visitor would have to find "the American country house, whether it is based on early or late English precedent, to excel in the practical and convenient aspects of the plan, as well as in comfort and efficiency in equipment."[5]

With such a sense of national identity, it is hardly surprising that the most popular of all styles in country house architecture was the Colonial Revival. In the gamut of historical styles this was one of the few which was wholly American, having come into

77. The ice-making room at Nemours, Delaware. The long, rectangular molds were filled with water and slotted into compartments for freezing.

being in the burst of national rediscovery that followed the Philadelphia Centennial Exhibition of 1876. However, the individuality of the American country house was more than a matter of style. The conditions under which it was created were, in some respects, so unlike those in Europe that typically American features emerged through a process of natural evolution. Some of the differences ran deep. One of the most basic concerned the very idea of the countryside into which the prospective country house owner was proposing to venture. It was likely to arouse strongly contrasting emotions on either side of the Atlantic.

Parts of Britain possessed thrilling and romantic scenery but little of it could be called genuinely untamed. Man had been living there too long: even the heather on the seemingly wild moors of Scotland was the subject of yearly burning by landlords eager to provide their young grouse with succulent new growth. Farming had not been financially attractive since the 1870s, but for the prosperous banker or industrialist thinking of building a house the countryside would probably seem (whatever the actual deprivation) a desirable, friendly place typified by small fields, green lanes, flowering hedgerows, cheerful cottages, and plenty of sport. And by 1870 nearly all of it was accessible by rail. The American experience, however, inspired more ambivalent feelings. On the one hand, because it was still a predominantly agricultural nation, there was a stronger identity with the land; most people probably knew a relative who still farmed. Even the new immigrants generally came from rural backgrounds in Europe, though once arrived they were often unable to escape the big cities. Growing industrialization made the nostalgia that many Americans felt for the land all the stronger. Yet beyond the confines of the farm the countryside was rarely the cozy, comfortable place it was in England. It was on an entirely different scale; perhaps it had only been recently broken, or not broken at all. Whole swathes of the American landscape seemed endless and empty of human life. It might be sublime in the eighteenth-century sense of the word, but even its beauties were, in their vastness, slightly terrifying. The English traveler Thomas Grattan clarified the differences in attitude between England and the United States in his somewhat chauvinistic book *Civilized America* of 1859: "The *improvements* of a country place in England, mean the copses or clumps of young trees, put into the earth and fostered in their growth to rural embellishment. In America the same word means the clearance of old timber, with half-burned and unseemly stumps defacing the sward."[6] So much of England's native forests had been felled in the Tudor and Stuart periods that, by the eighteenth century, the planting of trees had become both aesthetically and economically desirable. In much of late-nineteenth-century America, however, the clearance of trees to reach cultivable land had taken place within living memory; no wonder that trees were less highly regarded. As late as 1903 Desmond and Croly commented that "even the most habitable American country has not been so intelligently and consistently humanized as the greater part of England."[7]

It took some time before people thought of building houses for pleasure in this seemingly limitless, possibly hostile countryside; when they did venture out into it, they went in groups. In the years following the Civil War there was a boom in spas and watering-places to accommodate those Americans who wanted to escape the city but were not prepared to go too deep into the country. Enormous hotels, all plush and glitter, the biggest the world had ever seen, were built at Saratoga Springs, Newport, Elberon, Long Branch, Richfield Springs, Cape May, and Manchester-by-the-Sea. So, incidentally, were some elaborate private houses – little different from country houses, sometimes, except in their rejection of the country. With its carriage drives, its tennis championships, its *fêtes champêtres*, its costume balls, and in some cases its horse-racing and gambling, life at a resort often seemed preferable to the solitary existence of a landed estate. As astonished Englishmen often remarked, Americans actually seemed to like flocking together. For this reason the top resorts continued in popularity, and fashionability, long after country houses began to be built.

Resort people did not want to risk being left on their own. Nor, however, did the builders of country houses. Biltmore is exceptional in its apparently remote location, though, even so, the town of Asheville was a fairly flourishing resort. Most other owners wanted, not unreasonably, to be within striking distance of family and friends and neighbors. In England this happened almost inevitably, because the countryside was already full of greater or lesser country houses, manor houses, rectories, *cottages ornés*, and villages, and it had an established social framework based on the county. But in America the network had to be invented. Consequently nearly all American country houses can be found in a few places where an owner would not feel lost: the Berkshire Hills, the Hudson River Valley, the shore of New Jersey, the Brandywine Valley, the Philadelphia Main Line, and certain places outside the big industrial cities. Beyond these regions lie vast tracts of country – many tens of thousands of square miles – in which not a single country house can be found.

In some cases the group spirit inspired even more tightly organized clusters of houses, based on the family. The family compound, where several households had independent dwellings on the same estate, was an entirely American phenomenon. A factor in its development must have been the absence of the British system of primogeniture, under which the eldest son takes all. Perhaps the rich American preferred to see his family gathered around him during his life rather than found a dynasty after his death. It also helped promote the elusive cause of family unity through several generations. The architectural effect was described by *American Homes and Gardens* when it visited Nathaniel Thayer's house in Lancaster, Massachusetts, unconsciously echoing the third vision of Macbeth: "Further on are houses of other Thayers and still others, each a spacious mansion and each provided with spacious grounds."[8]

The prime example of a family compound is Pocantico Hills, for after the main house of Kykuit was built half a dozen other Rockefeller houses sprang up on or around the estate. Each of Junior's sons – except the unhappy and rebellious Winthrop, who sought to escape family pressures by building a ranch in Arkansas – erected a dwelling there. To begin with these households operated independently, but their proximity expressed – and encouraged – a remarkable family solidarity that has persisted through three generations.

In England the Rothschilds bought neighboring estates in Buckinghamshire in order to gain position in the county. No such consideration weighed with the Rockefellers. They already had all the prominence they needed, and more. Indeed, one reason for remaining loyal to Pocantico Hills was that it offered greater privacy than they could have achieved individually. By the 1930s the park in which most of the houses were situated had to be fenced and patrolled against scroungers, party crashers, lunatics, potential kidnappers, scandal-mongering journalists, and a generally over-inquisitive public. This only enhanced the apparent secretiveness and mystique of the Rockefellers and inflamed the curiosity of people already excited by those very qualities.

On Long Island an even more elaborate family compound had been conceived by John D. Rockefeller's associate in Standard Oil, Charles Pratt. Beady-eyed, goatee-bearded, short, stout, frugal, cautious, and rich, Pratt bought eight hundred acres at Glen Cove in 1890. The architects Charles Lamb and Hugo Rich converted an old house for Pratt and built two new ones for his children. An agricultural school was founded as a rural

78–79. Two of the substantial country houses on Dosoris, the Pratt family compound on Long Island. John Pratt's house (left) is by Charles Platt.

extension of the philanthropic Pratt Institute. Every weekend Pratt came to inspect work at Dosoris, as the estate was now called, but he died in the spring of 1891 before it had had a chance to come to fruition. His heirs continued the enterprise and eventually there were twenty-one Pratt homes (Plates 78 and 79) and over a hundred ancillary buildings on the estate. More clearly than the Rockefellers, Pratt saw Dosoris as a means of keeping the family together. It worked. Several of the houses there were built by his grandchildren and the estate continued in operation for half a century. After the Second World War the estate succumbed to the development pressures of Long Island and was broken up, the larger of the houses becoming institutions. In the 1920s, however, the compound served no fewer than eighty-nine family members.

The manner in which Dosoris developed was not entirely according to Pratt's vision. "Averse to all flaunting or squandering of wealth," as Pratt was described by the *Dictionary of American Biography*, he had originally intended that each house would cost no more than twenty thousand dollars. Gradually this rule was bent, departed from, and finally forgotten. Pratt's progeny went to more fashionable architects than Lamb and Rich. They included Delano and Aldrich, Charles A. Platt, the latter's son William Platt, and Carrère and Hastings (Thomas Hastings was a family friend). The final accolade came in 1914 when *Country Life in America* annointed George D. Pratt's Killenworth, a large, stone-built Tudor mansion, as "Best House of the Year" (see Plate 23).[9] The architect Alexander Buell Trowbridge was Pratt's brother-in-law.

But economy did rule in one respect. Concentrating the family at Dosoris had the practical benefit that some of the services of the houses could be shared. Thus the stables and garages were centralized at a point known, from the layout of the drive, as the Oval. Operationally this was the heart of the estate, with a splendid building complete with clock tower to house the administration. It seems to have replaced the original Pratt administration building, typically no more than a wooden barn, which burned in 1903. In the first three decades of this century the Pratts at Dosoris employed some four hundred staff.[10] Near the Oval were the cowbarns built in 1899 for the Jersey herd. All these buildings were designed by William B. Tubby, a Pratt architect of long standing. He had not only built Charles M. Pratt's town house in Brooklyn but the mausoleum in which Charles Pratt senior is buried at Dosoris.

The distinctive grouping of American country houses, whether in a family compound or just near other houses, was a response to the geography of the country: it seemed too enormous for most people to set themselves up on their own. Those who did so, however, could often locate themselves amid spectacular natural surroundings. "Most of our country houses are differently built, placed, and surrounded from those of other countries," wrote Marianna van Rensselaer in 1903. "Our large parks and private domains are often laid out upon virgin soil instead of upon sites which have been used for other purposes, while in the west of Europe such a thing as a virgin site hardly exists."[11] While Biltmore, Olana, and Kykuit all stood on estates that had been farmed, they were placed bravely on mountaintops and commanded peerless views. In these mighty settings it was appropriate that the park should be planted naturalistically: avenues and marble statuary would have looked puny. But by 1900 the immediate surroundings of more and more country houses were being treated formally, with terraces, arbors, pergolas, pleached alleys, and box hedges. The hope was to turn the garden into an outdoor room, in the manner of the Renaissance gardens of Italy and the more modern ones of England, and to ease the transition between house and landscape. Under the hand of Beaux-Arts architects like Carrère and Hastings the elaborate geometry of the plan acquired a beauty of its own. Planting was necessarily subject to the American climate, and Guy Lowell, generally an advocate of the formal garden, counseled against too great a reliance on architectural features: "we must always remember how comparatively short our American summer is, and how bare and out of place they are apt to look during the winter months."

Inevitably climate also had a direct influence on the shape of the American country house. Without doubt the most striking native feature was the porch or piazza. "The veranda of a country house is its most important external feature, as far as convenience, comfort and general appearances are concerned," wrote one author in 1903.[12] In the same year Mrs. van Rensselaer went so far as to state, "it is hardly needful to-day to affirm that an American country house without a piazza is in every sense a mistake and a failure."[13] Even Henry James, usually such a severe critic of American life, called the porch "the happiest disposition of the old American country house."[14]

James had in mind the porches of Federal mansions, formed by the tall columns of the portico. They proved to be such an attractive extension of the living space of the house, and so useful in shading the main rooms from sun, that they became a necessity for most subsequent country houses, whatever the style or date. In the *Architecture of Country*

80. The classic image of the veranda from Greyfield on Cumberland Island, Georgia.

81. The veranda was such a popular feature that one was even incorporated into Gillette Castle in Connecticut, home of the actor William Gillette, famous for his stage portrayals of Sherlock Holmes. Built in 1914, Gillette Castle was inspired by the castles on the Rhine.

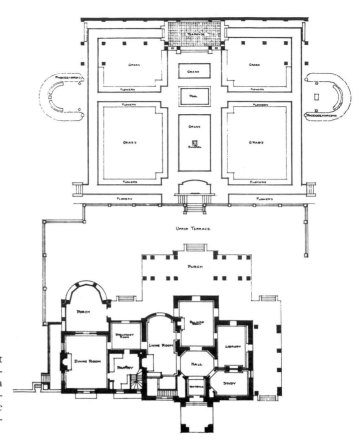

82. Plan of Gellian Court at Tarrytown, New York. A simple mid-nineteenth-century villa which was enlarged and enveloped in porches. Note how the porches are reflected in the pergola on the lower terraces.

Houses Downing drew attention to the "noble veranda" that he gave to his Southern Villa in the Romanesque Style. He imagined that it would be "the lounging place, *conversazione*, and often dining-room itself."[15] Queen Anne was the style friendliest to the porch, because it was informal enough to allow one to sprout on any side; porches were wrapped around corners and bays and sometimes enveloped houses completely. Later, more formal styles called for greater restraint. Architects of the Colonial Revival had a particular problem, because what the early colonists termed "porch" was really " a sort of entrance hall within the bulk of the house."[16] To add a porch of the more accepted kind would have been a solecism, though one frequently committed, so purists were better off choosing another style. But what were they to do when restoring a historic structure? "Ten to one the first thing that the average person thinks of, upon becoming the owner of an old house, is the addition of a piazza," lamented Charles Hopper.[17]

Even in new buildings the porch could be hard to contend with, as Myron Hunt discovered when meeting Henry E. Huntington's request that one measuring forty by sixty feet be attached to the east side of his San Marino Ranch in Pasadena. "Our piazza life," as one writer called it, was too beguiling to forego.[18] Combining English and national enthusiasms, J.D. Sawyer felt that a New American style could be created by adding porch and veranda to the Elizabethan country house.[19]

Appropriate furnishings for the veranda, according to *Country Life in America*, included flowers boxes, hanging plants, swinging seats, awnings, grass or rag rugs, steamer chairs, rockers, stools, floor cushions, lanterns, desks, and wicker in a thousand varieties. Some of these had evidently found their way onto the piazza of Henry Flagler's

90

83–84. Two country houses designed by Wilson Eyre for sites in Connecticut. Though the style of Mrs. Charles B. Curtis's house is strongly influenced by the English architect C.F.A. Voysey, plenty of allowance has been made for shady arcades. In the Melbert B. Cary house the same purpose is served by tall porticos. Architectural Archives of the University of Pennsylvania

Whitehall in Florida, to judge from the description his private organist, Arthur C. Spalding, gave to his family. "It is an enormous piazza about 25 ft wide and extending along the side of the house for fully 75 feet," he wrote in January 1907. "There are big rugs, divans, swinging chairs, rocking chairs, tables and everything to make one comfortable." It was in fact "by far the most attractive spot about the place."[20]

The sister of the piazza was the awning, another means of keeping the sun out of rooms (Plate 85). For strict utility it would have been more sensible to have internal blinds, as in England, since these could be adjusted without going outside in the rain. However, they would not have made the brave show that striped blinds and awnings did on many houses in the later part of the nineteenth century. From old photographs the effect is reminiscent of the shutters painted in the heraldic colors of the estate seen on French and German castles. Beaux-Arts pedants may have found them a distraction, since they disrupted the architecture, but they must have been the salvation of many less distinguished houses. They gave an air of jollity to even the gloomiest pile. Some houses look quite literally bare without them. "The squareness and plainness of the various openings, together with their simplicity will be materially altered by the form, and any slight coloring which will naturally enter into the awnings," wrote Myron Hunt about Huntington's San Marino. The extensive use of both awnings and also ivy – elements that have generally disappeared – may explain why the wall surfaces of some houses now strike one as surprisingly plain.

The fierceness of American summers had another architectural consequence by giving prominence to the ice house. It was a minor genre of building, but much discussed. At a surprisingly early period visitors to the United States were struck by the ready

85. Awnings prominently displayed at Shelburne Farms, Vermont. The house was first built by R.H. Robertson in the late 1880s, then trebled in size a decade later.

availability of ice. "The winter produces it in ample quantity," wrote George Makepeace Towle in 1870,

> the summer makes it a universal need. There is ice everywhere; ice in the great metallic "pitcher" on the breakfast and dinner table, ice on the butter, ice on the radishes, ice for the meat and fish in the cellar, ice for the beverages – the water and claret and punch, the "sherry cobblers" and "Tom and Jerrys". It is dirt cheap; for twopence you get a large lump of it, beautifully green and crystalline weighing five or six pounds.[21]

Ice could be bought in blocks, as Towle indicated, from one of the highly efficient companies that cut ice from the great rivers during the winter; the prudent householder had an opening in his outside wall so that it could be placed directly into the refrigerator (initially simply a box with ice round it) where food was stored. Or it could be had from damming a stream or diverting water into specially prepared beds. The principles of the ice house in which it was stored, packed in straw, were simple: perfect drainage, complete insulation by means of double walls crammed with straw or sawdust, and total exclusion of air. Once even a tiny draft penetrated, the ice was as good as lost: it started a funnel which quickly grew as the ice melted and fell in. However, if the basic principles were observed it was not necessary for the ice house to be constructed under ground.

86. Compressors for the ice-making room at Nemours. Alfred I. du Pont, owner of the house, insisted on having two of every kind of machine in case of breakdown.

None of this meant, of course, that the ice itself would be pure: on the contrary it was all too likely that it would be contaminated in some form. Consequently the arrival of what one magazine article called "ice by wire" – still something of a novelty even in the 1920s – was to be applauded (Plates 77 and 86). The new machines did away with the "mess, the damp smell and germ-laden air from melting ice, the constantly varying temperature in the refrigerator with spoiling of food, the dependence on the ice crop," according to a 1914 advertisement for the Brunswick Household Refrigerating and Ice-Making Plants.

In the first years of the twentieth century some sentimentalists continued to advocate the spring house as a place for storing food. The idea was that the air would be kept cool and fresh by the water as it bubbled out of the ground. Though the spring house had long been old-fashioned – indeed obsolete for large houses – it acquired a certain mystique among Arts and Crafts folk. A variant was the trough of cold water, freshly drawn from the well, in which the milk churns were placed at Frank Lloyd Wright's Taliesin in Wisconsin.

Naturally, climate had a great influence inside the country house. Larger door and window openings than would have been found in Europe were the traditional means of encouraging cross breezes, especially in the South. Often there were no doors between hall and rooms for the same reason. This openness in the plan was also encouraged, paradoxically, by the severity of northern winters, for which the heating of American houses had, of necessity, to be better than that of English ones. It was a matter of preference, too. English country house owners seemed almost to have reveled in Arctic temperatures: certainly they took relatively few pains to mitigate them. This was not the case in America, and one of the most frequent comments of travelers was on the luxurious warmth of its dwellings. Central heating was developed earlier, and used to greater effect, than in England. Predictably, Grattan, writing in 1859, took a censorious view of the exotic temperatures that the unfamiliar hot-air systems generated, which he thought dangerous to health.

> The method of heating many of the best houses is a terrible grievance to persons not accustomed to it, and a fatal misfortune to those who are. Casual visitors are nearly suffocated, and constant occupiers killed. An enormous furnace in the cellar sends up, day and night, streams of hot air, through apertures and pipes, to every room in the house. No spot is free from it, from the dining-parlour to the dressing-closet. It meets you the moment the street-door is opened to let you in, and it rushes after you when you emerge again, half-stewed and parboiled, into the wholesome air. The self-victimized citizens, who have a preposterous affection for this atmosphere, un-doubtedly shorten their lives by it. Several elderly gentlemen of my acquaintance, suddenly cut off, would assuredly have had a verdict of "died of a furnace" pronounced on their cases, had a coroner been called, and had a jury decided on fair evidence.[22]

In the 1870s central heating had only just begun to penetrate the main rooms of English country houses, even new ones.[23] But its use was quite simply universal in the United States, where even in southern Florida, James Deering, building Vizcaya in 1911–17, insisted that there should be a furnace capable of heating the whole of the house.

Towards the end of the nineteenth century the hot air which Grattan so much feared, pumped out through grilles, began to decline in popularity. It was thought that the various enclosed systems formed by pipes and radiators, which circulated hot water or preferably steam, created a kinder atmosphere. But the most sophisticated writers on houses were also coming to the conclusion that central heating did not provide the

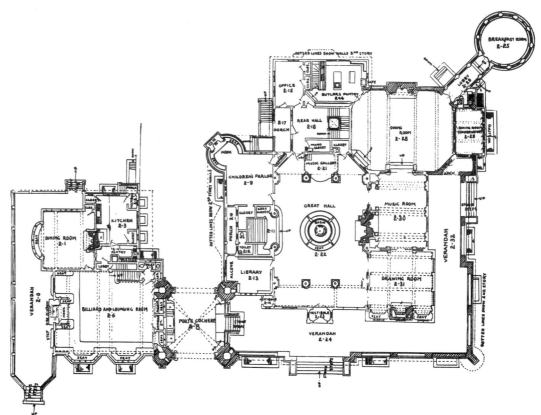

87. Plan of Kildysart, Daniel O'Day's house in New Jersey. Not only is the house engulfed by verandas, but the plan is very open. The children's parlor and the library are among the few rooms shown with conventional doors.

complete answer. The open fires that were so much a feature of English houses had some benefits. One was that the escape of heat up the chimney enforced the circulation of air: it drew fresh air into the room if the conditions for ventilation were right. (In this respect ill-fitting doors and windows were a positive boon.) Then there was the sheer joy of the thing. "What epicure could ask for a greater pleasure than to open his eyes in a winter or autumnal morning upon the soft sunshine streaming in at his window, and to listen, during the few moments that he allows himself for argument as to the precise time when he shall get up, to the light crackling, sizzling and whispering of the newly lighted coal in the grate!" wrote Clarence Cook in 1881.[24] Elsie de Wolfe, who believed that steam heat ruined complexions, furniture, and temper, wrote that in her own houses she had a fireplace in every room. Naturally she burned wood, which was considered the most elegant and attractive fuel. She still had her furnace in the basement, however, since it was recognized that no amount of open fires could cope effectively with an American winter.

Without efficient central heating, every room would have had to be closed by a door, as in northern Europe. Henry James for one would have been pleased. "This diffused vagueness of separation between apartments, between hall and room, between one room and another, between the one you are in and the one you are not in, between place of passage and place of privacy, is a provocation to despair which the public institution shares impartially with the luxurious 'home,'" he wrote in *The American Scene* in 1907. "To the spirit attuned to a different practice these dispositions can only appear a strange perversity, an extravagant aberration of taste."[25] To James, living off the nuances of intimate conversation, open planning was anathema because it made talking *à deux* so much less interesting: one never knew when one might be overheard. But to other Americans the openness of their houses seemed to correspond to the greater informality of their lives. Again the Queen Anne style was well suited to it. Sheldon praised Theophilus P. Chandler's, Chestnut Hill, Pennsylvania, for its "fine and free" interior:

> you can stand at the dining-room fireplace, at the extreme west end of the building, and have a view of ninety-two feet, through library, hall, and parlor, to the fireplace of the parlor, with its mantel and seat, at the extreme eastern end of the house; or you can stand at the fireplace of the hall, at the extreme northern end of the building, and look across to the stained-glass windows on the first landing.[26]

Kildysart, the so-called farm at Deal, New Jersey, built by Standard Oil's Daniel O'Day, seems to have been even more open (Plate 87). The music room and the drawing room give both into the great hall and into each other; the former also opens directly into the dining room. Only the library (where quiet was at a premium) and children's parlor (where noise had to be contained) have conventional doors. It is likely that the other openings had sliding doors that could be pushed right back into the walls – an American innovation – but this is not clear from the published plan. Note also the large L-shaped veranda enclosing two sides of the main block.

A free style was by no means necessary to the free plan. One could hardly wish for a more formal piece of architecture than Biltmore, yet, as we have seen, all the main ground floor rooms open into a gallery that is in turn separated from the winter garden by no more than an arcade. The taste for the portière curtain happily coincided with that for a greater ampleness of space. "Doors are ugly things at best," wrote Mabel Tuke Priestman in 1906; "draperies possess lines of beauty."[27] One wonders whether she would have said this of the portières at Vancroft in Ohio, made of elaborately riveted elephant skin.

The spatial generosity of Biltmore was not possible in the smaller country houses built after the First World War, and in 1919 Fiske Kimball observed that plans of "formal regularity" were the norm.[28] Here the sliding door came into its own. Anyone who entertained large numbers of guests was likely to appreciate the chance of opening one room into another. Frank Lloyd Wright, who never missed a trick in advancing his cause, claimed that open planning made life easier for servants. The servants themselves might not have agreed: without doors the whole house was on view and no work-in-progress could be concealed.[29]

Even the most free-flowing of plans could not entirely do away with closed compartments. One of the most revealingly American of rooms was the office or den. Perhaps because equality between the sexes was greater than in Europe, perhaps too because the social machine was run by and for the women rather than the men, it is rare to find a full-blown male preserve of the kind seen in English houses, composed of billiard room, smoking room, and gun room on the ground floor with bachelor bedrooms above.[30] For one thing there was not the supply of more or less unemployed younger sons to make up the shooting parties: in America even the sons of the wealthy generally worked. Nevertheless, the country house owner retained one room as his sanctum. The den was his equivalent of the boudoir, wrote Lillie Hamilton French in 1908; from its privacy she was inclined "to believe that the inherited instincts of primitive man, guarding the approaches to his cave, are being exercised again."[31]

The Moorish-style smoking room was on the whole less popular than in Europe, no doubt because it seemed rather effeminate. The chief attribute of the den was, after all, its assertive masculinity. "The average American has lost in a measure, perhaps, the old habit of the smoking jacket and slippers, much more of the long dressing gown," wrote Charles Hooper in 1913. "He prefers to sit with his chair tilted back and his feet on the mantel and talk shop, rather than to lose himself in the dreamland of Oriental laziness."[32] Stuffed ducks, arms and armor, and tribal art were popular themes for decoration. It was not essential to have hunted or bought the real thing. "Have you a den?" asked an advertisement for the Milwaukee Papier Mâché Works, Inc., in 1903. "Send for pamphlet of reproductions of Game Fishes, Armors, Indian Subjects and Unique Decorations." With the masculine character of the decoration went masculine habits of behavior that would not always have been tolerated in other rooms. "It has just occurred to me that I haven't a cuspadore [spitoon for chewing tobacco] for Whitehall," Henry Flagler wrote to William Pierre Stymus, Jr., his decorator. "I wish you would order for me one for each of the offices, two for the billiard room and one for the library. Mrs. Flagler says she doesn't want any elsewhere in the house."[33]

Elsie de Wolfe maintained that men did not like their dens, but the evidence is against her. Not only was it probably, from a male point of view, the most comfortable room in the house, but it was the one that most closely resembled the owner's working environment; and that, as numerous critics of the American scene observed, might well have been where his heart was. Without the example of a leisure class who had made the spending of money a fine art, the American millionaire found it more difficult to dissociate himself from business than did his European equivalent. He had no wish or incentive to do so. Consequently, the den probably had a desk at which he could work

88. An elaborate pipe organ, such as this one at Great Barrington, was one of the great status symbols of the American country house.

89. Pipe organs continued to be built long after the arrival of the gramophone. This advertisement for the Estey Residence Pipe Organ appeared in *Country Life in America*, May 1922.

90. The tower at Hammond Castle in Gloucester, Massachusetts, was designed to contain the pipes of the mighty organ.

91. Doors to the Welte-Mignon organ at Vizcaya, Florida, made from a Neapolitan altarpiece.

or play at working. The male camaraderie of office or golf course was also important, and in the 1930s it found a further locale with the rise of the tap room or bar. In order to preserve the authentic atmosphere of good fellowship, genuine bars were sometimes brought in from favorite but defunct watering holes: the Cicardi Winter Palace in St. Louis, Missouri, furnished John Ringling's at Ca'd'Zan in Florida. At least this was more appropriate than the Tavern Room at William J. McAneeny's house at Palm Beach, whose paneling came from an Italian church.[34]

Like the den, the reception room is another typically national provision of the American country house. In English usage "reception room" is simply a generic term for any of the main rooms of the house. This is not so in the United States, where the purpose of the reception room, as its name indicates, is solely that of receiving visitors – the kind who come on business. Its appointment was formal, probably in one of the French styles. Comfort was not aimed at, and some authorities even maintained that there should be no fireplace, to discourage those being received from staying too long.

An inescapable feature of many American country houses was the organ (Plates 88 and 89). It was the ultimate status symbol, highly expensive and excessively complex to install – so much so that it was best ordered at the same time as the house was designed, so that it could be literally built in (Plate 90). Jacques Gréber, the Frenchman who landscaped Harbor Hill and Whitemarsh Hall, was struck, in his *L'Architecture aux États-Unis* of 1920, by the prevalence of the organ. Hiding the pipes behind richly carved screens or tapestry was, he wrote, "extremely happy from the point of view of the acoustic, although it costs more than the most expensive panelling."[35] So conscious was the Aeolian Company of the organ's architectural role that in 1904 it issued an advertisement specifically to describe its decorative possibilities. "As an artistic triumph, the AEOLIAN PIPE-ORGAN stands preeminent," gushed the copy.

It may be so designed and treated as to provide either the most conspicuous or the least conspicuous of the house's furnishings – being specially constructed in each case, it is easily adapted to either the music-room or hall, and the architectural treatment

97

can harmonize with the period in which the room is designed, or its presence may be emphasized by having it correspond with the furnishings of the room.

Special artists were engaged to execute Louis XIV, Louis XV, and Empire models. The instrument itself could be operated either manually or by a perforated paper roll, the *Aeolienne*, marked so that the person at the keyboard could pull the appropriate stops. There were whole operas on roll, and a notable feature was the merry crashing of cymbals and rattle of drums that accompanied them. Because of this, indeed, the player organ was best suited to the more rousing kinds of music. It was typical that, after visiting three New York showrooms, John Ringing was impelled to purchase his Aeolian-Skinner organ for Ca'd'Zan when he heard a German march from a Broadway show, *The Parade of the Wooden Soldiers*. Needless to say, John D. Rockefeller, Jr., was more scientific when it came to chosing the organ for Kykuit. He consulted an expert – the organist at the Fifth Avenue Baptist Church – as to the relative merits of the Aeolian and the less-tried Steinway versions, deciding, with typical conservatism, on an Aeolian. Besides the main console downstairs there were echo and solo keyboards on the third floor. At $50,000 (the price of the Ringling organ) one might have expected these spectacular but costly instruments to have been rapidly superseded by the gramophone, but they were still being advertised in the 1930s.

It is a far cry from organ pipes to the other pipes that ran through country houses, but for the well-being of the inhabitants the latter were somewhat more important. They probably had more than a little to do with the Duke of Windsor's observation: "Compared to the creature comforts Americans took for granted, the luxury to which I was accustomed in Europe seemed almost primitive."[36] For to most Europeans luxury, in its most naked sense, meant plumbing. "Plumbing, as we know it," trumpeted the *American Architect and Building News* in 1878, "is essentially and almost exclusively an American institution."[37] No one who visited America could fail to remark on the bathrooms. It was not that, by the late Victorian period, new English country houses did not have bathrooms: they did, though not in great numbers (partly because the idea persisted that it was actually more pleasurable to have hot water brought to your bedroom in jugs). But many older country houses had yet to enter the age of plumbed-in hot water, and such bathrooms as did exist were generally bleak affairs compared to those known in the United States. "To the foreigner there is frequently something disagreeable and effeminate in the completeness of these arrangements for personal comfort," wrote Desmond and Croly of American bathrooms and bedrooms, "but they have become such a necessary part, not merely of the ease of American life, but of its economy, that the neglect of such arrangements is inconceivable."[38]

It was not always so. When Harriet Martineau visited America in the 1830s she was surprised to find that bathtubs were a rarity in private houses. The spread of bathing may have had something to do with the promotion of water treatments at spas, though even at the end of the century Mrs. William K. Vanderbilt thought daily bathing would harm her children.[39] The internal water-closet was, in its early days, almost an emblem of the two views of luxury reflected in the American country house: some saw it as an advance in civilization, others maintained that it would sap the moral fiber of the nation. One person in favor was the phrenologist and advocate of the octagonal house, Orson S. Fowler. While "squeamish maidens and fastidious beaux" might prefer the seclusion of an out-of-doors privy, "matrons, the aged and feeble" would certainly find more comfort than offence in a water-closet placed under the stairs.[40] Only the year before this was written in 1853, however, Lewis F. Allen had maintained in *Rural Architecture* that

92–93. Ogden Codman, Jr's, designs for the marble bathroom at F.W. Vanderbilt's Hyde Park, New York. The Metropolitan Museum of Art, New York

water-closets had "no business in a *farmer's* house. They are an *effeminacy*, only, and introduced by *city*-life."[41] Though many of Fowler's quackish notions would become discredited by the end of his life, his views on the water-closet were prophetic. Both bathrooms and water-closets were not only, it would seem now, an obvious benefit to the master and mistress of the house: they also saved labor.

Or so Louis H. Gibson argued in *Convenient Houses* of 1889.[42] Economy, however, is not the whole story, since, as foreigners such as Gréber noted, the American bathroom was more than just utilitarian. "La salle de bain est un chef-d'oeuvre," he exclaimed.

Low and inviting bathtub; well-placed towel rail, where the towels warm themselves while you are taking your bath; large washbasin; shelf of accessories of which the distance is well calculated so that one does not wound one's forehead during one's ablutions; tap of rapid discharge; hot water under pressure, naturally: the bath, in

America, does not become the long ceremony that it often is in France, for the geyser and its caprices are unknown. Finally, the presence of a *water-closet* belonging to each bathroom is a great *commodité*.[43]

In some instances the owner went so far beyond mere utility that the bathroom was turned into a resplendent work of decoration. One of the finest is James Deering's bathroom at Vizcaya (Plate 94), with its inlaid marble floor, tented ceiling, Empire metalwork, and handsome plumbed-in shaving stand, with goat's feet and swans,

94. James Deering's bathroom at Vizcaya, Florida, designed in the Empire taste.

placed so that he could look out over Biscayne Bay. Gilded swans dispensed fresh and seawater into a bathtub exactly the same length as its owner. Ringling's bathroom at Ca'd'Zan, its tub hewn from a solid piece of Sienna marble, pales by comparison.

Less opulent clients were likely to make do with white tiling (for hygiene) around the walls and a porcelain or iron enamel tub, square at the feet and round at the head. Built-in tubs were preferred to the kind on little feet because of the difficulty of cleaning underneath. After 1900 the shower made its appearance, its advocates stressing its hygienic and health-giving properties. Some stood over the tub, but the most elaborate were freestanding structures with pipes that surrounded the bather like a cage. By means of dials it was possible to chose one, or a combination, of half a dozen options in which water sprinkled or deluged down from above, was projected from the sides or rose up in a jet from the floor – an alarming moment for someone not expecting it. Near the sea hot and cold salt water was often offered as an alternative to fresh. Mixing chambers prevented sudden changes in temperature, and the shower might have had a testing device to avoid "an unpleasant shock of cold or hot water, which often occurs when the valves of an ordinary shower are first opened."[44]

Bedrooms were less flamboyant than bathrooms, but they were considered equally carefully, particularly in the provision of closets. This was, as Gréber commented, "enormous" by European standards. In the first years of the century a common arrangement was to have a pair of deep closets between bedroom and bathroom. The specialization of closets was considerable. "We now know clothes closets, linen closets, shoe closets, cell, attic, and storeroom closets, and others in large variety," reported *Country Life in America* in the 1920s.[45] Ideally the design of each was adapted to the articles being housed. "Ordinarily for *lingerie* there are very large wardrobes with shelves," another author had observed twenty years earlier.

The shelves are first entirely covered with perfumed silk sachets. When the doors are opened, one sees dainty lace-trimmed and be-ribboned articles piled in sets. Nightgowns of silk or linen-lawn and lace, filmy corset-covers, skirts, etc. Every shelf holds ravishing snowy heaps of delicately-tinted silk underwear. In drawers below, lying upon the ubiquitous sachet, are my lady's silk stockings of every hue and style, matching her endless gowns. Another wardrobe is appropriate to bonnets and hats.[46]

Costumes, skirts, and long wraps found their home in a highly polished, dust-free gown room. The linen room was made of hardwood because of the costly nature of its contents: sheets, pillowcases, bath towels, tablecloths, napkins, and tray covers, piled up by the dozen and color-coded by ribbon as to grade and use. Much of it was embroidered, provoking the bitter comment: "No other part of the house more potently emphasizes the contrasting life of the great world of toilers and the other little world of ponderous wealth and fabulous luxury."[47] The linen room may well have had its own closet for scented soap, colognes, bathsalts, and so on. Rugs and woolen things were stored in the cedar room against moth. When the contents of all these closets were in place and the doors were closed, order prevailed. The more order, the less housework.

Saving labor was a preoccupation of the American country house. "What a difference would it make in this country, if it could be supplied with nice, clean, dutiful English maid servants!" William Cobbett had commented in 1818.[48] But there was little tradition of domestic service in the New World. Even in Colonial days the supply of servants, other than slaves, had been inadequate and the quality poor. In the post-bellum

South the old generation of skilled black servants was disappearing, or so it was felt. The supply of labor, industrial as well as domestic, was one of the crucial differences between the economies of the United States and Britain. In Britain it was still possible as late as 1914 for an observer to ask rhetorically: "Has there ever in the big towns at least been a time when employers could not get practically at a moment's notice all the labourers they required?"[49] It is true that house owners, particularly in the country, were experiencing difficulties in finding servants, partly because the traditional surplus labor of the countryside was drifting to the towns. But the position was far more critical in the United States, where there had always been greater difficulty in obtaining workers. Rural areas, far from supplying a surplus of young people from which servants could be drawn, were precisely those which put most value on retaining their sons and daughters for the farm. Not only could the latter afford to do without (in the English term) "going into service"; they despised it.

The extreme reluctance of native-born Americans to make their living from household work was recognized throughout the nineteenth century. In 1904 Hugo Munsterberg, professor of psychology at Harvard, saw the spirit of self-assertion, of equality, as being "everywhere the background of social conceptions." Because the work that a man did was not thought to affect his social personality, almost any form of employment was acceptable except that which involved personal dependence. "The chamber-maid has generally much easier work than the shop girl; yet all women flock to the shops and factories, and few care to go into household service. . . . Even the first generation of children born in the country decline to become servants."[50] Since at least 1850 this sensitivity had been recognized by adopting the euphemism "help" or "hand." It was perhaps for the same reason that a footman was called a "waiter" and a lady's maid even a "sempstress."[51] As a result of the shortage, American servants received higher wages than those in England; and some people believed that, because of their greater freedom, they were also better educated, more independent of thought, more able, and more willing. This was not, however, the majority view. Most writers (not just English ones) lamented their lack of training, familiar manners, and ideas above their station. Hardly ever did they wear livery: in fact they dressed much like their employers.

Fortunately for house owners, successive waves of immigration supplied a workforce with less egalitarian ideas. First came the Irish, then the Italians, the Germans, the Swedes, and the Chinese. By the turn of the century a third of domestic servants were foreign born. Even so, supply did not keep pace with demand. In 1890 there were 1,216,000 servants in the country; ten years later this number had risen to 1,283,000 – an increase of 5.5 per cent. During the same period, however, the population had gone up by 20.7 per cent. Domestic service was not badly paid, but it held out no chance of promotion and offered little free time, besides being deeply unfashionable. It suffered from the lack of status reflected in a remark made by an advocate of cooperative housekeeping in 1907: the servant girl, he wrote, "is generally a servant because she is not clever enough to be a factory girl, nor attractive enough to be a prostitute."[52] Others with more direct experience of the servant's life were more charitable. According to Mary Carter, whose *Millionaire Households* of 1903 scarcely preached socialism, the lot of a laundress was "toilsome . . . indeed, exhausting to strength, while consuming the best years of a woman's life, and never adequately paid for."[53] It was difficult for her to save more than a pittance for her retirement.

Some Americans hesitated to work with the foreigners who made up such a large proportion of the workforce; in California the Chinese were thought to make particularly difficult colleagues. Everywhere training schools were failing to supply qualified staff

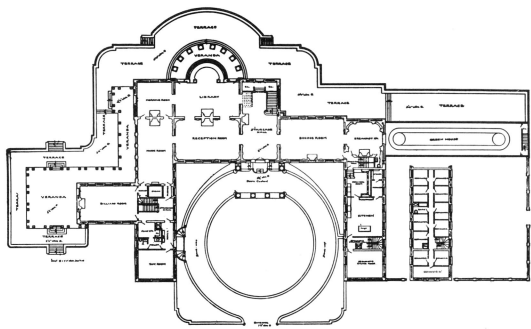

95. Plan of Indian Neck Hall, Long Island, built by Ernest Flagg for Frederick G. Bourne, president of the Singer Manufacturing Company, in 1897–1900. The service wing on the right is a mere shadow of what might have been found in a contemporary British country house. In this case, however, there seems to have been no shortage of domestic help. The bedrooms of the men servants (shown here in the courtyard) occupied the second floor of this wing.

in anything like sufficient numbers. The crisis was particularly acute for those country house owners who, aspiring to a fully aristocratic style of life, were bent on reintroducing the hated word "servant" to describe their domestic staff. "The present use of the word has come not only from the almost exclusive employment of foreigners in domestic service," wrote the authoritative Lucy Salmon in her study of *Domestic Service* in 1901, "but also because of the increase of wealth and consequent luxury in this country, the growing class divisions, and the adoption of many European habits of living and thinking and speaking."[54] Or, as Miss Carter commented more placidly: "In order to establish an unmistakable air of ease in a millionaire's mansion the butler should have *at least* four men with him."

There were two ways of tackling the servant problem. One was to improve the conditions in which servants worked and lived so that they would be less likely to leave. Efforts were made to provide generous bedrooms for servants and to make them attractive. Writing of the Adirondacks, where the supply of staff must have been particularly thin, Augustus D. Shepard wrote: "Anything that the architect can do in arranging the plan to make it possible for camp owners to keep servants satisfied, he should do."[55] In this connection he put the architect's role on a par with that of the family doctor in promoting the well-being of the household. Though a magazine article of 1909 urged every householder "to regularly visit her servants' surroundings and, to use the old Yankee term, to 'poke around' a little occasionally in her servants' bedrooms," most writers wisely took the contrary view, for lack of privacy was one of the strongest objections to being a servant.[56] The other course was to reduce the level of housework so that fewer servants were needed. This exercised the architect's imagination in every department of the country house from the roomy vestibule, where overshoes could be removed so that mud would not penetrate further, to the plumbed-

103

in sink in the kitchen (better than a dishpan on a table to which kettle and waterbucket had to be carried).

The small number of servants created the most obvious of all differences between the English and the American country house. "In looking at the plan of a modern English house," wrote Frank Miles Day in *American Country Houses of Today*,

> the American is struck by the fact that half or more than half of the first floor is given up to housekeepers' and butlers' rooms, to kitchens, larders, sculleries and to little rooms for knives, lamps, boots etc. a vast array of "kitchen offices." The Englishman is equally surprised to find that in an American house of similar size some of these services are quite lacking and the remainder compressed within a third, perhaps even within a fourth part of the area of the first floor.[57]

The one indispensable room was, of course, the kitchen, and most large houses had a pantry and serving room (or butler's pantry). There was likely to be a servants' hall of some kind, because servant maids found that their young men did not like to sit in the kitchen and leave by the back door; closets for refrigeration were given greater prominence than in England; and two or three further closets or larders would be

96. The drying room at Biltmore, where sheets were slid into heated chambers.

necessary for storing food. To have many more rooms than these, however, was distinctly unusual (Plate 95). This in itself implied a different principle of organization from that of England.

The idea behind the planning of English houses was separation of function: every activity should be allocated a special room for it to be performed in. In the United States more rooms simply meant more work, and even the scullery, where vegetables were prepared and dishes washed, was done away with. This threw greater emphasis on the kitchen, yet all professional architects were agreed that, even for a large household, a big kitchen was probably less convenient than a smaller one. "What Every Kitchen Needs," ran the headline in *House and Garden*, " ... Economy of Space that Saves Work."[58] Owners possessed a healthy disrespect for the deep-seated fear of cooking smells which caused the kitchen in an English country house to be separated from the dining room by a long corridor with at least two intervening bends and doors. The American country house rarely had more than the serving room to separate them. On this subject, however, it may be that the English architects had the last laugh. "I also note what you say about the kitchen odors," wrote Charles Schneider to Frank A. Seiberling of Stan Hywet. "I knew that this was giving you trouble last spring for Mrs. Seiberling called it

97. Central heating boilers at Nemours, made by the Kewanee Company in New York.

98. Shields Automatic Bottling Machine. Like J.D. Rockefeller, Alfred I. du Pont bottled his own mineral water.

to my attention and I ordered Palmer to put checks on several doors and made inquiry after these had been placed and was told that the condition had been improved wonderfully."[59] But the smells continued to enter, and there was not a lot that could be done to stop them.

The laundry, as at Kykuit, could be some way from the house, and one would have thought that this would have made the job of laundry maid one of the more desirable below stairs occupations, because of the relative freedom that it brought. However, we have heard Miss Carter on the subject. The hours of the country house laundry were long, starting early and continuing until eight or nine in the evening. When all the work was done by hand – the washing, the scrubbing, the wringing, the ironing – it was hot,

99. Waterwheel at Nemours for pumping water through the gardens, made by the Diamond State Machine Works in Wilmington, Delaware. The hub bears du Pont's name and the date 1931.

wearisome and, for the head laundress, responsible. But this was one area of activity that would be alleviated by mechanization (Plate 96). Happily for servants, the Americans were, as Clarence Cook commented in 1881, a nation "in love with machines and contrivance."[60] The priorities of the American industrialist, who was far more likely to put capital into labor-saving machinery than his counterpart in England, were transferred to the country house. That is hardly surprising, since the industrialist and the country house owner were often the same person. It was for this reason that the technology of some houses took on a beauty of its own, perhaps exceeding that of the architecture it was meant to serve. One rarely has the opportunity to share in the joy that the most mechanically minded owners took in their domestic apparatus, for what has not been scrapped is generally to be found in a derelict, dust-gathering condition. But where one does see a brace of boilers, blazing in a livery of pillarbox red (Plate 97), or a pair of shiny black belt-driven compressors, surrounded by a full supporting cast of flywheels and generators, it is hard to escape the conclusion that, in more ways than one, these represent the heart of the home. The two examples just mentioned are taken from Nemours in Delaware, designed by Carrère and Hastings for Alfred I. du Pont in 1909. Only seven years before, du Pont had joined two of his cousins in buying out the family company, and had then compounded his notoriety by divorcing his wife and taking yet another cousin as his new bride. He was both a successful industrialist and a strong-minded man whose new house can be read as a

101–02. The new domestic technology was one means of easing the servant problem, as these advertisements of 1915 and 1916 show. Significantly a comparable telephone advertisement in England, where domestic labor was still more plentiful, shows the servant racing up and down the stairs.

Calling Mary

Do you shout through the hall, race up and down stairs, wear out your body and nerves? Or do you have an Inter-phone in your bedroom by which you can talk to the servant in the kitchen—give orders and instructions in a way that saves your time and energy and that of the maid?

Western Electric Inter-phones

can be quickly and easily installed in any home—old or new. The illustration shows a connection between bedroom and kitchen. Such a set costs only $15 and can be purchased at your local electrical store, or direct from us.

Send us the $15 and we will ship a two-station outfit by parcel post with full directions for installing. Sets can be had to connect as many rooms as desired, also for communication between buildings, such as house and garage.

Write for our illustrated booklet, "The Way of Convenience." Ask for booklet No. 31-B.

WESTERN ELECTRIC COMPANY

New York	Atlanta	Pittsburg	Chicago	Kansas City	Denver	San Francisco
Buffalo	Richmond	Cleveland	Milwaukee	St. Louis	Salt Lake City	Oakland
Newark	Savannah	Cincinnati	Indianapolis	Dallas	Omaha	Los Angeles
Philadelphia	New Orleans	Detroit St. Paul	Minneapolis	Houston	Oklahoma City	Seattle
Boston						Portland

Send 10c in stamps for new game, "Going to Market"

The New Answer *to the* Servant Problem

She's leaving! Leaving her position—disgruntled; leaving you—discouraged. And you had just congratulated yourself on getting at last a maid who really suited, and who seemed satisfied to stay.

But—you have been all through such experiences time and again. You'll call the Employment Bureau and have them send around another girl. You'll hope for the best—and let it go at that, knowing full well that it will be a repetition of past experiences.

What are you going to do about it?

Listen:

Electricity will make it easier for you to get servants and to *keep* them—by making housework more attractive. And it will simplify your own work if left without a maid.

There's the Washer and Wringer to do the week's wash on a Monday morn, and the Electric Iron to follow it up in the afternoon of the *same* day.

There's the Electric Toaster to make appetizing toast at the table and to keep it crisp and warm.

There's the Electric Range rapidly coming into more general use for cooking through the attractive rates now being made for current in many parts of the country.

And after your electrically prepared meal is over, there is the

Electric Dish-Washer to clear it away.

Then, too, there are the Vacuum Cleaner, the Fan, the Inter-phone and the dozen and one other conveniences—all to be had with the quality mark—Western Electric.

These devices are easy to buy and each one is an investment which soon pays for itself. Exclusive of the Electric Range, the cost of current to operate them all per month is less than your monthly bill for light alone. For while other necessities of life are *increasing* in cost, electric current is steadily decreasing.

If you have a servant problem in your home, why not find out now how electricity can help you solve it?

Write our nearest office today for your copy of Booklet No. 73-B, "The Electrical Way."

WESTERN ELECTRIC COMPANY
INCORPORATED
195 Broadway, New York City
Houses in All Principal Cities of the United States and Canada

Western Electric

America's Electrical Week, December 2nd to 9th

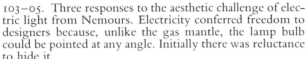

103–05. Three responses to the aesthetic challenge of electric light from Nemours. Electricity conferred freedom to designers because, unlike the gas mantle, the lamp bulb could be pointed at any angle. Initially there was reluctance to hide it.

gesture of defiance to the many other members of the du Pont clan which dominated Delaware. He was also something of an inventor, who numbered Thomas Edison among his friends. This, of course, explains the splendor of the technology, which includes an entire room for making ice (Plate 77), a plant to bottle his own water (Plate 98), and a waterwheel designed by du Pont with his name prominently emblazoned on the hub (Plate 99). All the domestic machinery was made in duplicate so that there was a back-up in case the first system failed.[61]

Just as du Pont's cast-iron trolley for moving trees, again designed by himself, is so heavy that it requires a tractor to move it an inch, the efficiency of du Pont's machines has to be considered in a special sense. They were, one suspects, the below stairs equivalent of thoroughbred racehorses: sleek, beautiful in motion, one-off, but not necessarily the epitome of cost effectiveness. It seems a safe guess that the expense of making and running them in this case outweighed the cost of the wages they saved. Elsewhere, however, the benefits of technological advance, particularly in reducing labor and making life pleasanter for such servants as there were, were undoubtedly real.

First, gas made work in the kitchen easier and more efficient, since, unlike the old range, it did not need to be alight all day. Then electricity presented itself, according to a Western Electric advertisement of 1916, as the "New Answer to the Servant Problem" (Plate 101). Vacuum cleaner, fan, washer and wringer, toaster, electric range, telephone (Plate 100) – all made it easier "to get servants and to *keep* them." Even the kitchen of William Randolph Hearst's San Simeon possessed an automatic electric device for boiling eggs. While the person who benefited most from these inventions was the struggling middle-class housewife, who would before have employed just one maid but now had none, the difficulties of the country house owner battling to keep staff were also eased. The more that the lot of his servants improved, the more did his own peace of mind.

109

100. With the house telephone, messages could be delivered without walking.

— 7 —

"Along that green embowered track"
THE PHILADELPHIA MAIN LINE

PROBABLY THE BEST place to savor the subtle blend of English and American tastes that gives zest to the American country house is in that area west of Philadelphia known as the Main Line. The very name – derived from the Main Line of Public Works that connected Philadelphia with Pittsburg, but popularly associated with the main line of the Pennsylvania Railroad – indicates a pattern of organization that knows no direct parallel in Europe. For without the railroad's services, not to mention its promotional activities and even sales of land, there is no reason to suppose that the area would have become celebrated for its numerous rural estates. But veiling this uniquely American – one might almost say uniquely Philadelphian – form was a gauze of other influences, its threads selected, sometimes, from the finest that the rest of the world could offer.

"It is elevated; its atmosphere is pure; it is thoroughly drained by numerous streams; its soil is fertile; and it is in a striking degree picturesque," declared a far from impartial source – the office of the railroad's General Passenger Agent – of the region through which the railroad passed. "Nature – the great landscape gardener – has carved and molded it into rolling hills and placid vales, and so studded it with trees and interlaced it with crystal rivulets, that the picture everywhere is lovely to look upon. Added to all are the improvements made by the Pennsylvania Railroad Company."[1] The PRR's main purpose in driving its lines westward to Cincinnati was to take its share of the traffic of an expanding continent: in the 1860s, gentlemen unfortunate enough to miss the last train home to their country estates were forced to take a crowded, evil-smelling night train called the Emigrant. But the potential for local traffic had also been foreseen as early as 1832, when the old Columbia Railroad ran a stopping train to Paoli. The Paoli Local, as it was known, became more than an ordinary service. With its obliging conductors, ready to help with bags or even take messages for passengers whom they probably knew by name, it was the symbol of a way of life. The General Passenger Agent wrote of "station-houses that are models of beauty and comfort" and luxurious trains that catered for every need. No wonder then that it later seemed the emblem of a golden, unhurried world:

> Along that green embowered track
> My heart throws off its peddler's pack
> In memory commuting back
> Now swiftly and now slowly –

111

106. Rathalla at Rosement, home of the manufacturer and banker Joseph F. Sinnott, designed by Hazelhurst and Huckel.

107. Perspective drawing of Bardwold by Benjamin Linfoot, 1885. It was the home of the widow of Matthew Baird of the Baldwin Locomotive Works. Many of the early residents on the Main Line had an association with the railroad. The Athenaeum of Philadelphia

> Ah! lucky people, you, in sooth,
> Who ride that caravan of youth
> The Local to Paoli.[2]

The combination of country estates and commuting would reappear, decades later, in Lake Forest and Lake Bluff, where rich Chicagoans increasingly sought refuge after the vicious labour disputes of the 1870s. Arthur Meeker, the novelist whose family owned Arcady Farm in Lake Forest, captured the semi-country, semi-suburban atmosphere in his book *Chicago, with Love*:

> the scene on the Northwestern railroad platform each week-day afternoon when the 5.55 came in, bringing husbands and fathers back from the city, was like an informal outdoor reception. Of course, with the constant coming and going and many close links to Chicago, it was hardly a rural existence in the English sense: they wouldn't call our country, country, any more than we'd call their life, life. But it was all extraordinarily agreeable.[3]

However, though some estates ran to several hundred acres, these Illinois communities were geographically more limited than the straggling Main Line.

Sometimes the Local would make an unscheduled stop at a private halt, placed there by one of the PRR's directors. It must sometimes have seemed that nearly all the rich residents up and down the Main Line had some connection with this wondrous fount of wealth. President George B. Roberts – "this useful and unassuming man," as he was described in typical language of the time[4] – occupied a farmhouse that had been in his family for five generations. Alexander J. Cassatt, soon to become third vice-president, built a substantial house, Cheswold, at Haverford in 1872–73 and bred horses on his farm at Berwyn; it was during his presidency of the railroad that McKim, Mead and White's Pennsylvania Station in New York, based on the Baths of Caracalla, was built. Other PRR men felt more or less compelled to follow Cassatt's lead. Those not directly employed by the railroad might well have been associated with the Baldwin Locomotive Works. A partner was Matthew Baird, whose widow built a massive house called Bardwold, of which the porte-cochère is shown in Plate 107. It is of course an illusion to suppose that every country house was built with railroad money, but equally there can have been few successful lawyers or bankers who failed to participate in the enormous riches that it brought.

That so many people wanted to establish themselves in the country is less surprising in Philadelphia than elsewhere. William Penn himself, hoping both that city-dwellers would think about the country and farmers understand the city, had granted plots within the city to those who bought large tracts of country land. The region became one of the few with a native tradition of country house building that continued after Independence. Country houses developed along the Schuykill River and around the Lancaster Turnpike, the line of which was almost exactly that later taken by the railroad. In the mid-nineteenth century additional prestige was given to landownership by the founding of the Farmers' Club. Whatever the value of the papers read at the Farmers' Club's monthly meetings, held when the moon was full to facilitate night driving, the club's significant feature was that membership was limited to twelve. This had precisely the effect that its founders must have anticipated, and to be elected was soon regarded as one of the highest social honors.

Country houses there already were around Philadelphia, but it was not only through them that most new owners were introduced to the pleasures of country life. As in so many places, the era of building large country houses was preceded by one of boarding in hotels. Philadelphia, the "Red City," was thought to be particularly stuffy in the summer because the brick of which it was built retained the heat. In later years families would go north to Maine, but in the 1860s they preferred a remedy more close at hand. They traveled no further than the old turnpike inns, where they could walk and drive and ride, play sedately at croquet and quoits, and read novels. Of these inns the most fashionable was the White Hall Hotel at Bryn Mawr, with its overflow, the Wildgoss Boarding House, run by a lady and daughters of that name. Several country house builders had been Wildgoss boarders.

The development of Bryn Mawr lay with the PRR. In the late 1860s, wishing to straighten out a kink in the line, it bought a large farm as an alternative to paying heavy compensation. On this land it not only built the large Bryn Mawr Hotel but began erecting houses and selling plots. Great was the rejoicing when, according to official government figures, the railroad station at Bryn Mawr was found to be four inches higher than that of the Main Line's airy rival, Chestnut Hill.

From earliest days a point was made of English, or rather British, associations. Several estates were given names such as Chetwynd, Thorncroft, and Leighton Place after English progenitors of the family or the houses which they had owned. Cricket thrived – and, as the Rev. S.F. Hotchin observed, "bats and balls and wickets and gloves and flannel abound."[5] The Merion Cricket Club was founded in 1865 and furnished by Frank Furness with the present large clubhouse, confusingly at Haverford, thirty years later. The rolling hills of Chester County, crossed by post-and-rail fences, were well suited to chasing the fox, and the Radnor Hunt Club – the very center of existence for some country house folk – was established in 1883. Landscape that spelled sport to some eyes suggested gardening and planting to others. Many owners emulated Clement A. Griscom's example in creating a garden at Dolobran. It was largely woodland with thirty acres forming an American Wild Garden stocked with native plants and trees. Like many Main Liners, Griscom, a member of the Farmers' Club as well as president of a transatlantic steamship company, seemed the very image of a country gentleman, keeping a model farm on which, according to *Fads and Fancies*, "the cowpens and the sheepfolds are as perfectly appointed in their own way as one of the International Navigation Company's ocean greyhounds."[6]

Influences were not only English but Welsh. This may seem strange, since Wales was at that time generally regarded as a poor and unfashionable corner of the British Isles. But parts of the country around Philadelphia had been settled in the seventeenth century by Welsh Quakers, and this early history gave Wales and things Welsh a certain glamour. Naturally the settlers had brought with them one or two names from their homeland, such as Merion. But when the PRR, largely under the unassuming, Welsh-descended President Roberts, began to dominate the region, a serious new outbreak of Welshness occurred. Names such as Bryn Mawr and Wynewood appeared out of nowhere. Old names such as Elm Corner vanished to be replaced by the spuriously Welsh ones of Narberth and Radnor. Soon the Welsh game was being played by private people – Dolobran, for instance, having been named after an estate in Wales owned by the Lloyd family, Griscom's maternal forebears.

The Main Line's exaggerated identity with Wales was captured by Margaret B. Harvey in Her *Song of the Dames of Merion*, to the tune of *Men of Harlech*:

> Merion hath sturdy yeomen,
> Sprung from race of cymric bowmen,
> Ever quick to scorn the foemen,
> Ready for the fray!
> Merion hath beauty!
> Dames alive to duty!
> All their hearts despise the arts
> Of spoilers bent on booty!

It would be interesting to have a closer definition of "spoilers bent on booty" and know if any of them had settled on the Main Line. Respect for ancestry, or supposed ancestry, rarely extended to Quakerism, and the popular pattern of church building was that later replicated in Maine: a rich Episcopalean edifice for the masters, a larger Roman Catholic one for the staff.

All this Welshness seems to have had little direct expression architecturally, but it is evidence of the Main Liner's intense consciousness of his past, and this is reflected in a reverence for old buildings. Thoughts were turned to Colonial architecture by the Centennial Exhibition, celebrating the hundredth anniversary of the nation, held in Philadelphia in 1876; and it was not long before farmhouses were being bought and restored with varying degrees of sensitivity. Rodman B. Ellison's Linden Slade Farm, bought in 1886, may have been one of the better examples, since the addition of library, billiard room, and bedrooms was made in the form of two "cabins" which did not impair the existing structure. The house that B.F. Clyde purchased in Radnor in 1892, once Washington's headquarters, probably fared rather worse. Hotchkin revealed more than he intended when he wrote: "As we look to-day upon the interior of this modern and beautiful summer home it is hard to realize that the old stone mansion is of historic

108. Bloomfield, home of George McFadden, a characteristically suave work by Horace Trumbauer.

interest."[7] More successfully, perhaps, care was also taken to make new houses look as though they had been settled in the landscape for many years.

It took some time for the Colonial Revival to gather steam. Philadelphia architects of the 1870s and 1880s – Addison Hutton, George Hewitt, Theophilus Chandler, and Frank Furness – favored boldly eclectic architecture (Plate 109), full of vigor, a little whimsical, often with towers hinting at Scotland. In this as in other ways A.J. Cassatt's Cheswold, designed and many times altered by Furness, set the pace, though, had it survived, the interior, hung with Impressionists bought on the advice of Cassatt's artist sister Mary, would have been more memorable. "Hold on to your Monets, I am only sorry I did not urge you to buy more," she wrote from Paris as their price rose.[8] From Europe, too, came some of the furnishings, though not enough to satisfy Cassatt's pretty, bird-brained wife, Lois: "I have been to all the principal dressmakers here and I must say they are too awfully dear to buy much. . . . To do what we want to do properly for the house and all we ought to stay the entire time in London and Paris."[9] Eclectic houses continued to be built into the 1890s. A monumental example, Rathalla at Rosemont (Plate 106), was designed by the firm of Hazlehurst and Huckel for Joseph F.

115

109. Carved timber gable of Wooton, an example of the boldly eclectic architecture favored before 1900.

110. Lynedoch, W.P. Simpson's estate at Overbrook. So great was the fashion for Virginia creeper and other climbing plants that wall surfaces were often left plain, being lost to view.

Sinnott, manufacturer and director of the First National Bank. "It is on the crest of a hill and quite noticeable from the Pennsylvania Railroad," observed Moses King in his *Philadelphia and Notable Philadelphians* of 1902.[10] With its splended white towers, just asymmetrical, and vigorous silhouette, it must have impressed and inspired the commuters. Shortly, however, it would come to look out of date, as Horace Trumbauer introduced his suaver historicism (Plate 108).

Trumbauer himself was something of a rare bird in Philadelphia. His large, showy mansions still offend the prevailing canon of taste in which an important factor is reserve. So reluctant were owners to make a too-flamboyant architectural display that they often all but hid their buildings under ivy or Virginia creeper. Generally the ivy has now been removed, but old photographs show that at the turn of the century some houses became virtually one with the landscape, great haystacks of greenery with only the protruding window awnings to signal the presence of a dwelling underneath (Plate 110). The fashion for creepers may explain why wall surfaces were often kept unusually plain and decoration was concentrated above the level of the gutters. Creepers did much to soften the appearance of the buildings they covered, thus prefiguring the use of more sympathetic building materials that would become a hallmark of Philadelphia architecture after 1900.

"He was absorbingly preoccupied with textures – textures achieved by everyday materials used in countless ways," wrote an obituarist of Wilson Eyre; "varying the bonding and the mortar width in stone and brickwork, adze-dressing of timber, roughness in plaster surfaces. He was continuously interested in craftsmanship, and full of ingenuity in obtaining good work with the craftsmen at hand."[11] Born in Florence, Eyre was a man of discriminating taste who regarded architecture as an art. His example

116

was followed in the 1920s by such architects as Robert Rodes Goodwin, Arthur Ingersoll Meigs, and David Knickerbacker Boyd (Plate 111). Their work is distinguished by the use of local materials, particularly the attractive local limestone. They did not necessarily use the region's own historical styles, preferring the Tudor, Cotswold, and Normandy idioms. What unites them is an eye for proportion, a feeling for picturesque composition, and a sympathy for the materials with which they worked.

Even more extreme and more Philadelphian is Richardson Brognard Okie (Plate 112). More than anyone, Okie epitomizes the Philadelphian country house owner's reticence and attachment to the past. He himself was a countryman who enjoyed living on his ninety acre farm near Devon, Pennsylvania, and was proud of the horses that he exhibited at the Devon Horse Show. He hated the modern world, mechanical devices, and motorcars, and it is ironic that he should have met his death in a motor accident in 1945. "Colonial Revival" is too strong a term to be applied to his architecture, which is more a continuation of the tradition of the old Pennsylvania Dutch houses which he intimately knew and thoroughly understood. The keynotes of his style were undressed fieldstone walls, door and window frames of solid oak or cypress, and substantial chimneys reflecting equally substantial fireplaces inside. Where he could get away with it, he also favored wide floorboards, handmade nails, oak door frames pinned with oak dowels, and hand-split cypress shingles. In the old farmhouse manner, rooms were placed one after another like a row of beads. Simplicity was the ruling principle.

In the novelist Joseph Hergesheimer he found an ideal client. Okie must have been delighted when his first set of plans for restoring Hergesheimer's old farmhouse was sent back with the comment that it was not nearly simple enough. The second set was

111. Gatelodge to Walmarthon, home of the leather manufacturer Charles Walton. This work of the 1920s is by David Knickerbacker Boyd.

112. Appleford at Gladwyn, R. Brognard Okie's enlargement of an early-eighteenth-century farmhouse. Okie specialized in country houses based closely on old Pennsylvania traditions.

113. The Radnor Hounds at Brookthorpe, seat of the avid sportsman and author of foxhunting books J. Stanley Reeve, painted by Charles Morris Young in 1922. Private Collection

accepted, and Hergesheimer described the resulting building work in his book *From an Old House* of 1925. Restoration involved stripping the walls back to the stonework, inserting a concrete floor, and adding such un-Colonial features as a sleeping porch, bathrooms, and modern kitchen; in fact the house was virtually rebuilt. But for all that, as much as possible of the old fabric, including paneling, was retained and – according to Hergesheimer – the spirit of the old building was not dispelled. It kept its ghosts. When he watched his wife "seated on the floor and drawing over milk-white legs the sheerest of stockings," he was still able to wonder "what different women, with that same movement in that same room, had put on what different stockings, thick and home-made! What different men, in the dimmest morning, had hurried into stout breeches there!"[12]

It may seem that Hergesheimer's enthusiasms were just those satirized by the novelist John P. Marquand in *So Little Time*: Beckie wanted the old Connecticut farm that she and Fred had bought to retain "the atmosphere of those dear old people who had lived on it and who had made things with their hands, such as pail yokes and wooden scoops and sap buckets, and those dear little cobblers' benches that you could stand in front of the fireplace to put things on, such as cigarettes and cocktail glasses and what have you."

118

Soon the architect Simpson Bolling had persuaded her to add on stone wings and a tower in the Normandy *manoir* style, since "Norman-French and New England were really the same thing, basically, and she and Simpson had not done a single thing, either, to spoil the spirit of the old house." But the mood inside remained distinctly "old, farmy and kitcheny," as Beckie called it.

In taking your place at the seventeenth-century trestle table, which Fred had found on Madison Avenue, you had to be careful not to stumble over spits and pots and candle molds and pestles and mortars and other ancient implements which had been collected on the old kitchen hearth. An old pine dresser, very old and very battered, was filled with pewter. Candles burned in pewter candlesticks and the central table decoration was a great mound of small multi-colored gourds, all varnished and heaped on an enormous pewter platter. Around the platter and among the candles were ears of red and yellow corn, and a few small pumpkins to show that it was autumn. The chairs were simple wooden kitchen chairs which Fred and Beckie had been collecting over a period of years, constantly discarding one when they found a better one, until all of them now had a fine patina. Fred had once said that he hated to think how many pants seats had been worn out, and how many spines had been curved, giving those chairs their present luster.

Of course, it is easy to make fun. Hergesheimer may have been at times a little too fanciful for modern tastes, but his feeling for the past had a solid foundation in the knowledge that old country buildings, and the customs and countryside that went with them, were fast disappearing. As he wrote in the introduction to a collection of photographs that had recorded pre-Revolutionary architecture around Philadelphia:

> Month by month, almost day by day, better roads, laid in concrete, were taking the place of the old country lanes with, in spring, their banks dark with violets. Day by day, it seemed, the cities were reaching out into the country with their hideous and inappropriate houses, suburbs of villas.... Lovely serene buildings were torn down, to make way for the villas and bungalows, without any faint realization of the fatality that ignoble destruction was bringing about.[13]

Hergesheimer's indignation was that of the artist, but his instinct for the old ways of the countryside was not so different from that felt by many country house owners since the 1880s. Moreover, he shared an identity of interest with people who were very far from arty, who perhaps had never read his books. In 1930 the Radnor Hunt Club (see Plate 56) was forced to leave its old premises at Bryn Mawr and move out to the greener pastures of White Horse. The dedicated rider to hounds J. Stanley Reeve, author of *Red Coats in Chester Country, Radnor Reminiscences*, and other books of foxhunting lore, felt obliged to take the same route. Having built Brookthorpe at Bryn Mawr in 1921 (Plate 113), he now constructed a "small but comfortable hunting-box" called Runnymede in 1931 and transferred his stable there, cursing the encroachment of the suburbs, the conversion of soft roads to motor highways, the increased use of barbed wire, and the onward march of the twentieth century in general.

— 8 —

"Everything here grows wonderfully"
WINTERTHUR

THE DIFFICULTY of disentangling the cultural ideals that influenced the American country house are illustrated succinctly by a house that lies a few dozen miles to the south of the Main Line, Winterthur. This surely would seem to be the most American of houses, since it is celebrated for its unrivalled and exquisitely displayed collections of American decorative arts. One might add that the form that the building ultimately took externally – more like a sanitarium than a country house – has no obvious parallel in European architecture; it expanded outwards and upwards under pressure from the collections inside (Plate 120). But in other respects it appears the very ideal of the British- or at least European-style country house. It was surrounded by a large working estate in which successive owners took pride (Plate 139): even Henry Francis du Pont, who finally turned the house into a museum, was devoted to it. It is surrounded by woods and naturalistic gardens that owe much of their ultimate inspiration to the English gardener Gertrude Jekyll. Above all it grew organically over a period of a century and a half, thanks to the varying needs, enthusiasms, obsessions, and priorities of several generations of one family of owners. This alone serves to make it a very rare thing in the history of the American country house, which, as we have seen, was seldom expected to serve the purpose of a dynastic seat. Clearly it is a phenomenon that must be looked at in some detail.

To discover the origins of Winterthur we must look back beyond the time frame of this book, to the early nineteenth century. For the first of the two owners who principally shaped the house before Henry Francis du Pont was James Antoine Bidermann, known as Antoine, the son of a rich Swiss financier whose family enjoyed long associations with Winterthur in Switzerland. Bidermann *père* had been one of the largest investors in Éleuthère Irénée du Pont's infant gunpowder company, founded in 1802, and in 1814 the young Antoine, aged only twenty-four, was sent to America to investigate a failure to pay dividends. His financial skill complemented du Pont's technical knowledge and manufacturing ability. Having declared the books to be in order, he moved in with the family and before long had married du Pont's daughter, Evelina. The couple lived in Hagley House until du Pont's death in 1834, upon which Bidermann took control of the company. Within three years he had reorganized it so that succession could pass to du Pont's sons; he himself was ready to retire and become a gentleman farmer. Hagley House was literally on top of the powder works – so close that it was possible for the severed limb of a workman to land on the front lawn after an

114. Henry Francis du Pont's dining room at Winterthur, Delaware.

115. Winterthur. The original Greek Revival box can be seen beneath the steeply pitched roof and tall chimneys added in 1884.

116. The new entrance front added by Colonel Henry Algernon du Pont in 1902. The old slate roof was replaced by one of Spanish tiles; the interior had something of the masculine feeling of a gentleman's club.

explosion. Bidermann's farmland was further removed, in the valley of a fast-running stream called Clenny Run. It was overlooking this stream that he built Winterthur.

Plans were acquired from the French architect N. Vergnaud during a long visit, partly for business reasons, that the Bidermanns paid to Europe in 1837–39. They were considerably simplified during execution, however, and the house that arose was austere and square, enlived only by window shutters and ennobled by a Greek Doric porte-cochère, the columns placed somewhat illiterately on plinths. To the *Delaware Republican*, writing in 1858, it seemed a "splendid mansion," and, if this judgment seems suspect, one has less difficulty in sharing its view of the landscape. The approaching visitor was "astonished and delighted at the romantic appearance – first at the beautiful fields, as he wends his way on the serpentine road, next passing through the beautiful forest which is decked in various directions with graveled walks, until he arrives in the valley where the stupendous tenant house, large barns and out buildings attract his attention, surrounded with timber."[1] For Bidermann, with his long financial experience, farming was a business as much as a hobby. But like so many of the du Ponts and their associates, the family were also active gardeners. "I have dahlias planted and in bud. The roses and pinks are also just opening, the strawberries shaping," wrote Evelina to her son in France. And again: "Everything here grows wonderfully."[2]

As Bidermann left it, Winterthur, designed as it was by a Frenchman, was virtually indistinguishable from houses that could be found in Europe. It was Colonel Henry A. du Pont, the father of Henry Francis and known universally as "the Colonel," who transformed it into something unmistakably American. One of the Colonel's passions was the landscape; another was family history; another books. Guests would be shown every book in the library, one by one, causing them to run dry of admiring adjectives. Architecture seems to have held less fascination for him. Nevertheless, that did not stop the Colonel remodeling the house on three separate occasions. The first campaign took place while he and his bride were away in Europe following their wedding in 1874. Work was supervised and no doubt paid for by his father, General Henry du Pont, who kept a tight rein on expenses. This did not entirely discourage the architect Theophilus Chandler, du Pont's brother-in-law, who buoyantly despatched progress reports, probably expecting that more would be done when the Colonel returned. "Do not laugh at the grand display of walks and terrace that I have just scribbled," he wrote of one scheme that the General showed no inclination to pass. "And now while I mention terrace, you will see so many pretty examples of just such arrangement of terrace and lawn in France, and better still in Italy – Why not make a memorandum? – and find photographs of such as you see, in a similar situation."[3] Elaborate precedents were scarcely needed for the work then in hand. It included inserting an arch into the ground floor hall, relocating a fireplace, installing a dumb waiter and creating a new bathroom – nothing that greatly altered the external appearance of the Bidermann house.

In this form Winterthur served for a decade. With a growing family (though all but two of them died in childhood) and the rewards of a successful business career, more space was required. The answer was to place a steeply pitched slate roof on top of the Greek Revival box (Plate 115). "I don't believe I shall recognize your much changed house with its gables, and tiles, and turrets," a friend wrote to Mrs. du Pont. "It must look quite a castle."[4] It did not; it looked merely incongruous, rather as though a stovepipe hat had been placed on top of a classical statue. When in 1902, thirteen years after the death of the General, the du Pont company was sold to three du Pont cousins, the Colonel lost no time in undertaking a more full-blooded remodeling. This time the architects were the little-known Philadelphia firm of Robeson Lea Perot and Elliston Perot Bissell. Their work was gorgeously mixed in manner, though heavy. The old building was completely obscured behind a new front and wing. The front comprised

117. The marble staircase built for Colonel du Pont. Henry Francis du Pont reacted against the heavy, somewhat charmless taste of his father, and this staircase was ultimately replaced by the Montmorenci staircase (Plate 122).

123

118. Sandwich glass at Beauport, Massachusetts. This somewhat theatrical back-lit arrangement displays the gentleman-decorator Henry Davis Sleeper's sure eye for color in appealing but relatively humble objects.

drawing room, entrance hall, stair hall, and office; the wing, which was next to the office, contained a squash court, billiard room, and library. The emphasis was on masculine needs and the decoration had a similarly clubby feel; a high point was the marble stairs (Plate 117). Outside, the former slate roof was replaced by one of old Spanish tiles that sorted oddly with François Premier dormers and weighed so much that virtually all the walls of the Bidermann house had to be rebuilt to support it (Plate 116). "The house seemed enormous!" recorded Marian Lawrence, a young visitor in 1905. "The hall was solid marble with marble pillars and staircases with bronze railings all the way up to the third story. Large azalea trees in full bloom were set about in the hall in pots."[5]

It was in this house that Henry Francis du Pont, or Harry, grew up. The unyielding masculine character of the building reflected his father's character, which remained sternly martial. Du Pont and his sister would be sent to bed without supper if they forgot the Latin names of their father's plants. The Colonel was extremely attached to his gardens and trees. When an ancient chestnut was struck by lightning, he wrote that he would "feel terribly if this injury should kill the poor old tree."[6] One of his lasting contributions to Winterthur was to lay out the Pinetum, inspired by examples he had seen in England. Saddened by the expensive failure of the architecture, Miss Lawrence was delighted by the underplanting of dogwoods and azaleas that seemed to shimmer in the woods. "Harry Dupont told me to pick all the lilies of the valley I liked, write the addresses of people to whom I wanted them sent and the butler would box and send them. This is a luxury! I picked until I was tired and sent them to the family and aunts at home."[7]

Despite the severity over names, it was gardening that brought the father and son closest together. Mrs. du Pont died in 1902; in 1906 the Colonel was elected to the U.S. Senate and spent part of each year in Washington. As a result, the running of Winterthur fell increasingly to Harry. At Harvard he had studied horticulture at the Bussey Institution, situated near the Arnold Arboretum. When he had the opportunity to apply his knowledge at Winterthur, he combined botanical science with a feeling for the soft color harmonies of Gertrude Jekyll. He showed the restraint of the artist in limiting his palette, though equally something of his father's character emerged in the precision he demanded even when organizing naturalistic effects. Detained in Paris and unable to supervise the 1911 plantings, Harry was glad that he had had someone make a plan showing "with greatest accuracy the position of each tulip."[8] A cousin, Anna Robinson, was detailed to supervise the planting of the new bulbs – probably about thirty thousand – following a complicated system of labels that du Pont had already placed in the ground. Poor Anna was required to annotate each of these labels with another of her own tied onto it.

Until the Colonel's death in 1926 the house and its decoration remained outside Harry's preserve. However, he had other opportunities. Having married in 1916, he maintained his own apartment in New York and built a house on Long Island. The house gave him his first taste of collecting and arrangement. Two events that took place within a few days of each other in 1923 aroused his passion for objects. The first was a visit to Mrs. J. Watson Webb's home at Shelburne, Vermont, where he saw her collection of early American furniture. As Jay Cantor has commented, it is not surprising that, his eye trained by years of gardening, he should have been particularly drawn to the color of such pieces as some Staffordshire plates in a pine dresser.

The second was another house visit, this time to Henry Davis Sleeper's Beauport near Gloucester, Massachusetts. Sleeper was a man in easy circumstances who had studied at the École des Beaux-Arts but became, instead of an architect, a set designer, decorator, and dealer. In Boston he knew Isabella Stewart Gardner, and the example of her Venetian palazzo there, Fenway Court, must have influenced Beauport, which was begun in 1907 and then grew and grew as new rooms were added almost continuously over the next three decades. But Sleeper's taste was less for the grand than for the intimate, the charming, the special, the unexpected. Though Sleeper's rooms were created for the accommodation of old paneling and old furniture, historical accuracy was not much aimed at. More important was the subtle coordination of color and light and the theatrical contrast of one room with another. Inevitably the piecemeal growth of the house created some odd corners and awkward passages; these only served to stimulate Sleeper's ingenuity and bring forth such happy ideas as a false, back-lit window filled with mellow-colored Sandwich glass (Plate 118).

Du Pont determined that his house on Long Island would be "American" and he

119. The new wing snakes around the hillside, 1929. The eccentric proportions were caused by the desire to minimize damage to the woodland and to incorporate period rooms.

120. Winterthur from the southeast. When work on the rebuilding was finished, the Colonel's house had been all but obliterated.

asked Sleeper to help him. The collecting of American furniture and even rooms was nothing new by this time. As early as 1850 Ben: Perley Poore had begun building old paneling, stairs, and mantels into his house, Indian Hill, perhaps inspired by Sir Walter Scott's Abbotsford which he had visited as a boy. The taste quickened after the Centennial celebrations of 1876, and in 1907, evidently influenced by Poore but more scientific in approach, George Francis Dow created a series of period rooms in the Essex Institute in Salem. Academic respectability came when the Metropolitan Museum of Art in New York held the first major exhibition of American furniture in 1909. The same year a group of gentleman collectors founded the Walpole Society, to which du Pont would belong. They took their name from the eighteenth-century English collector Horace Walpole because "he was the discoverer of English arts and crafts at a time when polite society could appreciate only the foreign";[10] in a similar way the Walpoleans sought to boost the status of Americana. With collecting went a concern to preserve old houses, seen in the Society for the Preservation of New England Antiquities, which was founded in 1910. (In the fullness of time Beauport itself came to be recognized as an outstanding expression of New England culture and was acquired by the SPNEA soon after Sleeper's death in 1934.)

After the First World War the interest of Henry Ford and John D. Rockefeller, Jr., was aroused. In Ford's case the spur had been the restoration of his family home, finished in 1919; he went on to amass enormous quantities of artefacts judged to reflect the American spirit for the Henry Ford Museum and Greenfield Village in Dearborn, Michigan. "A rather doubtful compliment, I think," commented du Pont when told by Ford's curator that his collection was equally as good.[11] When du Pont saw the first photographs of Williamsburg in 1934, it struck him as looking "terribly new. . . . If I had been Mr. Rockefeller I would rather have done less to the little houses on the main street and done more to the main building in order to convey the illusion of age."[12]

By 1925 du Pont had already bought several hundred American pieces as well as some architectural details. He called his new home Chestertown House after rooms that he installed from various houses in Chestertown, Maryland. It was not an especially large building and the furniture tended to be of the simpler kinds, made from oak or pine: Sleeper enjoyed the contrast that light-colored wood made with dark paneling. Inheriting Winterthur offered larger possibilities. The way his mind was working can

126

be gathered from a letter written to one of his favorite dealers, J.A. Lloyd Hyde, in 1927: "Should you run across a large American room, or know of one, I should be much obliged if you would let me know, as I might need one for this house here sometime."[13] However, that seemingly casual comment hardly prepares one for the scale of the addition that he undertook in 1929, which trebled the size of the house. A new conservatory was applied to what had been the entrance front, while a long thin wing ending in a kink projected southwards from the back (Plate 119). New entrances were made on each side of this wing (Plate 121); the old roof was replaced by one of flat tiles. Externally the Colonel's house could now barely be discerned.

Like his father, however, du Pont had been anxious that his enormous additions – nine stories tall in places – should disturb the existing landscape as little as possible. This partly explains the curious massing of the house, which seems to be all spine and no flesh. For so large a building it is extraordinarily understated. It has no controlling accent; even the main entrance door, hidden behind old trees on the terrace, fails to command attention (Plate 120). For someone who became so preoccupied with decoration, du Pont had peculiarly little interest in the external appearance of his house. His architect was a local man, Albert Ely Ives, and it seems that his main task was to incorporate the old rooms that du Pont had assembled. Efforts to create a coherent exterior were handicapped by the need to build in cornices and windowsills, doorways, dormers, and quoins from two eighteenth-century country houses – Woodlands and Port Royal – near Philadelphia. They dictated detailing of a more delicate scale than could ever be appropriate for so large a building.

121. Exterior of Winterthur, looking towards the Port Royal entrance. The entrance was adapted from the Port Royal House built near Frankford, Pennsylvania.

But the justification lay inside. The obvious inspiration for a series of period rooms was the recently completed American wing at the Metropolitan Museum of Art, which had a profound effect on many collectors. "Those who know their American Wing," commented *Town and Country* of Colonel H.H. Rogers's shooting-box at Southampton, would recognize "a magnified reproduction" of the Old Ship Meeting-House at Hingham, built in 1681, which was conscientiously installed in the gallery on the third floor.[14] Initially, however, du Pont hoped to continue to receive advice from Sleeper, who had been a shaping influence on his taste. An illustration of the Sleeper approach is provided in a letter about two carved eagles which du Pont had bought:

> They are very good of their kind and although not exactly alike, are almost so, and to my way of thinking more attractive and real looking for not being absolutely a pair . . .
>
> I think you could make a very attractive and interesting room by planning niches to fit them at the end of a low barrel vaulted ceiling. I should be inclined to make the latter a flat arch, such as you often see in the out-buildings of colonial houses. No doubt the architect might resist this idea as not being perfectly regular, but unless you insist upon the seeming eccentricities I think the room might look too Georgian and ordinary.[15]

Regularity and ordinariness were to be avoided, even at the expense of authenticity. But by now Sleeper was an old man and unable to give du Pont the attention that he needed; they parted company. Fortunately du Pont had on hand another expert with whom to discuss every detail of the project. This was his widowed friend Bertha Benkard, a recognized authority on eighteenth-century furniture, notably Duncan Phyfe, and president general of the Colonial Dames of America.

Guided by Mrs. Benkard, du Pont bought literally thousands of objects for Winterthur. He possessed the four ideal attributes of the collector: knowledge, money, passion, patience. He was always prepared to wait for the "perfect" object or piece of textile. He trusted Mrs. Benkard to the extent of sending her detailed shopping lists – often several pages long – of things to look out for among the New York dealers. Often shopping expeditions were made together. When they were not, du Pont would pursue her from Florida and elsewhere with telegrams. "PREFER GIMP IN RED AND WHITE PARLOR. USE WHATEVER FINISHED NAILS WOULD LOOK BEST IN RECEPTION ROOM. LET US GET THE WHITE BROCADE WITH GREEN VINE AND SMALL RED ROSES FOR ENTRANCE HALL SOFA," he cabled in March 1931. "USE PEACOCK CHINTZ IN GOLF ROOM. ALL THE EXTRA CHAIRS TO BE USED IN DINING ROOM. SIXTEEN IN ALL. SHOW THEM WHERE YOU WANT THE EAGLES IN BADMINTON COURT." They shared a passion, not just for furniture, but for upholstery, always preferring old fabric to new and fussing anxiously about the details (Plate 123). Fringes could cause agony: "It is absurd, but really modern fringe kills every kind of antique material," wrote du Pont. "There is a certain queer, standing-out harsh quality about it which is unbelievably bad."[16] Decorators were instructed to give paint surfaces a "rubbed look" and "sort of antique finish." The beauty that du Pont sought to achieve was one of complete harmony and repose. He was fond of the maxim that "if you go into a room, any room, and right away see something, then you realize that it shouldn't be in the room."[17]

Paneling, doorcases, and mantelpieces were given as much personal attention as furniture and fabrics. These, however, were not Mrs. Benkard's special field. For advice he was first driven towards books; later he came to rely on the young architect Thomas T. Waterman. Both took du Pont in a somewhat different direction from the one he had

128

122. The Montmorenci staircase, installed in the 1930s. The stair, from Montmorenci, North Carolina, was originally circular and went up only one flight.

123. The Cecil Bedroom. The counterpane is believed to have been inherited by John Hancock from his uncle Thomas, a stationer and bookseller in Boston during the first half of the eighteenth century.

been traveling with Mrs. Benkard. Waterman was a contrast to his worldly friend from New York. "I hope you aren't having any very fashionable guests as I am down to one suit, one linen suit & evening clothes (!) and a much darned bathing suit," he wrote before one visit. "My finances are so precarious I can't get any new ones, so I will have to be admired for myself."[18] Waterman had been employed as a draftsman for a firm of restoration architects working on Williamsburg. In 1932 he organized a tour of old Southern houses for du Pont and Mrs. Benkard; three years later he was given the job of fitting some old paneling from Warren County, North Carolina, into Winterthur. Soon he was working on du Pont's most ambitious piece of reconstruction: installing the staircase from Montmorenci.

For many people the Montmorenci staircase (Plate 122), sweeping lightly upwards on its elegant ellipse, is their most vivid memory of the Winterthur Museum. In du Pont's campaign to extirpate his father's taste it represented a triumph, since it took the place of the Colonel's marble stair. Nevertheless, it caused heart-searching on the architect's part, if not the client's. Montmorenci was a house in Shocco Springs, North Carolina, dating from about 1822. In its original form the staircase was circular and went up only one flight; to adapt it to the proportions of the stair hall at Winterthur, it was made oval and given a second flight. Waterman's conscience was uneasy. "I must confess I feel a

130

little sad and guilty when I think of Montmorenci, but the stair hall should be glorious and I have reached the conclusion that any sacrifice is worth while to make Winterthur complete," he wrote to du Pont in 1935. "It is so extraordinarily perfect otherwise, each time I see it I am amazed to think anyone could achieve so flawless a thing."[19] The extent of the alteration worried du Pont less than it did his scholarly young friend. "It is much better to have it all in this house than scattered by bits in different houses all over the country or more probably burned."[20]

The Montmorenci staircase was typical of the struggle between authenticity and eye. Increasingly, authenticity won. Two years after the staircase Waterman carried his point when installing paneling from Morattico, a 1715 house from Virginia: it was fitted, not into the French parlor, but into the billiard room (a room hitherto popular with guests), because the window openings corresponded more closely. As time went on some of du Pont's earlier rooms, such as the Pine Kitchen, which itself replaced the working kitchen of his father's house, were replaced by better and above all more genuine examples – in this case the parlor of the Kershner farmhouse near Reading, Pennsylvania. As the collection expanded, more and more rooms were pressed into service. By the end of the 1930s all the recreation rooms, including the bowling alley, badminton court, squash court, and ping-pong room, had disappeared. The arteries of the house were hardening. Two visits of the Walpole Society record the process. The first took place in 1932 and elicited a glowing response:

> We have seen restored houses, beautifully done, like that of Mr. Perry, or new houses like Mr. Palmer's, other unforgettably delightful homes. Yet never have we seen so many old American rooms under one roof.... Nor could we imagine that there could be put into one house so many rooms so different, in size, period and character, in such way as to make it liveable – to make a home of it. But Mr. du Pont has done it. Here are rooms that welcome the guest, furniture which seems glad to receive him. There is nothing of the museum in the air. We are not among the dead.[21]

On the second visit in 1948 Waterman explained how the Dancing Room, lined with paneling from the Ritchie house at Tappahannock, Virginia, and pleasingly furnished with vernacular furniture of different dates, had been improved. "In deference to their great importance as among the oldest of Virginia paneled rooms du Pont had them reconstructed last year, in exact accordance with their original state."[22]

It could be said that du Pont's relentless drive to create an American house finally crushed the life out of it, turning it into a museum. But the museum idea had come early to du Pont: he had played with the thought of making one of Chestertown House. If his rooms seem like beautifully contrived stage sets, they were. They existed to be enjoyed. "I am sorry that it makes you feel depressed," he wrote to a collector discontented to discover that his own collection did not match up to du Pont's, "as one of the joys of having the furniture in the right setting is to give pleasure to other people as well as to myself."[23] As a museum Winterthur has continued to evolve, in many cases sacrificing the period room settings, now considered inauthentic, that du Pont created. There is, however, a point beyond which creative evolution ceases to be possible without an owner to breathe life into it, and it is only in reading the descriptions of the entertainments du Pont gave – often in the garden, with the pool transformed into fairyland by means of silver paper or blue cellophane and lanterns – that one can envisage the role that decoration played in a larger vision of life. Whether these pleasures of landed life strike one as essentially American or a foreign import will depend on which of the two views of the American country house, described in chapter 2, one happens to share.

124. Needlework hanging of Ardrossan, Pennsylvania, by Kathrine McKean, 1936. It shows the owners, Colonel and Mrs. Robert Montgomery, surrounded by the activities of the estate. Private Collection

When the weekend comes
All my dearest chums
To the country go tearing off,
To improve their frames
Playing damn fool games
Such as polo and Tom Thumb golf.

While they're breaking ground,
Biffing balls around,
And perspiring to beat the band,
I am sitting pretty
In the great big city
With a cool drink in my hand.

From Saturday until Monday,
I'm what the sportsman abhors:
A week-end hater,
Thanking my creator
For the great indoors.

While all the others are rushing
From bathing suit to plus-fours,
I'm glad I own a
Comfortable kimono
For the great indoors.

ACTIVITIES

Cole Porter
The Great Indoors
from *The New Yorkers*, 1930

— 9 —

"More fun than a yacht"
THE FARM BEAUTIFUL

IN 1914 HARRY DU PONT assumed responsibility for the Winterthur farm. It had been built up to two thousand acres by the Colonel and included a pedigree Holstein herd. There were also two hundred and fifty Herefords, a hundred hogs, a hundred Dorset sheep, forty-five horses, and over two thousand poultry. A spanking new string of dairy barns, giving the cows a complete change of air every six minutes, was built in 1918 (Plate 139). Though his Holsteins consistently won prizes, du Pont the farmer is an aspect of the man which now tends to be overlooked. To fellow country house owners, however, it would have been at least as interesting as du Pont the collector, for an essential element of the American country house was the estate on which it stood. This could be just as true of a small place as a large one. "The land foremost," Joseph Hergesheimer had written in *From an Old House*; "I had not expected that." What surprised him was the intensity with which he identified, not only with the old Philadelphia farmhouse he had bought, but the ground beneath it and the orchard and vegetable garden that surrounded it. To express this solidarity with the soil many country house owners built farms.

Economically these farms were often something of an illusion. American country estates, unlike English ones, rarely, if ever, supported the house. But ample justification was thought to lie in the pleasures of land ownership and the opportunity to enjoy active, outdoor pursuits. This larger idea of the American country house, in which the dwelling-place itself, however costly, formed only a part, was enthusiastically endorsed by Barr Ferree in his *American Estates and Gardens* of 1904:

> this great new building energy is not due to an interest in architecture as architecture, perhaps hardly to gardening as gardening, but to an entirely new conception of country life, and a new appreciation and realization of its manifold joys and pleasures. The movement countryward is not, in fine, a Renaissance of architecture, important as is the place architecture takes in it; nor is it a Renaissance of the gardening art, important as that is likewise; but both these factors testify, and in a most impressive way, to a Renaissance of country life.[1]

A glimpse of this Renaissance is provided by Thomas W. Lawson's estate at Egypt, Massachusetts. Lawson, a stockbroker who also wrote poems and books, could survey the entire enterprise from an artfully tumbledown cottage called the Nest – a gazebo smothered in wisteria and trumpet vines. In the foreground are the gardens; beyond

135

125. The Ring Barn at Shelburne Farms, Vermont. Dr. William Seward Webb decided to create an estate after visting the Duke and Duchess of Marlborough at Blenheim Palace, in Oxfordshire. The Duchess was Mrs. Webb's niece, Consuelo Vanderbilt.

them, the many buildings that housed animals and fowl – all in the estate livery of gambrel roof and gray shingled wall with green blinds and white trim. They stand out briskly against fourteen miles of picket fence picturesquely overgrown by rambling roses.

Horses predominate: three hundred of them. There are barns for stallions, brood mares, farm horses, and carriage horses; also a foaling barn, stallion service building, hospital, racetrack, and riding academy. Equal thought has been given to the needs of the Jersey herd. The cowbarn is in the form of a deep, south-facing U, so that the gutters dry quickly. In front of the cows, who stand two to a stall for company, is a track wide enough for the wagon to pass down as farm hands fork feed into the mangers. Water arrives by an automatic system. Two thousand hens occupy a show hen house, enjoying what now seems like the notable luxury of ten-foot-square wire-framed scratching pens on the sunny side of the building. The bantam house is a charming structure, cross-shaped, with four porticos and a shingled cupola. Pigeons coo in their dumpy tower of a dovecot, surrounded by a crinoline of chicken wire.

Nearby stands a Dutch windmill for grinding grain and cutting up silage. Nor have the ducks and geese on the pond been forgotten: their huts have large windows for light and ease of cleaning. A tall conical-roofed water tower rises out of the ground like a giant firework. Farm office, farmhouses, post office, and blacksmith's shop make up the final complement of buildings which house, as well as animals, some thirty men.

Dreamwold was the name that Lawson gave to this community of man and beast, rushed up in double-quick time (the riding academy was completed in fifty-six days). There had been little except briers and boulders on the land when he bought it, and it took him and his architects, Coolidge and Carlson of Boston, not much over a year to make the desert bloom. He himself had a house on the estate, Dreamwold Hall, but, reflecting the priorities of the place, it did not dominate. It almost seems to have been one of those buildings designed to look smaller than it was, the entrance front – three hundred feet long – having been broken down into the different elements of guest house, service wing, and central block. Each section pulled its gambrel roof well down over its ears. Of the interior fittings *House and Garden* commented: "in a well-designed house no detail or fixture must be too prominent, too insistent."[2] They hardly seem inconspicuous today. To light the dining room the Lawsons chose a chandelier in the shape of a huge golden pumpkin entwined with bell-like flowers, and elsewhere the wall lamps take the form of brass heads blowing bubbles made of glass, each bubble enclosing the light bulb. Curious though these Art Nouveau fantasies may seem, there was a logic to them, since they continued the organic theme of the estate. Farm produce provided the subject of burnt-work panels; grapes, rabbits, and oxen decorate chimney-pieces. Another reference, however, was made in the Russell Crook andirons of the dining room, ornamented with bears and bees. They were not intended to evoke Nature so much as the stock market, epitomizing its two sides. One bear gets the honey, the other bear gets stung.

Architecturally, Dreamwold was an unusually complete example of the kind of farming enterprise that many American country house owners chose to indulge in. In England it would have been called a "model farm"; the term generally used in the United States was "farm group." Rearing livestock was a hobby that appealed to men who, though they had withdrawn from the sharp-edged world of business, missed the excitement of managing men, creating systems, and bending the world to their will. It had a competitive element that challenged them. Yields could always be increased, hygiene might be improved, experiment and innovation could open the way to greater

126. Agricultural trophies at Harvey S. Firestone's farm in Ohio. Competition with neighboring landowners could be intense.

efficiency. There was rivalry with neighboring landowners for the trophies at the agricultural show (Plate 126). Farming in America was doing well at the turn of the century, thanks to the bumper harvests of 1897 and 1901. But generally it was not the thought of profit that attracted the country house owner to it. Healthy food, particularly milk, could be difficult to obtain in remote areas, and, even in the city, produce might not always be trusted. What was grown on country estates was often sent to the family's town house as well. From Eagle Nest in the Adirondacks a battered tin box containing eggs would be sent weekly to the owner's New York apartment.[3]

And less tangible benefits existed. A farm was thought to be wholesome for the children; it suggested a point of contact with the nation's agrarian past; and above all it rounded out the image of country life created by the house and dependencies, providing a useful objective for a morning's visit with guests (just as the slave cabins of Southern plantation houses had done before the Civil War). To someone brought up in the country, like Frank Lloyd Wright, farm life might well seem to be one long round of "pulling tits and shoveling shit."[4] It appeared otherwise to the weary city dweller, who could even, in his more maudlin moments, have been tempted to agree with E.P. Powell's observation in *The Country Home* that "all animals love the beautiful."[5]

The farm group reflects the country house owner's role in a movement whose roots struck down far deeper into American society than his own stratum. Ever since the Civil War a profound nostalgia had been felt for the early days of the country's history, when its economy was based on the land and the great war machine had not been called into existence. Henry Holly, author of *Holly's Country Seats* (1866), was one of many authors to evoke a sense of epic decline, looking back as far as the ancient Greece described by Homer to prove the comparative puniness of modern man. He was in no doubt as to what had caused the degeneration. "The secret lies in our artificial lives. We do not breathe enough of the pure, fresh air of heaven."[6] Increasingly, and with reason, the life of the cities came to seem undesirable. Though the Civil War had been fought for an

127–28. Haymaking and a flock of sheep at Shelburne Farms. Early photographs often emphasize the pastoral quality of estate life.

industrial society and a pure moral order, the cities that industrialization had brought into being were crowded, dirty, disease-ridden, and corrupt. The problem was compounded by immigration: it was calculated that over ninety per cent of arriving immigrants remained in the cities even if they had been country people in their homelands. Meanwhile the countryside itself was becoming more mechanized, and growing numbers of young people were drifting away from the land. "It is a common complaint that the farm and farm life are not appreciated by our people," wrote John Burroughs voicing the national sense of loss. "We long for the more elegant pursuits, or the ways and fashions of the town. But the farmer has the most sane and natural occupation, and ought to find life sweeter, if less highly seasoned, than any other. He alone, strictly speaking, has a home. How can a man take root and thrive without land?"[7]

By the turn of the century thoughtful people among the middle classes were wondering what could be done to reverse this trend, and in particular how they themselves, and their families, could escape the baneful conditions of urban life. The answer was simple: a small landholding, close enough to a city to commute if needs be.

Numerous books and articles appeared explaining how to make ten or twenty acres pay. All agreed that, with the advent of the rural telephone and free rural mail deliveries, the country had become easier to live in. It was generally assumed that the husband would be away at his desk during the day, so that much or all of the farm work devolved upon his wife. But it was not necessary to go far away from the cities to establish the farm; in fact the nearer one was, the better the chance of specializing in flowers, raspberries, or other exotics for which prices were high. This might be done on Long Island. New York was also the leading dairy state and a few Holsteins, more productive than Jerseys and less mischievous than Ayrshires, could be made to give a satisfactory return.

Some people were tempted by beekeeping, but by far the most popular investment for the man with little land or capital was poultry (Plate 129). What breed to raise? In *How to Make a Country Place* Joseph Dillaway Sawyer described lyrically how he had tried

wild squawking brown, also white, Leghorns, ... the phlegmatic, good-natured partridge, buff and white Cochins, feathered to their toe-nails; the barred and white

138

129. Cover of *House and Garden*, August 1939. Poultry of all kinds, including decorative pigeons and doves, was a favorite of country house owners. Profit was often a secondary consideration to the healthy effect of outdoor life on the children.

House & Garden

DOUBLE NUMBER
Complete Midsummer Issue
PLUS
Separately bound Book of
30 HOUSES AND PLANS
costing under $10,000
•
2 magazines for the price of 1
35c

130. This photograph from *Country Life in America*, June 1904, captioned "A cow-barn fit to dine in," demonstrates the hygiene of modern farming methods. It had been realized that tainted milk was a frequent cause of disease.

> Plymouth Rock, the strutting, tufted Poland; the silver penciled Wyandotte, the aristocratic white, buff and black Orpington, the jet black Minorca, the sprightly, trim Rhode Island Reds, the dignified Houdan, its illustrious descendants, the Faverolle, blue blooded Andalusians, staring white faced Spanish, and the tiny demure Bantams, who proved more intelligent than their pompous neighbors, notwithstanding the statement that a chicken's education ends when a day old.[8]

That Sawyer enjoyed it is obvious, and he felt that it did him good, "forcing pure country air into half-expanded city lungs." But he had to confess that, financially, chickens were considerably more bother than they were worth. Part of the trouble was that, by 1910, there were too many people doing it. One New Jersey man who knew what he was doing wisely gave up the unequal struggle and instead took a job running the Rockefellers' poultry operation at Pocantico Hills.[9]

Typically, Jack London had more ambitious ideas when he set about creating his Beauty Ranch in the Somona Valley, California, after 1905, "I have just blown myself for 129 acres of land," he wrote exuberantly that June, not realizing that this was the first of many purchases that would total over eleven hundred acres over the next eight years. "Also, I have just bought several horses, a colt, a cow, a calf, a plow, harrow, wagon, buggy, etc., to say nothing of chickens, turkeys, pigeons, etc., etc. All this last part was unexpected, and has left me flat broke." Before long his experience of farming had developed into a political message for the American nation which he delivered in his novel *The Valley of the Moon* of 1913. "In the solution of the great economic problems of the present age, I see a return to the soil," he summed up three years later. "I go into farming because my philosophy and research has taught me to recognize the fact that a return to the soil is the basis of economics." If London was not particularly early in advocating this agrarian creed, he made up for it by the zeal with which he went into every aspect of the farm. He not only built a dwelling of boulders, Wolf House, which tragically burned before he could occupy it, but erected barns, dammed a stream, terraced hillsides, and planted sixty-five thousand trees. The spirit which animated him was not very different from that which persuaded Frank Lloyd Wright to build Taliesin with chicken coop and goat pen attached, or Cyrus McCormick to buy a thousand acres in Lake Forest.[10]

140

Some farm groups were fully commercial. In New York, Briarcliff Manor in the Pocantico Valley and Brookside Dairy Farm at Newburgh were each established by a man who had previously made a fortune in business. They themselves became highly successful businesses, offering a top-quality product at above market prices. Even so, they were unable fully to satisfy demand. They gave the public its best chance of obtaining uncontaminated milk, at a time when it was realized that tuberculosis and other diseases could be transmitted through dairy products (Plate 130). At Brookside, Samuel L. Stewart's war against dirt extended to the design of tight-fitting duck overalls for milking (no baggy or coarse-fibered material to harbor filth), which were not only changed and laundered every day, but sterilized in steam lockers when not in use. Both Stewart and Briarcliff's owner, Walter W. Law, employed methods learned during their business careers in their new occupations. In order to enrich the singularly unpromising fields that he bought in 1890, Law negotiated a contract to clean the streets and stables of New York, thus achieving an endless supply of free manure.[11]

But the minutiae of economics were not always important. There were owners who did not intend to produce anything from the land they acquired. "What do I raise on my farm?" asked Samuel Clemens (Mark Twain) who bought a Connecticut farm, Stormfield, at the end of his life. "Really nothing but sunsets and scenery."[12] Or as another writer put it: "Fresh air was the largest product of the scrubby, abandoned farm that [he] purchased and whereon he built a home for both summer and winter."[13] Farmland often seemed very cheap and its principal function for the new owner might well be, in modern parlance, recreational.

Between the extremes of running a first-class commercial enterprise and raising nothing at all lay, one suspects, the majority of gentleman farmers, who enjoyed keeping livestock as a hobby but had little serious hope of making it pay (Plate 132). As long ago as 1851, writing in his book *Rural Homes*, the architect Gervase Wheeler had recognized the propensity of some gentlemen "to raise potatoes at four dollars a barrel, when you can send to the city and buy them at three."[14] Half a century later market place economics had still failed to catch up with the farm group. Oliver Gould Jennings, the eighth generation of his family to live at Fairfield, Connecticut, spent rather more time on his hundred and twenty acres than other estate owners, but his house, Mailand, was conveniently placed for New York. The farm kept both town and country houses supplied with meat, vegetables, and flowers through the year, and Jennings was particularly proud of a prize Jersey bull with the happy name of Interested Laddie. Nevertheless, there was no suggestion that any of the Mailand activities should generate income. "This farming is a fad to which Mr. Jennings devotes much of his leisure,

131. Vegetables from the Perennial Gardens of Ohio Columbus Barber's estate at Barberton, Ohio. Agriculture was the entrepreneur's one failure.

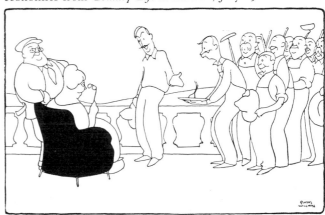

132. "The idea is to raise your produce with the minimum of Labor, not the maximum." A sharp reflection on farm group economics from *Country Life in America*, July 1908.

though he goes in for it simply as an amateur, the product being only sufficient to furnish his own table and satisfy the needs of the establishment."[15] For Washington E. Connor, formerly the chief henchman of Jay Gould, growing oranges and keeping a mixed herd of Holsteins and Jerseys on his Florida estate was again no more than the "favorite hobby of to-day."[16] Folly Farm was the name that the paper manufacturer Irwin N. Megargee gave to his model stock and dairy operation in Pennsylvania, because financially it had indeed proved to be a folly.

In the first full year of its existence, 1903, *Country Life in America* explained the idea on which the John Sloane estate, Wyndhurst in Massachusetts, operated: "No product of the farm is ever sold. Butter and cream are shipped every day to the family in New York. Vegetables and flowers are sent three times a week." Later in its life the magazine was even franker about farm group economics:

> The country gentleman of to-day does not farm for profit. He creates in the city and recreates in the country, and his herds and flocks are an investment in healthful diversion. He may, and usually does, exercise care in his expenditures and, once his establishment is equipped and manned, he maintains an orderly and economic plan of management. In the care and maintenance of his pedigreed herds, he is a specialist in a field which is little understood by the layman, . . . he is the man behind the pure-bred industry. . . . The dairy cow owes its present unequalled efficiency to him. He has been the largest single buyer and breeder. . . . He aspires to excel in the art of breeding great dairy animals – to attain the ideal which is ever eluding the grasp of the most persistent and skilful breeders. Regardless of what he may expend, his efforts result in quality breeding animals.[17]

Or, to quote an advertisement of the Louden Machinery Company, a farm was "more fun than a yacht." Colonel du Pont had made precisely the same comparison when the young Harry expressed a wish to improve the Holstein herd: "It won't cost as much as owning a yacht and it might do a lot for humanity." But after Harry's death in 1969 the Winterthur Foundation was unwilling to take such a large view: feeling unable to go on bearing the losses, it quickly closed the farm down.

With few of the usual economic constraints, the gentleman farmer could direct his energies at whichever speciality he pleased. Rare breeds had chic. At the beginning of the century, for instance, there was a vogue for Angora goats, though it was found that rearing them was more difficult than it looked. Later Clarence Lewis's twelve hundred acre Skylands Farm in New Jersey, completed in 1928, raised a not untypical mix: Guernsey cattle, Suffolk Punch draft horses, Berkshire swine, Hondau chickens, Black Chow dogs and Siamese cats. In Thorstein Veblen's somewhat sour view of the matter, the more exotic the animal the more it was likely to appeal to the conspicuously consuming owner, who would wish to avoid any imputation of "vulgar thrift." Naturally the barns and equipment of the farm group were of the best. "One emerges from the farm buildings in a somewhat dazed frame of mind, so numerous are they, so perfectly kept, so manifestly convenient, so entirely equipped with everything that could possibly be needed," rejoiced *American Homes and Gardens* after visiting Woodcrest.[18]

Were such farm groups of only dilettante interest? Not entirely. Estate owners pursued their farming with passion and, if they spent heavily, it could be to great effect in improving their stock. The benefit spread downwards to working farms. Through the estate owners' concentration on pure breeding, the quality of herds and flocks throughout the country was improved. "The finely kept places on Clairmont Farm are a

133. The Farm Barn at Shelburne Farms. "From a distance this great structure, with its wall and towers, looks like an old feudal stronghold with its castellated turrets and strong battlements," commented the local newspaper, the *Burlington Free Press*, 20 September 1899.

benefit to the neighborhood," wrote the Rev. Hotchkin of a large estate on the Philadelphia Main Line, "and the men employed upon it find use in the taste which leads a gentleman to strive to improve and elevate country life, while neighboring farmers gain information."[19] On Beauty Ranch Jack London hoped to show his impoverished neighbors that it was not necessary to farm the land to exhaustion. The herd at Arcady Farm in Lake Forest produced the first certified milk in the state: Arthur Meeker remembered that, as a child, he and the other young ones "were forced to drink so much of it that afterwards it was years before I was able to face another milk bottle."[20]

The public-spirited side of the farm group can be seen at Biltmore, where George W. Vanderbilt's object was to demonstrate model farming techniques to his backward country neighbors.[21] No doubt Vanderbilt influenced his brother-in-law Dr. Watson

134. Postcard showing the view from O.C. Barber's house at Barberton, Ohio. In the middle distance is the long, red-roofed "No. 3 barn"; beyond the trees to the right can be seen the smoking chimneys from which Barber's industrial wealth was accrued.

Seward Webb in establishing Shelburne Farms in Vermont. Webb, similarly hoping that his example would improve the quality of the state's livestock, bred hackney and French coach horses. He believed that they out-performed the Morgans to which the old Vermont farmers remained stubbornly loyal: even presenting the largest horse-raising towns with an imported animal and offering to buy back colts and foals did not overcome all resistance. Needless to say, he himself farmed on a princely scale (Plates 125, 127–28, and 133), with immense barns, breeding barns, and stables, equipped with "all the appliances which modern ingenuity can devise."[22] By taking down fences, laying fine macadam roads, planting between twenty-five and a hundred thousand trees each year, and putting thousands of acres down to grass, he was also able to create "a fine country place ... accomplishing in a few years what in England it has taken centuries to do."[23]

Biltmore may also have inspired Katharine Reynolds, whose husband owned the R.J. Reynolds Tobacco Company, to establish the model estate of Reynolda outside Winston-Salem in the same state. In 1917 a local paper commented that Reynolda was "destined to become one of the great factors in the development of rural life" in North Carolina.[24] While most farms in the area were devoted to bright-leaf tobacco, Mrs. Reynolds demonstrated the benefits of diversification, growing wheat, oats, corn, and vegetables. Agriculturalists from other states were called in to advise, and Charles Barton Keen designed the farm buildings, which Mrs. Reynolds wished to have "equipped with the very newest and best conveniences."[25] The showpiece at Reynolda was the barns for the Jersey herd. For these Keen could draw on his experience of designing Greystone Hall, the Pennsylvania estate of P.M. Sharples, inventor of the cream separator.

Perhaps the bravest attempt of this kind was made by Ohio Columbus Barber, the founder of Barberton, Ohio. This titan of industry was known as the Match King, from having organized seventeen independent match manufacturers into the Diamond Match Company, but his other interests included paper, pottery, metals, fire extinguishers, sewer pipes, rubber tires, boilers, paints, ammunition, and cereals. When he retired in 1909 he built a country house overlooking the smoking chimneys of Barberton and took up farming as a hobby (Plate 134). It was some hobby: by 1915 he had amassed a holding of three thousand acres, built a hundred and two structures and put thirteen acres under glass, creating a Perennial Gardens in which all elements in plant growth would be controlled by man (Plate 130). The centerpiece of the operation was a dairy barn eight hundred feet long. His aim, as he announced in a book that frankly declared his own genius, was "to demonstrate that scientific farming in a large way could be made as successful and profitable" as his other business activities.[26] Maybe, at the age of sixty-eight, he was too old to start; whatever the case it was predictable that this most overweening of farm groups should have consumed almost all his fortune by the time of his death in 1920.

Farm groups were built for both show and efficiency. They were therefore something of a specialized area of practice for the architect, and it is not as strange as it might seem at first that Alfred Hopkins, the doyen of farm group architects, was better known for designing prisons. Farm groups and prisons had this in common: they both required the tight coordination of a large number of different activities. Organization was of the

135–38. Farm hands at Winterthur.

139. Henry F. du Pont's dairy barns at Winterthur, placed on the brow of a hill to achieve the most striking effect.

essence. The size of a farm group did not always reflect the complexity of the architect's brief, since its partly ornamental and faddish nature tended to mean that more kinds of stock were raised than on a conventional farm. Thus, besides cows and hens, the estate owner might well keep a few sheep (for trimming grass) or a couple of pigs; and in addition there were the working horses of the farm. Feeding, milking, calving, dairying, possibly shoeing, the associated deliveries and collections – all had to work together smoothly. Generally the group would also include accommodation for the farmer; on a large estate there might well be a club for the hands, or even, exceptionally, a schoolhouse and church. So finely tuned was the running of Howard Gould's three hundred and fifty acre Long Island estate of Sands Point that it required no fewer than five separate teams of outdoor workers – for livestock, vegetable gardens, flower gardens, stables, and golf course. They slept in a two hundred bed dormitory in the castellated service building known as Castlegould, making the prison analogy even closer. But unlike a prison the farm group was also expected to please the eye. For as Hopkins himself commented apropos the farm group that he designed for James Speyer at Scarboro, New York: "A man is far more interested perhaps in ideal stabling quarters for his Ayrshires than in the number of quarts his dairy manager is selling a day."[27]

Estate owners prided themselves not only on their stock but on their equipment, and this was becoming increasingly sophisticated. But the machine aesthetic was rarely expressed in the architecture. The Frederick Pabst estate on Lake Oconomowoc in Wisconsin, built in 1906, was remarkable for being constructed entirely from concrete, for which fireproofing was a recommendation, but the style was loosely Tudor. Even in the 1930s few estate owners favored the Modern Movement. Hopkins, then in his sixties, was at first baffled when one client who manufactured glass bricks insisted that he incorporate them into the farm group; eventually they went in under the roof of the hay barn. Sometimes the style of the main house set the theme for the farm. But more often the cheapness and appropriateness of wood – it served equally well for all sizes of

146

140. Watertower at Nemours, Delaware. Towers could be both a symbol of power and a useful aid to design.

structure – suggested Colonial. This was perhaps the most popular but not the only idiom. Jacob Schiff's farm at Red Bank, New Jersey, recalled an English village, with shingle thatch and stucco walls imitating clunch: like a true *ferme ornée*, it included a tea house as "a retreat for afternoon gatherings."[28] In California the glass manufacturer Edward D. Libbey's thoughts turned to adobe. For his Long Island estate, Arthur Bourne chose Chinese. But the majority of owners shared Hopkins's view that historical flourishes should be done away with and the style kept as simple as possible. There were other ways in which the farm group could be enhanced. If it were placed on the brow of a hill, for instance, the long low buidings would be thrown into prominence against the sky. Harry du Pont followed this strategy at Winterthur (Plate 139).

Because groups largely consisted of one-story barns, towers were of great help to the architect in his design. Water towers were in any case often necessary to provide a head

141. King C. Gillette's barn group, composed around a tower, in California.

142. Dairy at the Fischer residence at New Canaan, Connecticut. The dairy was the pride of the farm group.

143. Hen house at the Fischer residence at New Canaan, Connecticut. Hens came into vogue as a central part of the country life movement.

of water, and in the flat landscape of Long Island estate owners vied with each other like the nobles of San Gimignano to see who could build the highest. The tallest of all was that erected by Harry Payne Whitney at his farm in Westbury, which is visible for miles around. Less dramatically, shorter towers were often attached to the barns themselves to give focus to a group (Plate 141). Often the ground floor contained the bull's quarters, thereby given pride of place. Generally there was a dovecot or pigeon loft at the top. Silos also lent themselves to being treated as towers. A prominent feature of many farm groups was the big roofs that contained the haylofts, and these required particular thought as to materials and silhouette. For the barns themselves, it had been discovered that ventilation was as important for cows as for humans. Louvres beneath the ceiling provided fresh air, and if they were additionally fitted with a baffle there was no draft.

The pièce de resistance of any farm group was the dairy, just as it would have been in eighteenth-century England or France. It illustrates the many practical considerations that governed this branch of architecture. The dairy had to be placed on one side of the group so as to be away from the traffic of the rest of the farm. The dairymaid or butterman probably required a cottage, which had to be near by but never contiguous. Fresh air could not be too plentiful, and a sunny porch was desirable for the drying and airing of milk churns. Romantic whimsy had no place in the interior, where strict principles of hygiene ruled: here at last the architect expressed the clinically efficient character of twentieth-century farming (Plate 142). This meant vitrified tiles for floor and wall – not marble, so frequently used in previous centuries, because "it is very absorbent and in connection with milk soon becomes greasy and foul."[29] Moldings and anything else that might catch dust were definitely out. The dairy room contained a separator, churn, and butter worker which were probably electrically powered, and next door the washroom had a refrigerator. The dairy also needed hot water and heating; steam was used for sterilization in large outfits.

It need hardly be said that Louis C. Tiffany's farm group at Oyster Bay, Long Island,

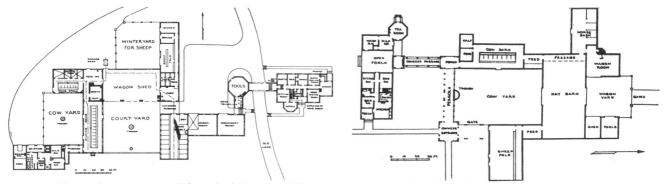

144–45. Plans of two groups of farm buildings by Alfred Hopkins. Louis C. Tiffany's estate at Oyster Bay, Long Island, includes an octagonal tower and (linked by a bridge over the lane) a house for the superintendent and hands. The partly ornamental intention of the Speyer group at Scarboro, New York, can be seen in the inclusion of owner's entrance, pergola, and tea room.

designed by Hopkins, was as artistic as any (Plate 144). It embodies many of the principles that have been described. First consideration was the setting. In order not to slice up the sweep of land in front of the buildings with roads, it was decided to make the entrance via an old lane at the back. To the right of the lane was the house for the superintendent and men; the latter entered by their own door. To the left of the lane rose an octagonal water tower with a pigeon loft at the top. But it was the hay barn that dominated the group: to achieve this effect Hopkins placed the storage area for hay over a shed, thus gaining extra height. The other buildings provided for horses, sheep, and cows; the dairy included a laundry where overalls could be washed. A manure cart on a track ran around each department and led to a communal pit.

Hens do not seem to have featured in the Tiffany farm group, but they were almost certainly kept elsewhere on the estate. Poultry houses were too small to offer much opportunity for architecture, though fashions in internal design changed frequently. On the whole, conditions for fowl seem generous by today's standards (Plate 143), but not everywhere. *Country Life in America* approvingly described the cruel system practiced on the Hyde estate on Long Island: "they are kept without exercise in a dark place and stuffed, by the aid of a French machine, with certain foods calculated to impart to the flesh so perfect a flavor that even the most fastidious follower of Epicurus must be pleased."[30]

Though Hopkins encouraged owners to think each center of activity on an estate had "its own individuality which must be respected" (Plate 145), there was one area in which even he had to admit a measure of defeat. As he put it in *Modern Farm Buildings*: "The author has not been as successful as he could wish in inducing the gentleman farmer to believe that in his piggery he has architectural possibilities of which advantage should be taken." Jack London proved the exception at Beauty Ranch, building what the *Santa Rosa Press Democrat* characterized as a Palace Hotel for Pigs (Plate 146).

Such was the symbolic importance of the farm to country house owners that many of them kept the word in the name of their house: Wawapek Farm, Foxhollow Farm, Firenze Farm, Hobby Horse Farm, Daisy Hill Farm – to name only a few. Grosse Pointe Farms was the name given to an entire residential district outside Detroit. And even here, in what appears to be a suburban enclave, farm groups can be found. Waterfronts onto Lake St. Clair were narrow, perhaps only a few hundred feet, but the plots could be very deep: that of Drybrook was a mile.

Sometimes houses called Farms genuinely possessed a working farm, sometimes not. Frequently such names perpetuated the memory of the estate's previous incarnation

150

when the land was worked by a small farmer, who, ironically, may well have wrung from it a greater net profit than his more extravagant successor. The taste for Farm names increased after the First World War, when life became simpler and the idea that a country house owner might himself farm did not seem as strange as it would have seemed at the turn of the century. This was also the period when the ranch and its out-of-doors lifestyle came into vogue (see chapter 13).

Before the First World War the farm group had seemed an agreeable adjunct of country life. In the 1920s it took on a new poetic meaning, creating an ambience of rural idyll in which the owner and his family might play a part, slightly in the manner of Marie Antoinette at her Versailles *hameau*. It was inevitable that sooner or later someone would headline an article ''The Farm Beautiful.'' It happened in *Country Life in America* in 1924. The farm group in question was Eagle's Nest on Colonel Jacob Ruppert's estate at Garrison-on-the-Hudson, New York. Designed by William La Zinsk, it has boulder walls and a somewhat French vernacular flavor from some angles. More striking than the architecture, however, is the magazine's soft-focus photography, which presented Eagle's Nest in the manner of an oil painting of the Barbizon school (Plate 147). Similarly lyrical photographs were used in the three individual articles which the magazine devoted to the Arthur E. Newbold, Jr., estate at Laverock, on the Main Line out of Philadelphia (Plate 148). Philadelphia, with its exclusive Farmers' Club, was well used to the notion of gentleman farmers. The Newbold place went further than other farm groups by not only glorifying the picturesque possibilities of the farm, but drawing the house itself into the bucolic fantasy.

146. The "palace hotel for pigs" built by the author Jack London on his Beauty Ranch in California

The Newbold estate was the creation of Arthur J. Meigs, an architect burdened with an excessively artistic temperament. "Your guts are more important than your head," he would say in describing the design process. "An artist has to work on his belly." This fiery approach must have been balanced by a more rational strain, since, more even than most farm groups, the Newbold estate had to be very carefully organized. But the premise was romantic enough. Moneymaking, he declared with fine Bohemian disdain, was tedious and this would always blight the character of commercial farms. On the other hand, livestock and the methods of farming could be beautiful, as long as they only supplied the family's own needs. If they were beautiful they should be brought close to the house. Having served in the American Expeditionary Force in France, he had got to know the traditional disposition of the French *manoir*, in which both house and farm opened onto the same courtyard. This had one drawback: the path to the house was permanently fouled by mud and muck. Nevertheless, he found the basic idea to be sound and, with modifications, adopted it for the Newbolds.

The plan in Plate 149, taken from the lavish folio volume which Meigs published on the estate, shows the ingenious solution. The driveway passes next to the farm court, but is separated from it by the goose pond, which keeps the beasts on their side of the divide (Plate 150). On the west side of the court the sheepfold forms another barrier, this time with the potager or decorative vegetable garden. Between the potager and the pasture Meigs was less clever, eschewing a ha-ha for a plain wire fence which shows in the photographs (Plate 148) – though in time this would have been covered by planting. The round cattle pond was designed with the deliberate intention of bringing the cows almost up to the drawing room windows, while it also served, coincidentally,

147–48. The camera as paintbrush: carefully composed views of the pigeontower and duckpond at Eagle's Nest, New York, and the cattle pond on the Newbold estate at Laverock, Pennsylvania. The cattle pond was designed to bring animals up to the edge of the garden.

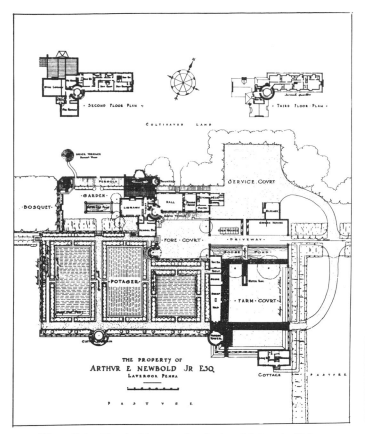

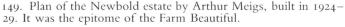

149. Plan of the Newbold estate by Arthur Meigs, built in 1924–29. It was the epitome of the Farm Beautiful.

150. The Newbold estate seen on the cover of *Country Life in America*, August 1925. It is in the Normandy *manoir* style popular in the 1920s.

as a paddling pool for the Newbold infants. The main house was not a farmhouse: a cottage was provided for the man who did all the work. But it was of the farm.

There was, initially, only one obstacle to the full realization of the scheme, and that was this house's very appearance. It had been built in 1914 by a different architect in a Colonial style. Eventually the Newbolds were brought to appreciate the incongruity, and half a dozen years after the farm was completed the house was encased in stone, with woodwork of soft browns and blues. So, appropriately, the style of the big house followed that of the farm, not vice versa. Meigs called the Newbold place "an American country house," since it fused elements from "England, France, Italy and Spain applied to the original block of what may be called American Colonial."[31] Yet perhaps its true national character lay in its being the apotheosis of the farm group.

"The workable, the expensively workable, American form of country life"

THE BERKSHIRES

THE IMPORTANCE OF the farm group is that it helped promote an image of country life, and there was no one area where this image was more sedulously cultivated than that frequently called by the guidebooks the "Inland Newport." In fact this title could hardly have been more of a misnomer. The Berkshire Hills in Massachusetts, to which it refers, attracted a fashionable element, if not quite such a worldly one as the Queen of Resorts; but the priorities of life there were conspicuously different. On his visits to Edith Wharton, whose estate at The Mount in some ways set the tone for the Berkshires, Henry James may have remarked to an English friend that here "everyone is oppressively rich and COSSU [well-to-do] . . . and 'a million a year' (£200,000) seems to be the usual income." But in *The American Scene* he also felt moved to acknowledge that it demonstrated "the workable, the expensively workable, American form of country life."

The principal attraction of the Berkshires was scenery. As one newspaper writer described it: "There are not autumnal pictures in any other part of our country more beautiful than those of Berkshire. The pictures the Great Master has painted upon the woody hillsides are inimitable."[1] Parts of this landscape had become, by the early twentieth century, quite thickly strewn with country houses, but the trees and the folds of land in the rolling countryside effectively conceal them from the roads. The feeling of the place remained rural; the views were superb. Often in the foreground were fields and farm buildings, perhaps a lake; in the distance rise the velvety blue mountains whose rounded form is reminiscent of Umbria. So at least thought the lawyer and diplomat Joseph Hodges Choate, as he looked out of the windows of Naumkeag (Plate 151): he called it "our Perugino view." To the sculptor Daniel Chester French, who had his summer studio at Chesterwood, Monument Mountain provided "the best dry view" he had ever seen. The summer colony came from Boston and New York, though sometimes not appearing until after the Newport season had ended, to enjoy the autumn colors.

There were two social foci in the Berkshires: the neighboring towns of Lenox and Stockbridge. It was typical of the growing nostalgia for the early history of New England that an article on the origins of Stockbridge should have appeared in *Harper's New Monthly Magazine* in 1871. "Few . . . are aware that this most beautifully set jewel

151. The view from Naumkeag near Stockbridge, Massachusetts, which, for the owner Joseph Choate, evoked the idyllic landscapes of the Renaissance artist Perugino.

of Berkshire was only a little while ago the wild hunting-ground of the Indian," wrote the author of the piece, N.H. Eggleston. "There are those alive today in Stockbridge who were living when the Indian tribe who owned the whole territory had not yet parted with it."[2] The first white settler was a missionary who, in the 1730s, followed the Indians into the woods and watched them make maple sugar: "it seems," wrote Eggleston, "that we are indebted to these Housatonic Indians for the discovery of that delightful sweet, so universally relished." So great was Stockbridge's pride in its history and appearance that it saw the founding of the first village improvement association in America, to lay out sidewalks, plant trees, introduce street lighting, and discourage litter.

But Stockbridge's younger sister, Lenox, was also her rival, both being anxious to preserve their differences. Named after Charles Lennox, Duke of Richmond, Lenox had become the shire town in 1787, and the county court attracted lawyers and judges. By the late nineteenth century the citizens of Lenox looked upon it as the social nonpareil of the region, and among the purchasers of new estates considerable premium was attached to finding land within the town limits. The residents of Stockbridge thought of themselves as taking a more relaxed, less competitive view of life, as befitted the elder sister. One of Choate's famous quips held that "In Lenox you are estimated; in Stockbridge you are esteemed."

Like so many places that attracted rich summer folk, the Berkshires' fashionable era had been preceded by an artistic and literary one. The first writer to draw popular attention to the region was Catherine Sedgwick, a Stockbridge native. In *A New England Tale* the dying Jane Lloyd, discussing where her body will be laid, declares a preference for "the narrow vales of the Housatonic" over "the broader lands of Connecticut"; and the gravity of the moment does not deflect her husband from delivering himself of a considered Picturesque judgment on the landscape:

> "I, too, prefer this scenery," said Mr Lloyd. . . . "I prefer it, because it has a more domestic aspect. There is, too, a more perfect and intimate union of the sublime and beautiful. These mountains that surround us, and are so near to us on every side, seem to me like natural barriers, by which the Father has secured for His children the gardens He has planted for them by the river's side."[3]

Elsewhere she characterized Stockbridge as a place without "ignorant imitation or fatuous aspiration," showing "a filial conservatism, a reverence for the past, demonstrated in a careful repair and scrupulous preservation of these ancestral homes."[4] Catherine's brother Charles transferred to Lenox, and his wife opened a well-known school for young ladies. (Sedgwicks of one kind or another became so ubiquitous that even the frogs were said to croak "Sedgwick, Sedgwick, Sedgwick.") Their friend the English actress Fanny Kemble was won over by the Berkshires and finally settled on Laurel Lake.

In 1838 Nathaniel Hawthorne arrived, bringing his family to "the very ugliest little bit of an old red farm-house you ever saw." Inspired by the "tangled woods," he wrote the *Tanglewood Tales*, which in turn gave their name to the gabled and bracketed villa built by Hawthorne's friend William Tappan, in whose grounds the Berkshire Music Festival is now held. By 1870 hundreds of tourists were visiting Hawthorne's cottage every year. Hawthorne's friend Herman Melville lived only a short carriage drive away at Arrowhead, a farm given to him and his bride by his father-in-law. In the old farmhouse he spent the mornings writing – five of the novels were composed there, including *Moby Dick* – and in the afternoon he worked on his land which produced food for the family and sometimes a cash crop of timber. The house itself appears in *I and my Chimney* and *Piazza Tales*.

When summer people began to express an interest in the place, they found that both Lenox and Stockbridge possessed inns – respectively the Curtis and the Red Lion – which ultimately grew into celebrated hotels, forming a nucleus around which the summer colony could coalesce. The very first of Lenox's summer residents is said to have been a Mrs. Lee of New Orleans, who built Fairlawn in 1837. Her example was followed by half a dozen other pioneers in the early 1840s. Most notable of these was Samuel Ward, the Baring Brothers American agent, who built Highwood. Ward was by no means a typical banker, though his personality foreshadowed that of later residents. A friend of Ralph Waldo Emerson, he enjoyed farming because it did not "interrupt the flow of meditation." He translated Goethe as a relaxation from growing potatoes, or perhaps vice versa. His farming interests presumably had a commercial motive, and he sold his land after failing to make it pay.

The rate of development remained leisurely until the 1880s. Then in the last twenty years of the century the property value of Lenox doubled, thanks to the building of big estates. Farmland that would have fetched fifty dollars an acre when it grew potatoes was making a thousand dollars an acre when required for an estate.[5]

From 1886 the area's advantages were boomed by a guidebook called *The Book of Berkshire*. Such factories as it possessed, mostly for paper-making, were hidden away in

152. The garden front of Bellefontaine, in Lenox, by Carrère and Hastings, illuminated at night.

narrow, deep valleys, which rendered them "in no wise offensive." Cholera had never penetrated the region, stopping on the outskirts. The bracing climate stimulated the lungs and blood and "gave tone" to the nervous stystem. Children thrived in the air, the drinking water was extremely pure, the roads were good, New York newspapers arrived by noon, and the "native people" compared "very favorably indeed, with those of any region or city in the United States."

In addition there were the usual amusements of archery and golf, horse-races and gymkhanas. Lenox was further remarkable for possessing a gentlemen's club, to which men could escape just as they might have done in cities; it held an annual ball. The social climax came with an annual procession of decorated carriages called the Tub Parade,

153. Brookside at Great Barrington, by Carrère and Hastings. The style of the house is curiously at odds with the garden.

supposedly originated by Fanny Kemble. But the pace in the Berkshires rarely if ever became breathless. To Charles Dudley Warner, describing the summer residents in *Little Journeys Around the World*, the summer folks' conversation ran to the peaceful rural atmosphere of the place. "They talked about the quality of the air, the variety of the scenery, the exhilaration of the drives, the freedom from noise and dust, the country quiet." Social activity was enticing but unhurried.

There were the morning calls, the intellectual life of the reading clubs, the tennis parties, the afternoon teas, combined with the charming drives from one elegant place to another; the siestas, the idle swinging in hammocks with the latest magazine from

154. Steps to the lake at Brookside.

155. Wheatleigh, built by Peabody and Stearns as a wedding present for Count Carlos deHereida and his wife in 1892.

which to get a topic for dinner, the mild excitement of a tête-à-tête which might discover congenial tastes or run on into an interesting attachment.[6]

What the well-behaved "native people" may have thought of the newcomers, who bought their farms and pushed land prices up, was satirized by a piece of verse, written in broad dialect, published in *Harper's Magazine* in 1880. It was called "Does Farming Pay?"

160

Them Yorkers come in thick, 'n' haow lan' riz [how land rose]!
They air some good, I tell ye wut it is.
Rich s'il [soil] t' sech ain't no consequence
Ner ain't clean crops, ner ain't a nine-rail fence.
Wut tickles them is traouts 'n' shutin', lots;
Nice air, red clouds, 'n' awful sightly spots;
Yer poorest pastur'hill where wind is ha'sh,
More'n likely is the one that takes their cash.

Throughout the following decade more and more land was acquired for country houses. The first of the monster size was Barrington House or "Searles Castle" at Great Barrington, down the road from Stockbridge. Both in its position and in its character it never seemed typical of the Berkshires. Built at legendary cost for Mary Hopkins, widow of one of the founders of the Southern Pacific Railroad, it was begun in 1885 by McKim, Mead and White. They were eventually ousted by the decorator (and later philanthropist) Edward Searles – not surprisingly, because before the house was finished he had married the widow who, at sixty-eight, was twenty-one years his senior. The massive silhouette of round towers and spiky roofs would be more at home in Newport, even though the forbidding blue dolomite from which it is built came from the East Mountain across the river. Typically, perhaps, the interior featured an organ of more than usual splendor made by James E. Treat, Searles's childhood friend. Evidently it was a success, because Searles went on to finance the building of two further organs on an even more majestic scale, in the Broadway Tabernacle in New York and the Serlio Organ Hall in Methuen, Massachusetts. Though Barrington House had grounds of sixty-five acres, there was no farm group.[7]

Nevertheless, Barrington House set the scale for the next decade. Some of the new houses were sited more or less in the center of Lenox itself. The most conspicuous is still Bellefontaine (altered after a fire in 1949) (Plate 152). Designed by Carrère and Hastings for Giraud Foster, it has a double-height Corinthian portico made of white marble from the paper-making town of Lee, a few miles away. In 1904 the same architects built Brookside (Plates 153 and 154) in Great Barrington for the inventor and electronics manufacturer William Stanley (who soon ran into difficulties with patents and had to sell).

For the banker and railroad director H.H. Cook, a descendant of Captain Thomas Cook who founded Portsmouth, Rhode Island, the Boston firm of Peabody and Stearns built Wheatleigh, a spreading Italianate villa of thin yellow bricks with endless colonnades (Plate 155). It is said to have been a wedding present for Cook's daughter, who married Count Carlos deHereida in 1891, the year before work began. In a completely different, picturesque-cottage style, Peabody and Stearns also designed Elm Court for William Douglas Sloane, owner of a Fifth Avenue furniture store who married a Vanderbilt. According to the weekly newspaper *Berkshire Resort Topics* in 1904, it was an example of "what the progressive modern spirit, backed up by abundant capital can accomplish." Certainly it was very large and work went on over a fourteen year period, from 1886 to 1900, including the farm group. Sloane's brother, John, built Wyndhurst in 1892; and in the first years of the new century John Sloane's friend Robert W. Paterson, a principal in the trading firm of Paterson, Dowling and Company and a director of the Manhattan Bank, constructed Blantyre. Both Mr. and Mrs. Paterson had Scottish roots, and the idea was that the house should recall Mrs. Paterson's family home in Lanarkshire; the name is that of Mr. Paterson's father's house outside Glasgow. For some reason the *New York Times* felt moved to fulminate:

While there are several imaginable explanations – chief among them, perhaps, lack of artistic instinct – why a wealthy New Yorker of Scottish descent should conceive the purpose of building at Lenox a summer home reproducing with some approximation to exactness a Highland castle of the sort constructed in the middle ages, it is not easy to understand why a New York architect, if he holds himself to be anything more than a boss of stone masons and carpenters, should peril his professional reputation among the enlightened by encouraging and assisting the wealthy New Yorker of Scotch descent to violate every one of the laws of artistic propriety.[8]

Since the architect, Robert Henry Robertson, also had Scottish blood, the rebuke seems a trifle hard.

As late as 1919 Margaret McKim Vanderbilt constructed Holmwood, replacing George Westinghouse's Erskine Park, where Mrs. Westinghouse reputedly insisted that everything, from the inside of the motorcars to the drives covered in tons of marble chips, had to be white. Old photographs give the lie to this legend. More remarkably, however, they also reveal that inside the house the walls and ceilings were covered in quilted or capitonné fabric and (in a bravura display of novelty by the owner, one of the pioneers of electric light) every cornice had a continuous frieze of light bulbs (Plate 156). But in scale if nothing else, the champion of the Berkshire country houses was Shadowbrook – an immense building again in a beguilingly inappropriate cottage style,

156. The dining room at Erskine Park. Note the capitonné or quilted ceiling and the frieze of uncovered light bulbs. The owner was the pioneer of electricity George Westinghouse.

all red-tiled roof and half-timbered gables (Plate 157). It was designed by H. Neill Wilson, a local man from Pittsfield, Massachussets, for Mr. and Mrs. Anson Phelps Stokes, and was later bought by Andrew Carnegie. One of the Stokes's sons, in the class of 1896 at Yale, is supposed to have telegraphed his mother from New Haven that he would like to bring "some '96 fellows" for a weekend; to which she wittily replied: "Many guests already here. Have only room for 50."[9]

It may seem that these and the other large Berkshire houses had little to do with rural simplicity. However, they were not all elaborate. In this, Naumkeag was typical (Plate 26). Despite the occasional craftsman-style flourish, such as pieces of glass pressed into the mortar over windows or a zodiac set into the stone floor of the entrance porch, it was thought of as no more than a summer home and this was reflected in its furnishing, which was comfortable but inexpensive. Even where houses were larger and stylistically more formal, the effort might well have been made to evoke a country feeling through the surroundings. This kind of pastoral had a long literary as well as aesthetic tradition; not surprisingly, therefore, its undoubted master was a novelist, Edith Wharton.

Wharton's first published book, written with Ogden Codman, had been *The Decoration of Houses*, so it was natural that she should have considered every detail of her house and its grounds with care. Her novels also exhibit an intense sense of place, whereby the houses that the characters inhabit often serve as an extension to their moral lives. As she

157. Shadowbrook, designed by the local architect H. Neill Wilson for Anson Phelps Stokes; it was later bought by Andrew Carnegie.

158. Edith Wharton's house, The Mount. This elevation of the east façade was drawn by Hoppin and Koen, the architects who replaced Ogden Codman, Jr. Avery Library, New York

159. Belton House in Lincolnshire, from Colen Campbell's *Vitruvius Britannicus*, clearly the model for The Mount.

declared in *The Writing of Fiction*, "the impression produced by a landscape ... or a house should always be an event in the history of a soul."[10] Certainly The Mount was consciously designed to reflect Wharton's own view of the ideal country existence and perhaps even its moral role, for she had come to the Berkshires in disgust at the artificiality of Newport. "At last I escaped from watering-place trivialities to the real country," she wrote in *A Backward Glance*. "The Mount was my first real home, and though it is nearly twenty years since I last saw it (for I was too happy there ever to want to revisit it as a stranger) its blessed influence still lives in me."[11]

The Decoration of Houses was published in 1897, just two years before the Whartons acquired the site of The Mount, then called Laurel Lake Farm. In it she and Codman had announced their devotion to the principles of Classical harmony, expressing a regard for historical accuracy that contrasted strongly with the muddled eclecticism of contemporary decoration (Plate 158). There is no question about The Mount's Classical pedigree, for it is nothing less than a miniature, pure white version of Belton House in Lincolnshire (Plate 159), then thought to be by Sir Christopher Wren. In England the "Wrenaissance" of Lutyens was already making a first appearance at this date, but such a literal quotation in the United States, where even the Colonial Revival as yet lacked historical purity, is remarkable.

Credit for the choice of Belton as the model probably goes to Codman, who had naturally been Mrs. Wharton's first thought as architect. At this time Codman knew Europe better than Mrs. Wharton did, having spent ten boyhood years in France while his family recuperated from financial losses suffered in the great Boston fire of 1872. Moreover, he appears to have used elements from Belton in his design of the Coats house in Newport in about 1884. This has a hipped roof, a widow's walk, and segmental headed windows and doorcase, though not the telltale cupola. When work began on The Mount, Mrs. Wharton had already collaborated with Codman in redesigning the Whartons' houses in Newport and on Park Avenue. But friendship cannot always survive being put onto a business footing, and she quickly quarreled with him over what she regarded as exorbitant fees. So she changed to another New York architect, Francis Hoppin of Hoppin and Koen. Once the leading draftsman to McKim, Mead and White, he had worked on other Berkshire houses; at The Mount he is reported to have followed Wharton's ideas closely.[12]

Just as the architecture was based on that of a great English country house, the approach also summons up the sensations of traveling through a landed estate – again in miniature. For as visitors followed the drive to the house they would have seen the estate at work in a number of ways. This was no accident; though the Whartons' resources were stretched and their land ran only to a hundred and twenty-five acres, these activities could easily have been hidden. But Mrs. Wharton wished to remind her guests that they were in the country. In describing The Mount in *A Backward Glance*, she makes no mention of the style of the house; rather, her thoughts seem first to have turned to the landscape. The first things she enumerates are the kitchen garden and farm.[13] The inspiration of the scheme, which was laid out by her niece Beatrix Jones, later Beatrix Farrand, designer of the landscape at Dumbarton Oaks, may have been less English than Italian, as one would expect of the future author of *Italian Villas and their Gardens*.

In Edith Wharton's time, the approach to the house began along a sugar maple *allée*. There were woods to the right, but on the left a succession of functional estate buildings appeared in view. First came the gardener's lodge, the greenhouse, and the potting shed, behind which could be glimpsed an orchard. Then, passing the kitchen garden, the drive reached the stables, a pretty Dutch-style structure. *Berkshire Resort Topics* called them "particularly fine."[14] A small spring house might also have been noticed, before the drive turned and picturesquely wound through the woods. The final sweep to the house ran past carefully tended lawns; but even once one had reached the terrace on the garden side, with its view over formal Italian gardens (Plate 160) and out to the mountains beyond, the farm was never far from mind. Its buildings were distinctly visible, situated between a pond and Laurel Lake.

Some of the farm buildings were inherited from the previous owners of the site. They were extended to form a quadrangle, one side of which included an ice house, while to the north were a hen house and piggery. It is said that the funds to build the piggery were gained when Mrs. Wharton dashed off a poem and sent it to a magazine. Part of the farm's purpose may have been to occupy her husband, "Teddy," with whom relations were strained. As regards its management, one suspects that Mr. Wharton's attitude was like that of all too many estate owners: apparently he liked the animals far too much to let any of them be killed. Edith meanwhile, though writing prolifically, still managed to attend committees for the Lenox Library, the Village Improvement Association and the Flower Show. She might have been a county lady from the English shires.

It was only to be expected that Ogden Codman's judgment of the house was critical. As he wrote to his mother on 8 October 1902:

> The place looks forlorn beyond my powers of description and it will take years and a small fortune in Landscape gardening to make it look even decent.

160. Walter Berry and dog in Odgen Codman's trellis niche for the Red Garden at The Mount. As with many American country houses, the garden was an integral part of the scheme.

161. Friends of the sculptor Daniel Chester French at Chesterwood, September 1915.

162. Curling at High Lawn House.

Inside it looks bare and poverty stricken, the walls are not properly painted as they were in such a hurry to get in . . .

The enclosed Courtyard is *to my* mind an utter failure, it looks like a clothes yard and is all out of proportion. There are regular rules for making courtyards and several of the old books in architecture give these rules and the reasons for them. Mrs. Wharton has at least *one* of these books but evidently neither she nor Hoppin can have read them.[15]

Edith shared none of these misgivings. However much she loved the polished, cosmopolitan life of the great European cities, the simpler attractions of The Mount remained, if anything, closer to her heart. "I would give up all this fine civilization," she wrote from Paris, "for a sight of my spring blossoms at Lenox."[16]

Despite appearances, many of the other Berkshire houses expressed similar priorities to The Mount. Quite a number were accompanied by farm groups. The Shadowbrook estate, for instance, was seven hundred and fifty-eight acres, and the buildings for the home farm comprised three cottages, a cow barn, tool barn, horse barn, hay barn, duck and poultry houses, carpenter's shop, blacksmith's shop, sheds for wagons and tools, a large ice house, and a dairy. Frederick Vanderbilt Field remembered the farm that his father, William B. Osgood Field – son-in-law of the Sloanes at Elm Court – had at his house, High Lawn (Plate 162). It was stocked with a fine herd of Jerseys – often the rich man's choice because of their low, deliciously rich yield of milk. Hay, corn, and alfalfa were grown to feed them, and there was a large vegetable garden to supply the house: "The setup was about as feudal as you could get back to in the first quarter of the twentieth century."[17] It was not expected to make money, but the losses had their advantage when taxation began to bite. Playing with the animals amused the children and the fresh country produce did them good.

High Lawn was not as relaxed as the Fields' other country house, Westerfield Farm on Lake Mohegan, but life there was less formal (despite fifteen indoor servants and two chauffeurs) than in the family's Fifth Avenue mansion. They all enjoyed picnicking in the playhouse:

> The picnic procedure never varied. In the middle of the afternoon preceding the outing, an observer would have seen the butler carrying a large tray of silverware, plates and linen from the big house. Sometimes later, he would be followed by the "fourth man" carrying cooking utensils, eggs, cream, salt and pepper. We participants would then gather at the appointed hour around the electric stove, and the picnic would get underway. An outstanding feature was that everyone was in a good humor. I wonder if that was not because we were, for a change, relatively on our own, away from the servants for a whole meal.[18]

It perhaps says something that even in this formal age – High Lawn was built in 1909 – Frederick and his elder brother Osgood were not punished one Christmas after depositing quantities of cow dung on the living room hearth in order to convince their younger sisters that Santa Claus and his reindeer had come in the night.

Cortland Field Bishop, a man of independent means who collected books and prints and sponsored the Wright brothers in their early flying experiments, is remembered for his terrifying appearances in his powerful French motorcar; but his young daughter enjoyed the gentler side of life on their estate of Interlaken. She would go "running by myself to the cow stable, where Francis the milkman taught me to milk cows and I drank the foaming warm milk, sometimes milking directly from the cow into my mouth. I loved the barn, too, where one could jump from the loft into a mass of loose, fragrant hay below."[19] In their own way the letters of Joseph Hodges Choate, owner of Naumkeag, suggest an equally pastoral vision. "What a luxury it will be to escape from the city, and to roll on the grass, ride over the hills, and float in Stockbridge Bowl," he would write from New York. "I do miss Stockbridge and every dear thing in it – wife, children, friends, houses, garden, lands, horses, cows, pigs, not to speak of the donkey."[20]

Yet one must also recognize that this façade of country life in the Berkshires was as elaborate and as civilized a fiction as one of Edith Wharton's own novels. It was decorative, wonderfully restorative, but not very practical. The test came in the First World War. Characteristically, *Country Life in America* wrote admiringly of the sacrifices being made in an article called "How the Lenox Folk are Helping to Win."[21] At Bellefontaine one of the largest greenhouses had been turned over from sweet peas to sweet corn. Only just enough coal was being burned at Wyndhurst to save the orchid collection. High Lawn was making do with thirty-six outside staff. The Lenox Horticultural Society announced that it would hold no more shows for the duration of the conflict: "This, be assured, means a good deal." But G.W. Ferguson, manager of Pinecroft Farm and known locally as "the wheat crank," had come into his own. For years he had been boring the neighborhood with how he had achieved thirty bushels of wheat annually on a small field. He had only done it to feed the chickens, but from now on productivity even in Lenox would be held in greater respect.

— 11 —

"One of the current luxuries that matters"
THE ARCHITECTURE OF SPORT

THOUGH THE FARM GROUP formed an attractive rural garnish to many American country houses, often the real meat lay elsewhere: in sport. Not all sports and games required architectural expression. Golf, croquet, skeet or claypigeon shooting, even the shooting of driven pheasants – popular though these were – had little need of buildings. But on some estates the provision for those activities that did benefit from roof and walls was elaborate. This profoundly impressed the Prince of Wales when he visited Long Island in 1924. Having experienced a dinner and ball at Clarence Mackay's Harbor Hill he later concluded: "paintings, tapestries, old china, and armour would have been commonplace enough in a British country house; what was surprising was to find on the same property a squash-racquets court, a gymnasium, an indoor swimming-pool, and a Turkish bath."[1]

And these were only some of the sport-related structures on the five hundred acre estate (Plate 164). Barr Ferree described the carriage house and its stables (Plate 165) as being "quite palatial, with magnificent appointments for the horses, a special suite for the head coachman, and comfortable quarters for the men."[2] In addition there were the polo stables, kennels, and an unusual device called the "deer run" – an artificial deer on rails which sped through clearings in the woods to give Mackay shooting practice.

The development of its sporting architecture is one of the outstanding features of the American country house. It reflects the enthusiasm for sport that consumed Americans in the late nineteenth century. For decades an ardent group of health campaigners, partly influenced by the English creed of "muscular Christianity," had inveighed against the evils of city life. In 1866 S.D. Kehoe, advocate of the Indian club, echoed the fears of many when he warned against the deleterious effects of excessive "mind work, by the ambitious student, the covetous and care-worn merchant, or the adventurer in political life."[3] The antidote was vigorous physical exercise, and there was much earnest discussion as to how this could be promoted among the poorer classes. Inevitably, however, it was the sons of the rich who most fully embraced the ideal of "manly sport." Their universities encouraged it as a means of conquering the unhealthy environment of the office. Theodore Roosevelt, small and asthmatic when he went to Harvard, showed what could be done. By sheer force of will he had overcome his physical disadvantages to box, wrestle, play tennis, and form a living example to the nation of the benefits of the Strenuous Life. Young women were not entirely excluded from this athletic world. Dress reform had begun to liberate them from the corset, and,

169

163. The basement bowling alley at Nemours, Delaware, made by the Brunswick Balke-Collender Company. Unlike skittles in England, ten-pin bowling was a fashionable game in the United States, equally popular with both sexes.

164. The court tennis building at Harbor Hill, Long Island. Court tennis was one of the many games for which some houses provided.

165. Detail of the stables at Harbor Hill.

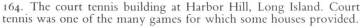

if they could not row or box, they might enjoy the supposedly gentler activities of bicycling, gymnastics, and hockey. These and other sports, such as football, basketball, golf, squash, racquets, lawn tennis, and polo, were virtually unknown to the young people of the 1860s: some had not been invented. In that benighted era the only exercise had been walking, riding, and carriage driving.

Foreign visitors frequently remarked on the determination with which sports and games were pursued in turn-of-the-century America. In more ways than one they could be seen as the obverse side of the business coin: the more arduously a man worked to make money, the more urgently he needed exercise. "We Americans are too officious about our diversions," observed Desmond and Croly in 1903; "and the appropriate habitation for a contemporary house-party, far from consisting of a series of well-fashioned rooms, would consist rather of a casino with billiard and card tables, bowling-alleys, a tank, and a tennis-court as the chief items of equipment. The office and the play room symbolize the two characteristic and natural extremes of American life."

Desmond and Croly's hint was soon taken up. In 1904 Mrs. William Astor had a private "casino" or playhouse built at Ferncliff in New York. The casino was a species of meeting place that enjoyed a vogue in late-nineteenth-century resorts. The term was used in its Renaissance meaning of pleasure house – as yet it was not associated with gambling. Its principal role was to provide somewhere other than church for people to see each other. There might be a small theater, otherwise just tennis courts and a dining room. The leading architects of the casino were McKim, Mead and White and it can be no coincidence that they were chosen by Mrs. Astor for Ferncliff. In one instance – the "pleasure dome" built by Lucien Hamilton Tyng at Southampton, Long Island, in 1930 – a private playhouse retained the artistic associations of the casino, being designed as a studio, theater, concert hall, and art gallery.[4] But this appears to have been unique.

The central feature of the Astor playhouse is an indoor tennis court the size of a small cathedral, vaulted, tiled, and top-lit, with an elaborate system of shades against the sun (Plate 168). Legend grew up that the Astors had originally asked for no more than a ping-pong court, "but the plan which [Stanford White] submitted included an indoor tennis court, two squash courts, swimming pool, great hall, living room, library, five bedrooms, two dressing rooms, three baths, a kitchen, and servants' quarters. This plan was accepted at once."[5] The idea had found its time.

170

Within a few years the playhouse had become such a recognizable feature of country house life that one became a turning point in Edith Wharton's novel *The Fruit of the Tree*, published in 1907. Gusts of enthusiasm were always liable to blow up the scale of these things:

"Why not build a squash court?" Blanche Carbury proposed [to Bessy Amherst, in need of winter exercise]; and the two fell instantly to making plans under the guidance of Ned Bowfort and Westy Gaines. As the scheme developed, various advisers suggested that it was a pity not to add a bowling-alley, a swimming-tank and a gymnasium; a fashionable architect was summoned from town, measurements were taken, sites discussed, sketches compared, and engineers consulted as to the cost of artesian wells and the best system for heating the tank.[6]

It was never erected, though by an ironic stroke of fate the same plans resurfaced after Bessy's death as a community building in the family's mill town. *Country Life in America* was somewhat behind the times when it reported in 1915: "The sports building is taking its place as a new and luxurious adjunct to the American country house."[7]

The playhouse is an entirely American phenomenon, which knows no European equivalent. The ingredients were usually a covered squash court or tennis court, swimming pool, and bowling alley, with grass tennis courts outside. When a tennis court is combined with a swimming pool the result is bound to be big, so one should not be misled by the apparent childishness of the term "playhouse," which was the one most commonly used at the time. These were very grown up undertakings indeed. The two-level playhouse on the Whitney estate of Greentree, Long Island, is actually larger than the main house. The Casino (as it was called) at George Jay Gould's Georgian Court, New Jersey, capped even this, having been constructed around an arena for exercising the polo ponies which was supposed to be even big enough to hold indoor matches. This was an American equivalent of the riding schools popular among the European nobility since the Renaissance (though associated less with polo than with the

166. George W. Vanderbilt's gymnasium at Biltmore House.

167. The du Pont solarium at Nemours.

168. Interior of the "cathedral of tennis" which McKim, Mead and White built for the Astors at Ferncliff, New York.

169. Human chessmen in the Casino of Georgian Court, New Jersey. The main purpose of this space was the indoor exercise of horses.

highly stylized disciplines of the *haute école*, still practiced by the Spanish Riding School in Vienna). The space could also be used for pageants, circuses, galas, and so on (Plate 169). Grouped around the periphery were a swimming pool, ballroom, bowling alley, racquets court, court tennis court, two squash courts, and a handball court.

The Rockefeller playhouse at Pocantico Hills, in a ramblng half-timbered style, was not as large as Gould's building, though still considerable (Plate 170). Built in 1925, it included a kitchen, and the grounds outside were gaily planted with flowerbeds. It therefore became an attractive and self-contained element of the estate – an ideal place of escape for the young. Perhaps it was too ideal in some ways, for John D., Jr., was compelled to circularize his children in 1930:

> Having in mind the churchgoing habit of the community and the traditions and attitude of the family and our joint responsibilities to the grandchildren as they come along, it seems best that the sport and game facilities of the playhouse and the place, including horses, golf, croquet and tennis, should be availed of on Sundays at hours other than between 10:30 and 12:30 in the morning.[8]

By this date there cannot have been many country houses beyond striking distance of a good country club, making it, one would have thought, less necessary for the owner to provide privately for sport. But the attraction of the private playhouse was precisely that it was private. As such, it remained "one of the current luxuries that matters," as *Town and Country* commented apropos an example outside Cleveland in 1931. "It is the most exclusive sort of club, without dues, the members composed of the friends of the owner."[9] Consequently, playhouses continued to be built until the Second World War. One of the most elaborate was constructed in 1939 on the Twin Peaks Ranch at Ojai, California (Plate 171). It served partly as a guest annex, and for those with artistic tastes the studio and bookbindery were close by. The sportsman was amply catered for. "Depending on your athletic tastes, you may swim or play tennis, have a strenuous game of badminton or a real workout in the bowling alleys," wrote William Randolph Hearst's right-hand woman, Ethel Head. "On the other hand you may prefer to swing a

170. (*above*) The Rockefeller playhouse at Pocantico Hills, seen from the air. Playhouses, often combining a swimming pool and tennis court, could be almost as large as the main house.

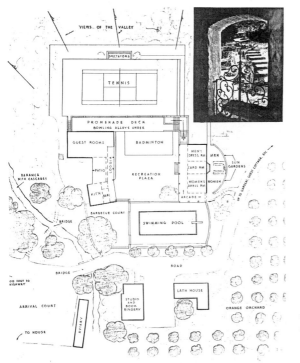

171. Outline plan of Mrs. Dickey's "sports plaza" in the Ojai Valley, California, 1938. Unusually it included an aviary, studio and bookbindery, and lath house.

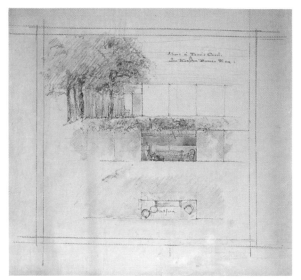

172. Alcove in a tennis court at J. Hampton Barnes's house at Devon, Pennsylvania. Even the simplest of structures could be carefully designed, in this case by Wilson Eyre. Architectural Archives of the University of Pennsylvania

173. Swimming pool at Lyndhurst, New York.

wicked ping-pong racket or merely sit peacefully over a game of contract." From the flagstone loggia less-sportsminded guests could easily reach "the attractive wormy chestnut bar with its inside cabinets wallpapered in bright geographic design."[10]

It was not absolutely necessary to have a playhouse to enjoy some or all of the activities found in one. At the turn of the century tennis was still thought of as an English game, though with the facilities available it is not surprising that American players were rapidly catching up (Plate 172). Grass courts were easier to provide than covered ones, and Olmsted suggested that at Biltmore there should be two, placed at right angles, so that play could continue throughout the day without the sun getting in anyone's eyes.

Swimming, on the other hand, was more popular in the United States, covered swimming pools being a rarity on English country estates. Oddly this was nothing to do with the weather, since open-air bathing pools were relatively common. Often these English pools were landscaped as rockpools to evoke the sylvan pleasures of a dip in the river; for many owners, this was how their swimming had been enjoyed in university days. By contrast the swimming pool of the American country house was more likely to recall the origins of water exercise in the Classical world, for, as *House and Garden* observed, "such a pool is only the revival, or rather the adaption to modern conditions of . . . the bathing pool or *impluvium* . . . of the Roman villa."[11] *Town and Country* likened the Whitney swimming pool at Greentree to the Baths of Titus, Caracalla, and Pompeii.[12] Architectural treatment was given to some open pools, such as Ralph Pulitzer's at Manhasset, Long Island, "built with a certain genuflexion to classical models,"[13] but a covered pool was the ideal (Plates 173 and 174). A handsome example, decorated with murals of seventeenth-century sailing ships, was built by James P. Donahue at Southampton, Long Island; it was attached to a large beach house whose style, in the ineffable words of *Town and Country*, derived from "the days of that jovially uxoricidal Eighth Henry of England." In this article Augusta Patterson went on to comment: "certainly it is gratifying to realize that Americans are learning to unite agreeable architecture with the minor athletics."[14] If you did not have a playhouse, the

174

pool could be put in the basement of the main house. It was a good idea to have it near the billiard room, perhaps with a separate staircase down from the owner's dressing room. This created a kind of masculine enclave. At Stan Hywet the Roman-style indoor pool is next to the large gymnasium (unusually, it is complemented by a natural-looking pool formed out of an old quarry, known as the lagoons). The danger of the basement swimming pool was that it could make the whole house damp, and for this reason some authors condemned it. In which case the obvious place for it was the conservatory. Conservatories were large, glassed-in, heated and fairly useless on the whole; and a moist atmosphere benefited the plants.

Bowling alleys were even rarer in England than covered swimming pools, since skittles was considered a rather low game. In America, however, bowling was not only fashionable but almost as popular with women as with men (Plates 163, 175 and 176). In 1895 a bowling alley was erected at Lyndhurst even though the house was then the home of George Gould's pious, as yet unmarried, sister, Helen. "The room at the south side is . . . a pleasant place while waiting for one's turn to play," wrote *Leslie's Popular Monthly*. "The room at the other end Miss Gould uses for a sewing room, and here, every

174. The Firestone swimming pool at Harbel Manor, in Ohio, decorated for Christmas, about 1940.

175–76. Bowling alleys at Biltmore, North Carolina, and Sagamore Lodge in the Adirondacks.

Saturday morning, she presides over a class of little girls."[15] However, a bowling alley could equally well double as a shooting gallery if desired.

Strictly speaking, these activities were games rather than sports. The importance of field sports such as fishing and shooting went beyond the buildings constructed specifically for them. They were central to encouraging that new interest in the country which persuaded people that they wanted to live there. The south shore of Long Island provides a paradigm of their influence. It had been little more than scrub and dune before being parcelled into estates, and without Eliphalet Snedecor's tavern, replaced after the death of "Liff" by the South Side Sportsmen's Club, there would have been little reason for rich men to explore it. But the deer hunting (Plate 177) and fishing were so good that, from the 1830s, one or two visitors decided to make a permanent base there. The first house of pretension was Dr. Alfred Wagstaff's Tallulah at West Islip, built after 1859. In 1879 William K. Vanderbilt constructed Idle Hour, and before long a little colony of sportsmen was established, each in his own country house, each a member of the SSSC. They included Christopher Robert's Peperidye Hall; Indian Head, home of Frederick Bourne of the Singer Sewing Machine Company; and Westbrook Farms, created by the tobacco brothers Pierre and Louis Lorillard and then rebuilt by William Bayard Cutting – a railroad magnate who was, unusually, a friend of both Vanderbilt and Edith Wharton. Before long the exclusive attitude of these new residents caused complaints about "the Millionaire nuisance."[16]

These Long Island estates fathered suburbs that eventually turned on their parents and devoured then. Occasionally, sport explains a sudden outbreak of country houses far away from urban influence. The most conspicuous example is Thomasville in Georgia, a little Greek Revival town which became a magnet for sportsmen around 1900. The newcomers were led by John Hay Whitney who had Greenwood Plantation. Here the

177. The development of Long Island was encouraged by its sporting potential: the activities of rich country house owners led to talk of "the Millionaire nuisance." This illustration of deer hunting appeared in *Harper's Weekly* in 1878.

main house dated from 1842, but other owners built anew, using architects from their home cities. For the financier Jeptha Homer Wade, the Cleveland firm of Hubbell and Benes designed Mill Pond in 1903. It is the most striking of the turn-of-the-century plantations – thanks largely to having been constructed around a hundred foot square courtyard with a movable covering of steel and glass. The popularity of Thomasville continued into the 1930s, with Delano and Aldrich building Box Hill for Alvah K. Lawrie, president of the Aluminum Company of America, and Abraham Garfield of Cleveland rebuilding Pebble Hill for Kate Hanna Harvey.[17]

As country life developed, the wild pleasures of wading through swamps in quest of game lost popularity to more organized pursuits, in which the horse took center stage. "You should have seen the trap that came for me at the Oakdale station this morning," bubbled the architect Richard Morris Hunt when he visited Vanderbilt at Idle Hour. "A jolly little omnibus, with a stunning pair of black French post-horses with bells and fox-tail suspended from the collar. Et puis le cocher!!! clack! et au château!!"[18] It was the horse in all its many forms – carriage horse, trotting horse, hunter, polo pony, racehorse

178. Stables and farm group at Hartwood Acres near Pittsburgh, Pennsylvania, designed by Alfred Hopkins about 1930. The Cotswold style was thought appropriate to the landscape of western Pennsylvania, which reminded the owners, Mr. and Mrs. John Flinn Lawrence, of England.

– that inspired the greatest triumphs of sporting architecture and made the deepest mark on country estates (Plate 178).

"One certainly gets the impression that more people keep horses for pleasure in America than in England," wrote a well-traveled writer in 1900.[19] Four-in-hand driving enjoyed a great vogue among millionaires: to keep several powerful animals pulling together required a cool head and iron will – attributes that had perhaps been developed to an exaggerated degree in the course of successful business lives. Driving was an expensive hobby, in which a smart appearance was everything. To make it really enjoyable there had to be a good number of well-made-up, preferably private, roads through pleasant countryside over which to drive. This was a spur to the landscaping of many estates. A coach-and-four stumbling along poorly maintained roads through ugly countryside would not have looked suitably picturesque. In Pennsylvania Alexander J. Cassatt and his friends went so far as to buy the neglected Lancaster Turnpike, the improvements coincidentally providing the community with, in the words of one

179. Theodore Roosevelt built the North Room of Sagamore Hill on Long Island in 1905, after his election as president for a second term. The decoration reflects his many sporting pursuits. "Really I like it better than any room in the White House, which as you know is my standard of splendor!" he wrote to the architect C. Grant LaFarge.

grateful clergyman, "the civilizing and comforting effects of proper highways between neighbors and friends, and uniting church and school."[20]

In some areas fox hunting was pursued with passion, and woebetide anyone who maintained that it was not appropriate to the United States. "To say [fox hunting] is un-American seems particularly absurd to such of us as are happy to be in part of Southern blood, and whose forefathers, in Virginia, Georgia, or the Carolinas, have for six generations followed the fox with horse and hound," wrote Theodore Roosevelt.[21] The sport underwent a renaissance in the 1880s when the best hunts were the Elkridge in Maryland, the Rosetree near Philadelphia, the Genesee Valley in central New York, the Meadowbrook and Rockaway on Long Island, and the unfortunately named Myopia outside Boston. There were some drawbacks to riding to hounds on Long Island, where Roosevelt was based, not the least being a paucity of foxes. As a consequence, the majority of days were spent drag hunting: this offered less of a challenge to the hounds but more of a test to the riders, particularly given the high wooden fences. At one meet of the

179

180–81. Polo at Georgian Court: preparing the field and watching the match.

Meadowbrook held at Roosevelt's Sagamore Hill (Plate 179), the master partly dislocated a knee, another man broke two ribs, and Roosevelt himself broke an arm. "I looked pretty gay, with one arm dangling, and my face and clothes like the walls of a slaughter house," he wrote to his hunting friend Henry Cabot Lodge.[22] Despite such hazards, *Vanity Fair* could report in December 1916 that "the sport is rapidly growing in favor" and, indeed, if the tide of popularity continued to swell "fox-hunting will soon be quite as much an American as an English sport." However, hunting folk continued to regret that fox hunting never received the broad support of the rural community it still enjoyed in England.[23]

Polo seemed even less egalitarian. It was first played in the United States in New York in 1876, but soon Long Island in general and the Meadow Brook Club in particular had become its American center: every player in the United States team in the dozen international matches with Great Britain between 1886 and 1939 had a country house on Long Island. Its appeal to the man of business was sung by George Gould: "The effect of the game upon the tired body is tonic. Also it stimulates the mind and leaves it tranquil. After a well-played match a man is at peace with the whole world. He can take up business problems with renewed vigor and mental clearness."[24] The Duke of Windsor noted with surprise that the term "polo player" was used in the press with almost the same opprobrious connotations as "playboy."[25]

Except in size, there was little outward difference between the design of the harness stable, the hunting stable, and the polo stable. Polo stables were the largest because of the number of ponies: a high-goal player might tire three or four in the course of a game, which meant keeping at least half a dozen in his stable, since at any one time half might be sick or injured. Inside the stable it had long been the practice to keep carriage horses in stalls and saddle horses, which are more high spirited, in loose boxes, in which they could move freely. The United States was a horse-loving nation and on the whole owners could be proud of their stables. "At no day since the domestication of the horse," averred *The Gentleman's Stable Guide*, "has he been so comfortably provided for as in the stable of the American gentleman."[26]

One principle was common to all thinking on stables: they had to be dry. Therefore a site on a hill or light soil was to be sought because it saved considerable expense in putting down drains. In the layout a courtyard of some kind was generally favored (Plate 183). For a large stables this was less economical than the usual commercial solution of two rows of stalls either side of a central aisle, but it was much more attractive. Some writers saw special merits, particularly for easy observation, in curving courtyards, and occasionally they were tried (Plate 182). Dreamwold had an interesting variant: a circular stallion barn with all the doors looking outwards. The idea was that no stallion would be able to see his neighbor and cause trouble. In an appealing piece of symbolism the stables on the Lathrop Brown estate at St. James, Long Island, took the form of a bar horseshoe, with the stalls occupying the curved U and the stud groom's

180

cottage, harness room, tack room, trophy room, and a pedimented gateway closing the mouth. But such experiments were rare, since it is the first rule of building that straight lines cost less than curves. In his own courtyard stable – a rectangle – the architect Thomas Hastings, of Carrère and Hastings, placed his dwelling house on the fourth side. Both he and his wife were devoted to thoroughbreds and wanted to live close to them. It was an extreme solution. For obvious reasons of smell, dirt, and flies most owners preferred the stables to be a little way from the house.

In construction, wood was praised for dryness. This pointed to Queen Anne in the 1870s and 1880s, Colonial thereafter. On the other hand so strongly were some horse activities associated with England that Georgian was almost equally popular, brick being a favorite material. After 1910 the Cotswold style – a cozy sub-species of Georgian – came into vogue, particularly around Philadelphia with its good supply of building stone. There was something about a cupola that most owners found hard to resist. It came close to being a cliché, and architects were hard put to ring the changes with squares and octagons, pillars and arches, domes, spires, and dovecots. Weathervanes were an open invitation to whimsy. Until about 1930 cupola and weathervane were likely to sail above tall roofs used as lofts (though some feared that feed stored directly above horses would be tainted by bad air). The need for these tall roofs declined when hay and straw began to be baled, making it more easily transportable.

The real test of any stable lay inside. This was not just a question of horse comfort but of life and death; and for the owner the death of a horse meant an expensive loss. Getting the right balance for the horse throughout the year was made more difficult by the extremes and uncertainties of the American climate. It sometimes seemed a case of reconciling opposites. The really useful stable had to be

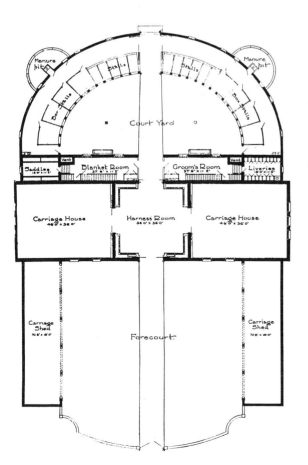

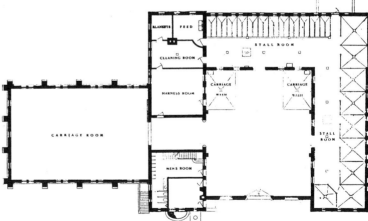

182–83. Plan of F.G. Bourne's stable at Oakdale, Long Island, by Ernest Flagg and F.W. Vanderbilt's stable at Hyde Park, New York, by R.H. Robertson. A vital principle of stable design was the separation of the stalls from the harness room and carriage house, because of the damage that ammonia fumes from soiled straw could do to leather.

perfectly cool, airy, and pervious to the atmosphere in summer; perfectly close, warm, and free from all drafts of external air, except in so far as shall be needed for ventilation, in winter; perfectly ventilated, so as to be pure, and free from ill odors, ammoniacal vapors and the like, arising from the urine and excrement of the animals at all times; perfectly dry under foot and well drained, since nothing is more injurious to the horse than to stand up to his heels in wet litter, decomposed vegetable matter, his own ordure, and slops of all kinds.[27]

184. A game wagon leaves the stables at Pebble Hill in Thomasville, Georgia, built in 1935.

How to achieve this delicate equipoise was no easy matter. As in all questions concerning the horse, opinions were strong and sometimes divided. Since direct sunlight could affect the horses' eyes, the stalls could not face south. But would not a north-facing stables invite fatal drafts? There again, according to the *Architectural Review*, "no stable gets enough air."[28] Heating was alternately advocated and deplored. Specially horse-minded owners liked to develop their own gadgets, from waterbuckets operated by pressure from the horse's nose to (in the case of Jock Whitney's racing stables at Upperville, Virginia) floor-mounted floodlights to facilitate treating leg injuries at night.

Most country house stables, even if they were intended principally for polo ponies or hunters, had a carriage house. Driving light traps and buggies was popular among all types of owner, not just carriage enthusiasts. It was even looked upon as a form of active exercise, one man saying to the author of Baedeker's *United States*: "I am really getting too stout; I must start a buggy."[29] Positioning the carriage house constituted one of the firm principles of stable design, since all were agreed that it had to be separated from the stalls. This was because ammonia fumes from urine-soaked straw damaged the sensitive lacquer of the bodywork and the leather harnesses and upholstery. The leather was another reason for absolute dryness. No opening was allowed between the harness room and the stall wing.

In first-class carriage houses the vehicles – two-wheeled phaetons, tilburies, and gigs; four-wheeled landaus, cabriolets, rockaways, curricles, and broughams – were drawn up, perhaps facing each other, with the precision of a military parade. Cocoa matting was put down the center of the room while the rest of the floor was dusted with white sand. Onto this, using colored sand, might be stenciled the owner's monogram or crest. Care of the carriages was only slightly less delicate than that of the horses. One corner of the carriage house contained a square with a drain for the vital operation of washing. Mud had to be removed as soon as the carriages returned home – but on no account with hot water or a hose, for both were ruinous to varnish. Particular care had to be taken to remove surplus oil, because it rotted the woodwork.

Whereas a spirit of simplification had triumphed below stairs in the main house, making the service quarters seem streamlined in comparison to the over-provision of the English equivalent, the working rooms in the stables were as specialized as anything in Europe. Division of function was the presiding rule, and remained in force until the Second World War. Lamp rooms and brushing rooms may not be found in American country houses, but cleaning rooms, tack rooms, feed rooms, blanket rooms, wash boxes, farrier shops, and trophy rooms were ever present in the best American country house stables. All were recommended by Richard V.N. Gambrill and James C. Mackenzie as late as 1935.[30] Polo stables also required a practice pit and a dummy horse.

A final consideration was the housing of the men. It was best if the stud groom had his cottage a little way removed, or he and his wife would never be able escape his work. On the other hand at least one man had to sleep on the premises to hear when a horse was taken ill. The hands or "strappers" were also provided with a club room or some other comfortable place to gather and enjoy a pipe after work. This represented self-interest as well as paternalism on the part of the owner, since it encouraged the strappers not to drift away. "There is nothing more annoying than wandering about on a freezing cold day trying to find a groom."[31]

The scale of the largest private stables is indicated by Georgian Court. Bruce Price, architect of Tuxedo Park, had the task of accommodating two hundred and fifty polo ponies attended by over fifty grooms. Because of the prodigious size of the stables he

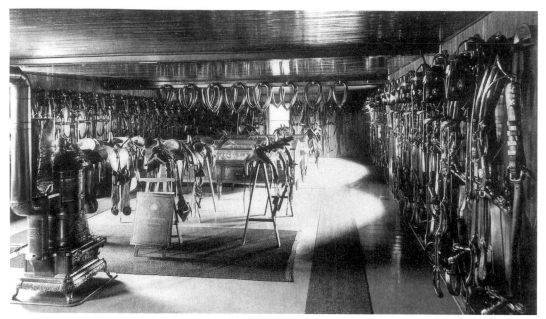

185. Gleaming tack and harnesses at Shelburne Farms. A French volume on stable management stands on the easel in the foreground.

abandoned the usual planning formulae and put up six blocks in the form of an **H**. The two in the center are connected by an arch, above which rises a tall octangular tower – the water tower for the whole estate. Despite the stables' vast scale, it was still necessary for the carriage house to be squeezed into an upper floor, with an electric elevator to take up the vehicles. Gould, dressed in "the high top boots, the baggy trousers, the hunting coat and stock of the cross country rider," owned forty polo ponies himself; the rest of the boxes were occupied by the horses of the American Polo Association, which used Georgian Court, with its three polo fields, to practice before the Internationals on Long Island (see Plates 180 and 181).[32]

The beauty of a well-kept, well-built stable was something the owner might well wish to share with friends. Gambrill and Mackenzie were fully alive to the pleasure, and seem to have understood the psychology of both owner and guest:

> There is nothing more delightful than the good old-fashioned custom of "morning stables" – generally indulged in after church on Sunday – when the owner and his guests pay a visit to the stables and inspect every horse and detail throughout. The stud groom in bowler hat and white coat with a basket of neatly sliced carrots under his arm, the smartly dressed grooms, who make the rounds on such occasions and strip every horse for inspection, are proud of their work and jealous of their reputations, and this weekly visit is the reward for work well done and the inspiration for even better results in the future.
>
> It is true that many city people dread to visit their friends in the country because of the necessity of just such visits to the stables, farm or kennels! But the interest in such things is growing so rapidly in this country and more people delight in well kept live stock and take a real interest in that side of country life.[33]

Racing stables and stud farms go beyond the scope of this book, since they are too big, too specialized, and too commercially organized to be considered simply as an adjunct to the country house. But, of course, racing formed part of the country house world: Saratoga Springs in New York and Aiken in South Carolina each served as a focus for building. Sometimes the sport was pursued on a private estate. In 1871 a Long Island newspaper reported that Augustus Belmont's racetrack and covered grandstand at Nursery Farm were "said to be the finest in the U.S."[34] Later John R. Macomber's appositely named Raceland in Massachusetts, built in the early 1930s, was one of the most complete of all sporting estates. "With its handsome stables, lovely lawns and formal gardens, steeplechase course, covered track and track for flat racing, kennels, nursery and miles of woodland bridle paths," it expressed the owner's "devotion to his lifelong friend, the horse."[35]

Dogs inspired an equal warmth of feeling in many owners. Their requirements were not dissimilar: kennels had to be well drained, well ventilated, but free from drafts. For some breeds sunlight was deemed important, though equally a patch of shade, perhaps from a tree, had to be provided in the runs. The largest kennels included a kitchen where fresh meat was cooked. Correct feeding was of the essence, and by the 1930s it was scientifically controlled. For his foxhound kennels at White Horse, Pennsylvania, M. Roy Jenkins introduced a system of individual feeding compartments by which the intake of every hound could be monitored. Another innovation was to put overhead sprinklers in the yards, so that hounds baying the moon could be quickly doused and sent back to their sleeping benches.

Where the master hunted four times a week the hunt kennels accommodated fifty couple of hounds; but like the racing stable such kennels lie outside the realm of the country house, since they were generally the common property of the hunt, paid for, at least in part, by subscription. On the other hand some private kennels were extensive. Jay F. Carlisle's Wingan Kennels, established on his Long Island estate of Rosemary Farm, was a canine village of many individual houses, built of redwood. There he bred labradors and pointers, breeds that do not work in packs and require to be treatd as individuals. One rule applied to all kennel types: they had to be placed out of earshot of neighbors.

Unpredictability was an attribute of both hound and horse that fascinated their owners. It was also found in large measure in the early motorcar, which is perhaps why motoring was initially regarded as a sport. Motorcars helped open up the American countryside; they removed the fear of isolation that haunted country house life in the horse and carriage days. "Remotely situated acquaintances" were turned into "neighbors."[36] By 1906 motoring enthusiasm had spread so far that, according to *House and Garden*, even horse-loving owners of country houses were likely to have at least one machine. The motor house raised special problems. The presence of gasoline vapor caused anxieties about fire to redouble. It was advocated that the garage floor should slope, so that cars could be made to coast out by their own weight in an emergency. Cranking the engine took too long a time. The heating apparatus had to be completely walled off. While large establishments would have a forge for making spare parts, this could never be placed in the basement, since gasoline vapor gravitated downwards. Equally, ventilation should be near floor level. A ready supply of fire extinguishers, hand grenades, or at least buckets of sand was suggested.

To most owners the obvious place for the motor house was in or next to the stables. There were some ways, however, in which horses and motors did not mix. It was even thought inadvisable to have the coachman double as the chauffeur or "machinist": their temperament and traditions were too far apart. Certainly in the combined motor house

186. The motor house or garage at Nemours. Faced in treillage, it was built in 1914.

and stable it was essential that animal and machine had their own courts. Motors were generally noisy (for this reason they were banned from Tuxedo Park); they were also prone to backfire. If that happened next to a horse being led to its stall it would shy and kick out. In fact it was not logical to have the motor house near the stable at all (Plate 186). Being less smelly than the stable, the motor house could be placed near the house. Eventually it was attached to it. Integration came first to suburban houses, where cost and space were at a premium. Despite the obvious advantages to the owner it did not become a standard feature of country house planning before 1930.

The size of the motor house naturally depended on the number of cars. The cars themselves were long and broad and, since they were always being adjusted, a certain amount of space had to be left around them for the machinist to work in. Maneuverability was a consideration in large motor houses: it was time-consuming to be forever moving cars around, especially when they took so long to start and warm up. Consequently, turntables made of steel plates on top of rollers were installed (Plate 188). Where there were only two to five cars it was possible to buy individual rollers that could be slipped under the wheels of the car like castors. Above the car there might be a swinging arm with a sprinkler or hose: it was just as important to clean the car as soon as it returned as the carriage, but the bodywork was a little more robust. The workbench was an important item in every motor house: self-sufficiency was a matter of pride. Gasoline was stored on site, preferably in a tank underground.

Eventually the motorcar helped destroy the homogeneous world of the country house, since it made travel just too easy. There seemed rather less point in staying somewhere for several days when the process of coming and going had become so simple. Even in the early days the range of the motorcar burst the confines of the estate. While the drives of a large estate might have been enough to satisfy the carriage enthusiast, the motorist needed greater scope. One of the most devoted motorists was William K. Vanderbilt II, builder of Eagle's Nest on the north shore of Long Island (Plate 191). In 1899 his honeymoon with "Birdie" Fair, heiress to a fortune from the

Comstock Mine, had taken the form of a motor tour through France, and the next year he won a motor "meet" at Newport in a French make called White Ghost. On Long Island he promoted two motoring initiatives which, though they did not take place on the grounds of a private estate, were backed principally by country house owners like himself. The first was the Vanderbilt Cup race, instituted in 1904. He gave the cup because he felt that "the United States was far behind other nations in the automobile industry" and he wanted to demonstrate to his powerful neighbors what foreign cars could do.[37] For three successive years the race was won by a French car; then it had to be canceled following the death of a spectator – hardly a surprising occurrence, since the crowds were huge and some people would amble out onto the track during lulls to see if another car was coming.

The second venture was more propitious. In 1906 Vanderbilt took the lead in establishing the Long Island Motor Parkway, Inc. The company built a concrete toll road from Lake Ronkonkoma in the dead center of the Island to the Horace Harding Boulevard on the edge of New York City. The newspapers may have been a little extravagant in hailing this as a "modern Appian Way," but care was taken to make it conform to the landscape and the twelve gatelodges and inn were designed by John Russell Pope. It was a road for men who took pleasure in motoring. Though it was overtaken by the development of public roads – part was ignominiously used as a bicycle track in the 1930s – its values anticipated those of the later state parkways. They were also the values of the country house, and Pope went on to build a gatelodge for Vanderbilt's first Long Island estate of Deepdale in 1910.

Like so many other members of his family, Vanderbilt was also passionate about the sea. His yachting career started with a little boat called *Osprey* when he was sixteen. By 1909, aged thirty-one, he had graduated to the steam turbine *Tarantula*, which was

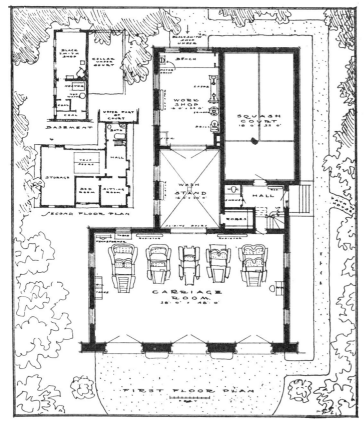

187–88. Two garages at Chestnut Hill, Massachusetts, by Andrews, Jacques and Rantoul, and Putnam and Cox. Turntables were frequently included to help move large automobiles, which needed several minutes to start and warm up. Both plans are to scale 1 mm = 1 ft.

189–90. Paths in the elaborate gardens of Georgian Court provided an ideal private track for motoring. In these photographs the chauffeur takes one of the children, while the physician from Lakewood Dr. Paul Kimball is accompanied by his dog.

succeeded by the first of his motor yachts, also called *Tarantula*, in 1913. Since 1905 he had been commodore of the Seawanhaka Corinthian Yacht Club. This love had determined the choice of the site of Eagle's Nest, on a long deep harbor. It also contributed to the style and form of the house, which he began building in 1911. His domestic routine at Deepdale was described as "the simple life of the country" by the *San Francisco Bulletin*.[38] Initially Eagle's Nest reflected this quiet regime. It began existence as a modest seven-room cottage, which Vanderbilt called the Bungalow. A serious young man with "piercing, sincere eyes," he was not fond of the social round and had deliberately chosen a site that seemed remote and unfashionable.

The Bungalow was designed by Warren and Wetmore, architects of both the New York Yacht Club (of which Vanderbilt was a member) and the outbuildings of Harbor Hill. In 1913 they erected a charming structure called, misleadingly, the Boathouse – very tall and located at the mouth of a narrow gorge. It never had accommodation for boats: because of the seven-foot tides on this shore, they were moored at the floating dock that was a standard feature of many Long Island estates. Instead the Boathouse was probably intended to provide extra sleeping rooms or perhaps a games room, with a stunning view over the water. By 1922 Vanderbilt's travels on the yachts had furnished him with enough scientific specimens to justify the building of a museum gallery, known as the Hall of Fishes. The style of the museum also reflected his travels – how else could one explain its flamboyant Hispanic doorcase and stucco facing, so impractical in the Long Island climate? Vanderbilt's motor yacht *Ara*, equipped like a hotel and carrying its own twenty-seven foot sailing cutter, was based in Florida, where he and Birdie had a house, Evidently he knew the work of Addison Mizner, whom he would soon back as part of the syndicate developing Boca Raton.

The Hall of Fishes foreshadowed the Mediterranean flowering of the house that began in 1924. The little Bungalow was engulfed in white stucco, extended round a cobbled courtyard, given red pantiled roofs, yellow Baroque doorcases of reconstituted stone, and wrought-iron balconies and window grilles. Over the entrance arch were placed

188

191. Eagle's Nest, Long Island, home of the motoring enthusiast William K. Vanderbilt II.

192. The country house of the yachtsman E.C. Bennedict. The telescope is a particularly nautical touch.

armorial bearings, a lubricious pediment, and a bell turret that strikes the hours. Vanderbilt's photograph albums contain pictures of some of the Spanish and South American sources from which the detail was taken. They were probably collected on yachting trips. Warren and Wetmore somewhat simplified the detail to suit the twentieth-century scale, for Eagle's Nest was never a palace. *Town and Country* justified the use of an Iberian style so far north by noting that Spain could be wintry as well as sunny.[39] Work finished in 1927, the year of Vanderbilt's divorce from Birdie and remarriage to the now also divorced Mrs. Barcley H. Warburton, whom he had got to know on a cruise on *Ara* the previous year. But Vanderbilt went on tinkering with the house, enlarging the Hall of Fishes to give it an extra story and a flat roof that served as the first tee to his golf course. In 1933 the family's devotion to the sport of motoring caused another addition, for alas that year William K. Vanderbilt III was killed in a car accident. The Memorial Wing, designed by Vanderbilt's friend the architect Ronald Pearce, was erected to house the young man's African big game trophies.

Though Vanderbilt's Boathouse was one only in name, other estate owners built the

193. (*above*) Boathouse on the estate of Herbert Dumaresq on Lake Winnepesaukee, New Hampshire, designed by Henry J. Carlson. From *Country Life in America*, July 1920.

8.30, PUTTING OFF FROM SHORE

COMMUTING
by
MOTOR YACHT

Mr. John W. Kiser commutes from Glen Cove, Long Island to New York daily in his yacht "Fillette"

8.35, THE OWNER COMES ABOARD

8.40, THE NEWS BEFORE BREAKFAST

8.45, AL FRESCO BREAKFAST

9.20, A GLIMPSE OF THE CITY

9.30, ASHORE FOR THE DAY'S WORK

194. "Commuting by Motor Yacht." For some yacht owners on Long Island and elsewhere, the need to commute was no cause to abandon sporting pleasures. From *Country Life in America*, July 1922.

195. An autogiro flies over Whitemarsh Hall, the enormous Stotesbury estate outside Philadelphia, designed by Horace Trumbauer.

real thing (Plate 193). It grew into one of the most attractive adjuncts of the American country house – by no means universal, but sometimes elaborate. The impetus for this development was the advent of the motorboat. "Necessarily, as in the case of the automobile, they have caused the evolution of a new form of architecture, the motor boat garage," wrote William Phillips Comstock, author of *Garages and Motor Boat Houses*, in 1911. "It is especially necessary to protect the high-powered finely-finished boats from the weather."[40] While motoring was regarded as a sport, motorboating was promoted by its enthusiasts as utilitarian. To a few people it made sense to commute by water (Plate 194). "Every week-day morning a veritable flotilla of able cruisers and marine runabouts streams into the metropolis from practically all points of the compass," wrote *Country Life in America* in 1927, "from New Jersey waters, the Hudson River, and from both shores of Long Island Sound."[41] Twenty or thirty craft would tie up at the landing stage of the New York Yacht Club each day. Detroit may have been the city of the automobile but some Grosse Pointe commuters still chose to make the journey by boat.

"As a sport, aviation certainly surpasses any other," said Mrs. Benjamin R. Holcombe of Newport in 1931.[42] She was one of an increasing number of men and women who took to the air, in planes or even in the new and erratic autogiro (Plate 195). Most people chose to keep their flying machines at the country club's airfield, but there were some country house owners, particularly in remoter parts, who had their own hangars. One was Elliot White Springs at Fort Hill, South Carolina. He put his flying experiences to good use in writing the popular novel *War Birds*. The most complete aviator's house, however, was probably Margrove on Long Island, home of the famous airplane designer Grover Loening.

Loening's house had no special provision for the aircraft themselves: they were all kept elsewhere. What the house does exemplify is the degree to which sporting imagery entered decoration. Loening was his own architect, and references to flight abound in the design of birds punched into the wall surrounding the flat roof, in the seagulls of the steel stair railing, in the photographic murals of Loening aircraft in flight, and perhaps (as a destination) in the exotic landscapes in silver on black glass by Roger Snediger.[43]

If quiet good taste is the ideal, the sporting influence on decoration was rarely benign, though it could undoubtedly be potent: some houses, like that of E.F. Hutton (Plate 74), became silted up with cups, trophies, and ribbons. Where the owner hunted big game, the display of buffalo heads and elephant tusks and tigerskins can verge on the terrifying, at Roosevelt's Sagamore Hill, for example (Plate 179). They did not come cheap. "In regard to the remaining moose heads which you strongly advise me to buy, and of which I understand you made a hurried inspection, you seem to forget the main point, viz: the price," wrote Clarence Mackay to Stanford White. "I know that this is a very small matter to you, and that you do not like to burden yourself with too many figures, but I look upon it in an entirely different aspect."[44] The figure that he had been given by the dealer was $3,500. Such parades of skin and horn naturally cause surprise on Long Island; further up New York State, in the Adirondacks, they form part of a fully developed style that symbolized some of the deepest instincts giving rise to the American country house.

— 12 —

"By far the most amazing thing in America"
THE ADIRONDACKS

ARCHITECTURALLY the sporting instinct achieved its most complete expression in the Adirondack Mountains of northern New York State. Here, in a region the size of Connecticut, largely inaccessible, forested and frequently covered in snow, the sportsman could expect to catch as many as twenty large trout in an hour, and the white-tailed deer were almost too plentiful not to be shot. One of the entries in the gamebooks of Litchfield Park records how one hapless stag came to inspect the owner, Edward H. Litchfield, when he was eating his lunch on a rock; he picked up his rifle, killed it ,and did not bother to inspect the quarry until he had finished his food. Sport was not entirely perfect. Moose had largely drifted away from the area before the hunters arrived, and attempts made to reintroduce them were unsuccessful, in part because the hand-reared beasts were too tame. (Litchfield complained that one bull moose, affectionately named Bolivar, would loiter around the kitchen door, drinking dishwater and annoying "the dog seriously by eating his meal as soon as brought.")[1] Black bears were common enough, but there were no wolves or panthers. Other areas of the country, from Georgia to Maine, could therefore claim to offer a greater variety and profusion of game. But nowhere else did the cult of hunting give rise to its own architecture, its own style of decoration, its own aesthetic – all of them uniquely American.

While one or two writers felt bound to make the inevitable comparison with Switzerland and the Highlands of Scotland, most people acknowledged that the Adirondack landscape had qualities unlike those of any other part of the world. "It is so new, so various, so contradictory, so vital, so un-European," gushes the fictional Lady Helen Pole, an Englishwoman visiting the region with her sick brother, in a turn-of-the-century novel called *The Aristocrats*.[2] Scarcely less ardent in his prose style, the philosopher William James sought to describe "the intense significance . . . of the whole scene" when he spent a night under the stars in 1898; one cause of tumultuous emotions was "its utter Americanism, and every sort of patriotic suggestiveness."[3] There were taller mountains in the world; individually some might have been considered more beautiful or dramatic. But in few other countries – at least ones that could be readily visited – did they extend over such a vast area of land, or seem so little touched by human habitation, or feel so remote. For a remarkably long time they were unknown. Only in 1836 was it realized that the Adirondacks, not the Catskills, possessed the highest peak in New York State. A detailed survey was not begun until the 1860s.

Unlike the Highlands of Scotland, whose purple hillsides were carefully managed for

196. Logs and lake: a corner of Sagamore Lodge in the Adirondacks.

the benefit of grouse, these forests were for the most part still unpenetrated by white man – a true wilderness. Early travelers and guidebook-writers romanced about the area's primeval state. "I love the freedom of the wilderness," wrote Joel Headley in his popular *The Adirondack; or, Life in the Woods* of 1849, to the Rev. "Adirondack" Murray, whose book *Adventures in the Wilderness; or, Camp-Life in the Adirondacks* of 1869 started a tourist stampede known as Murray's Rush; "the wilderness provides that perfect relaxation which all jaded minds require." Needless to say, it was not long before the wilderness was under threat from both commercial lumbering and tourism ("the desert has blossomed with parasols and the waste places are filled with picnic parties, reveling in lemonade and sardines," lamented the *New York Times*, somewhat hyperbolically, in the 1870s).[4] But so general was the appreciation of its character that in 1894 the constitution of New York State was amended so that the state's own landholdings "shall be forever kept as wild forest lands. They shall not be leased, sold or exchanged, or be taken by any corporation, public or private, nor shall the timber thereon be sold, removed or destroyed." In Britain, as in most other European countries, the opportunity to protect large areas of wilderness passed with the Middle Ages.

When James Jackson Putnam, a Harvard professor of neurology, invited Sigmund Freud to visit Camp Putnam in 1909, the great man's response was one of astonishment. He wrote to his family that "Of all the things that I have experienced in America, this is by far the most amazing." However, it was not only the "utter wildness of the American landscape" that impressed Freud, but the architecture of the camp.

> Imagine a camp in a forest wilderness situated somewhat like the mountain pasture on the Loser where the inn is. Stones, moss, groups of trees, uneven ground which, on three sides, runs into thickly wooded hills. On this land, a group of roughly hewn small log cabins, each one, as we discover, with a name. One of them is called the Stoop and is the parlor, where there is a library, a piano, writing desks and cardtables. Another, the "Hall of Knights" with amusing old objects, has a fireplace in the center and benches along the walls, like a peasant dining room; the others are living quarters. Ours with only three rooms is called Chatterbox. Everything is left very rough and primitive but it comes off. Mixing bowls serve as wash bowls, china mugs for glasses, etc. But naturally nothing is lacking and is supplied in one form or another. We have discovered that there are special books on camping in which instructions are given about all this primitive equipment.[5]

Camps like this one were conceived primarily as elaborate hunting lodges, and there was no end of hunting lodges in Freud's native Austria. The reason that he found Camp Putnam unfamiliar was that the log architecture and primitivism were intended to evoke two specifically American myths: that of the lone forest hunter and that of the pioneer. Neither had its equivalent in the imagery of the Hapsburg ruling class.

Camp Putnam, the nucleus of which was an old boarding house, was not especially distinguished architecturally. It had been established jointly by a group of intellectuals for themselves, their families, and friends who pursued activities of a vigorous but sometimes rather donnish kind. (The camp logbook, which guests took it in turns to keep, shows that a hike might be spent calculating the heights of mountains using surveying equipment; on wet days they busied themselves making toys and furniture in the workshop.) Nevertheless, organized as a group of separate structures, it reflected the ruling principle of decentralization behind even the most luxurious camps – the one exception being Litchfield Park, built as a French chateau of stone. Camp Topridge, built in the 1920s, was typical in having eleven cabins for guests and four for servants.

This was thought to be a convenient arrangement for both owner and guests, allowing them to come and go as they pleased, perhaps meeting only at meals. Plenty of space was "noteworthy in influencing the comfort of a house party during the stress of inclement weather."[6] The plan also had the practical merit of simplifying construction, for in this region of cruel winter frosts large buildings would have required deep foundations. Symbolically it perpetuated the idea that life here was one of the greatest simplicity, a regenerative "return to nature after ten months of wearying city life with ceaseless formalities and responsibilities."[7] Lieutenant Governor Thomas Woodruff was the embodiment of this philosophy. "He is a veritable steam engine in business or political life in the City," wrote *Field and Stream*, "but a boy-out-of-school-on-a-Saturday-near-a-swimmin'-hole when, after a long siege of the town's strife, he reaches camp and scents the fragrant balsam boughs on which he sleeps in an open lean-to."[8]

The illusion of simplicity, however, could only be sustained by a massive logistical effort. Even the *Craftsman* acknowledged that "a retreat in the Adirondacks ... shall have the privacy and the many domestic comforts which our civilization has changed from luxuries into necessities."[9] The very process of building raised special problems. Some of the largest camps were located on vast private domains, crossed by roads that were little more than tracks. Hauling sash-windows, doors, flooring, plumbing equipment, kitchen apparatus, and the like had to take place during the winter, when snow

197. Watercolor of an Adirondack lodge surrounded by flowers, from a guestbook. Adirondack Museum

198. Pen and ink drawing in the guestbook at Camp Pine Knot, signed P. Bigelow and dated 1878. It shows some of the activities of an early camp, including fishing, rowing, carrying a canoe overland, and bivouacking. Adirondack Museum

and ice provided a firmer surface than the bare ground. In any case it was desirable for everything to be on site when the snow melted in April and the short building season began. The workforce itself required accommodation while it was there, and the contractor would erect his own temporary camp for the men.

Nor was construction confined to the main lodge and cabins. Camp life would have been a poor thing without boats, so there had to be a boathouse, perhaps with the top turned into a platform for watching races on the lake or even made into a living room. Servicing the place meant constructing reservoirs and pump houses, sewage disposal tanks and filtration beds. Every camp had its ice house, and many had a farm. The latter was a practical matter, since meat sent up from New York was liable to spoil on the way. Alice M. Kellogg summed it all up when she wrote frankly:

> Dollars, of course, figure big in these camps. Cost is, indeed, one of their interesting features. Locations that seemed grotesquely impracticable for building purposes because of their primeval condition, had to be opened up, not only to secure the site for building, but also to lay new roads, provide a water supply, and introduce sanitary drainage – problems that exacted technical skill of a high order.[10]

By the 1890s the cost of even renting a camp was considerable. The Clarence Mackays may have eaten all the frogs from the ponds when they took the Stokes camp for six weeks, but they paid $12,000 for the privilege.

In some ways Adirondack life *was* simpler than elsewhere. While a couple was once sighted wearing full evening clothes in a canoe as they paddled their way to dinner with the Vanderbilts, such out-of-place formality seemed as ludicrous then as it does now. It was not uncommon for men to go off into the forests for a couple of days, hunting and sleeping under the stars. But, as Emily Post sternly warned the social ingénu: "Let no

199. The sitting room at Camp Comfort conjuring up the informality of early camp life.

one, however, think that this is a 'simple' (by that meaning either easy or inexpensive) form of entertainment!"[11] Running a large camp required the highest degree of domestic organization. Boy-at-a-swimmin'-hole though he seemed, Woodruff could entertain seventy guests at Kamp Kill Kare. The Garvans, who later owned the same camp, often invited the whole of the Yale and Harvard baseball teams, who would play each other, for the delectation of family and friends, beside the lake. On top of the house party there might be neighboring camp owners and *their* guests to entertain – for, typical of the American country house, these camps were unlike the hunting lodges of central Europe, built in sites of supreme isolation; though many owners possessed large estates, their lodges were sufficiently close to those of other camp owners to go over for luncheon or dinner. It could not have been done without servants, and sometimes they outnumbered family and guests by a ratio of three to one. Camp Topridge boasted a hairdresser, stenographer, masseur, dance instructor, and barber.

Some families expected to eat the kind of food they would have had in New York. When the doors to the dining room were flung open, one would see blazing fires and a "table well spread with all the delicacies one would expect to find at Delmonicos."[12] On 7 December 1912, for example, guests at Sagamore Lodge sat down to a dinner of *Huitres on the half Shell*, followed by *Consommé Palermo*, *Truite du Lac grillé m'd'hôtel*, *Quartier de Venaisson [sic] St Hubert*, and *Poulets rotis* – before the chef's already faltering French gave out with *Salade Grape Fruit*, *Plum-Pudding*, and *Patisserie*. Even picnics could be elaborate affairs. A guide described how, in the morning, "a man goes round to each guest asking whether he'd like squab or filet mignon and what kind of cold soup and dessert.... I need a guide for each two guests to cart the stuff so they can rough it."[13] The expenses of running an entirely private camp were somewhat mitigated if the owner belonged to one of the fifty or so sporting clubs that owned vast tracts of land; though club members built cottages, they could eat in the communal dining room – "a detestable arrangement," according to Lady Helen Pole.[14]

Perhaps the greatest extravagance of this supposedly woodsy existence was the transport needed to reach it. In the earliest days access was only by stagecoach and rowboat, but in the 1870s the railroads began to push laboriously and expensively north. By the turn of the century there was a choice of two lines, one to the west and one to the east, with comfortable sleeping cars from New York. Some owners possessed their own private railroad cars, with names like Vagabond, Wayfarer, and Wanderer, their walls piped with hot water to keep them warm. But if, for example, your destination was a camp on Blue Mountain Lake the railroad could only take you part of the way. It stopped at the settlement of Raquette Lake. From here you would have to get into a little steamboat (they seemed "to be of the pocket-edition size – one would think he could buy them for five cents"),[15] changing to another steamboat on Blue Mountain Lake, with your baggage pulled along in a punt-like vessel behind.

Between the two lakes ran a stretch of railroad known as the Marion River Carry. Three-quarters of a mile long, it was the shortest standard gauge railroad in the world, and was said to have the richest board of directors, including Chauncey M. DePew, Collis P. Huntington, J.P. Morgan, Harry Payne Whitney, Alfred G. Vanderbilt, William C. Whitney and John A. Dix. The carriages, covered in a cheerful striped awning, were old horse-drawn streetcars from Brooklyn. But two engines had to be tried and discarded – one was not strong enough, the other weighed too much for the track – before the problem of how to pull them was solved. In a later era guests en route to Camp Topridge would take the Merriweather, Mrs. Post's private airplane, to Saranac Lake Airport; then chauffeur-driven limousine brought them to the boat that

201. Bark-covered wigwam at Ne-Ha-Sa-Ne, owned by Dr. Seward Webb, provided an echo of the simple life in one of the most elaborate of the millionaire camps.

202. Guest cabins at Ne-Ha-Sa-Ne, linked by a boardwalk. Separate buildings scattered through the woods preserved something of the flavor of a primitive camp.

crossed the lake. The final part of the journey up the steep bluff from the shore was made by a little funicular railway (Plate 200). The modes of transport had changed, but the principle remained the same.

It was not only the millionaires in private railroad cars who came to the Adirondacks, or could lay claim to having a camp. The term was used comprehensively to "mean anything from a log fire in the woods to a hundred-thousand-dollar villa."[16] As this comment implies, some people literally camped out beneath canvas or a shelter made hastily out of branches and bark (Plate 201). They did so, on occasion, for a surprisingly long time, and their purpose had nothing to do with killing game. They were there for their lungs.

Somewhat disreputably, Murray had opened his *Adventures in the Wilderness* of 1869 with a highly implausible account of how a tubercular patient had experienced a miracle cure thanks to the Adirondacks' sparkling air. There was, however, much to be said for this air, according to a paper given by Professor Alfred A. Loomis to the Medical Society of the State of New York exactly a decade after Murray's book appeared. Granted, he said, the climate was damp, but the soil was well drained and the presence of so many trees meant that the atmosphere was heavily laden with ozone. His friend Dr. Edward Livingston Trudeau, himself a victim of the disease, would soon open a famous clinic.

The journalist Marc Cook, increasingly alarmed at tubercular symptoms, was persuaded to take "the Wilderness Cure," later writing about it first in *Harper's Magazine*, then in a book published in 1881. He gave an inventory of the semi-permanent camp in which, tended by a guide, he spent four months near Paul Smith's celebrated hotel:

A tent affording complete protection against rain and wind. A good bed in which you may sleep between sheets, and in proper night-garments. Two or three bark buildings, one of which may be used as a sitting and lounging room, when the weather is unpropitious; another as a dining-room, and a third as a kitchen. A small storehouse for garden implements, tools, etc. An open arbor, at the water's edge an ice-house. In your tent and buildings well-laid floors, a stove to take the chill off, if the night grows cold, tables, chairs, books, writing utensils, a student lamp, a clock, and such other conveniences as you may desire. A good table, with a menu embracing anything you want, from bouillon to ice-cream. A daily mail. Wine and lager beer, stowed in the

200. The funicular railway at Camp Topridge, taking guests to and from the lake.

cool bank of sand. A boat to glide over the picturesque lake when you feel so disposed. The great forest about you, through which the wind comes laden with the rare odors of pine and balsam. A cigar in the evening as you sit in front of a blazing log fire, which roars and crackles and makes fantastic shadows among the giant trees. Freedom – delicious, absolute freedom – from dust and noise, and the roar of city streets.

There is an idea of comfort.[17]

It might even be possible to keep chickens, certainly a cow.

Camp Lou, as Cook christened this habitation, was not very different from the camps that by this time some families had begun to build for the summer. They had no need of a specific cure, but they liked the idea of their children spending part of each year in surroundings of proven healthiness. (The children developed "courage, fortitude, resourcefulness" and went back to school "tanned, healthy and strong.")[18] It might have been from summer-long camps like these, made up of separate tents, that the idea of the permanent camp built of log cabins evolved. The moment of change is described by Mildred Phelps Stokes Hooker, remembering her parents' camp on Birch Island. In order to save labor when the camp was dismantled each year, her mother had little wooden storerooms built behind each tent into which the contents could be moved during the winter. "When the tents wore out it was a natural transition to add to these storerooms by putting cabins instead of tents in front. . . . Guide houses, carpenter shops, and ice houses all fitted well into this unit system, and pretty soon it became the accepted way to build, even if you had never had any tents."[19]

Yet the sudden appearance of what Alfred L. Donaldson called the Camp Beautiful, with a nearly fully formed architectural and decorative style, cannot be explained only as a gradual evolution. It was largely due to the sustained creative effort of one man: William West Durant, son of the railroad builder Thomas Clark Durant and owner, at his furthest stretch, of over a hundred thousand square miles of land. Credit for building "the first artistic camps the woods had ever seen" was awarded him in Donaldson's two volume *A History of the Adirondacks* of 1921. Though Durant had thirteen years still to live, the days of his Adirondack triumphs were long past. In 1904, following a lawsuit from his sister, divorce by his wife, and the death of his principal creditor, Collis P. Huntington, he went spectacularly bankrupt and was for a while, as manager of a hotel, reduced to serving some of his many hundreds of former employees. By then, however, he had passed three decades of lavish spending, lavish entertaining, and lavish building in the Adirondacks, and its architecture had been stamped in his image. The mainspring of Durant's activities was his father's Adirondack Railroad. This had been begun in the 1860s and it had to have traffic; traffic, Durant believed, would come in the shape of tourists, but for them the region needed opening up. His building schemes included hotels and clubhouses as well as private lodges, but all were in what would later be seen as the identifiable Adirondack style. Many of the elements of this style had come together in the first of the three houses that Durant built for himself (or for sale), Pine Knot.

Durant did not visit the Adirondacks before 1876, when he was twenty-six. Half his life before that date had been spent in Europe, whither his father had dispatched his family while he himself was engrossed in the heroic labor of building the Union Pacific Railroad. Schooldays were spent in England, at Twickenham, and it is intriguing to speculate on his exposure to the Picturesque movement, with its cult of the wilderness. Had he seen either the hermitages built by William Kent and others out of knotted tree

203. Birch bark, bent twigs, and stuffed animals all helped to conjure up the image of rough woodland life. This example is from The Hedges on Blue Mountain Lake.

trunks and moss, or the elaborate rockwork grottos constructed from rough stones, geological specimens, and shells? Of the latter there were several examples within easy striking distance of Twickenham, including the poet Alexander Pope's grotto at Twickenham itself. However, it would not have been necessary to travel so far from the family's main home in Brooklyn to see rustic architecture. Instances could be found in Central Park in New York, not to mention Brooklyn's own Prospect Park.

During his first two years at Pine Knot, from 1876 to 1878, Durant built a lodge, a couple of cabins, an open dining room, a kitchen building, and platforms for tents. Already the principle of dividing the camp into a number of different structures had

been established. The main building, known from old photographs, was a single-story structure, with low-pitched roof, very deep eaves, and rough walls built of logs still with their bark on. There were obvious Swiss overtones in this – sensibly enough, in view of the very heavy snowfall in winter – and the grander building with which he replaced it in 1882 was known as the Swiss Cottage.

Switzerland, however, was only part of the story. The key to the rest is given by the log walls which, whether load-bearing or merely a half-log facing on a timber frame, were to be an essential feature of nearly all the subsequent large camps. The log cabin was thought of as an indigenous way of building, the American equivalent of Vitruvius's primitive hut. It was not just associated with the pioneers of the western frontier. It had also become entwined with the imagery of the Pilgrim fathers, since it was assumed that their first dwellings must have been constructed of logs. This myth was exploded by later historians, but it retained respectability even in academic circles into the 1920s: see, for instance, the drawing of Jamestown in Yale University Press's *Pageant of America* of 1925. Not long before Pine Knot, the building type had been given further emotional currency by the "Log Cabin to the White House" presidency of Abraham Lincoln. When Chilston D. Aldrich added his *The Real Log Cabin* to a growing body of log cabin literature in 1928, he dedicated it to Lincoln.[20]

Pioneers built with what they found to hand; so did Durant and his successors. The straightest spruce trees were selected from the surrounding woods and removed with as little disturbance to the rest as possible. (By 1903 cutting had become so general that the magazine *Woods and Water* carried an article "The Destruction of Young Spruce for Rustic Architecture.")[21] Considerable care was taken to preserve the timber in its state of pioneer ruggedness. Trees could be felled only in the winter months if the bark was to stay on; conversely, if the bark was to be stripped, this was best done in June or July. The tree-trunks were then cast into the lake until the bark had soaked off. Once on site the logs were made to fit together like a puzzle. Kay Hochschild, who built Eagle Nest in the 1930s, remembered how the builders worked like "Benovenuto [*sic*] Cellini spacing and matching the young logs."[22] Where shaped timbers were used, the axe marks were left showing. Gaps between logs could be stuffed with moss or woodchips, or less authentically filled with Portland cement; but most large camps were sealed with inner walls of planks. They were left unpainted, and so of course were the logs. Shingle roofs might be stained dark green or red, the intention being, as the *Craftsman* characteristically put it, to seek "almost the coloration of a faded autumn leaf."[23]

Logs with their bark on were not the limit of Durant's interest in natural forms at Pine Knot. When he built Durant Cottage in about 1889, the principal room had a bark ceiling and the bedstead was made of rough cedar logs. The latter was probably intended to recall the rough-and-ready furniture that Adirondack guides made for early campers like Marc Cook. By the time he built the recreation building in the late 1890s, his rustic imagination had soared to new heights. The porch was surmounted by a screen of sticks, set in fanshaped patterns; and the sides of the windows, covered in the bark of white birch, were appealingly decorated with heart and lyre motifs made out of twigs (Plate 204). Finding exactly the right wood for Durant's purpose was a challenge. His entry in the *Encyclopaedia of American Biography* describes how "he would have his men search for days for timber with just the grain or texture which, polished, would best adorn some feature of a house. . . . He would take the native wood, polish it and treat it with a beeswax preparation so that its sweet scent stayed for generations."

At Pine Knot can also be seen that other icon of the Adirondack camp, the fireplace of native stone. Stone was also often used as a base, and for both purposes it was moved

204. Detail from Camp Pine Knot on Raquette Lake.

205. The correct style was maintained in every aspect of the estate, including, at Uncas, the entrance arch.

without, if possible, disturbing the moss. Owners never had to look very far to find a suitable quarry, but it could be unsightly if located too near the house. The boulders of the fireplace appeared to be in their natural state: if they were cut, it was only on the sides that could not be seen from the room. Consequently there was a considerable art to choosing and fitting the stones, the object being for no mortar to show. The boulders were rarely as massive as in the more exaggerated of the Mission Style buildings of California. On the other hand they acquired special intimacy from their local origins. Mrs. Hochschild decided that her bedroom fireplace would incorporate a seat. In her search she "sat on many large stones in what was then a cow pasture, trying them out for size and comfort and finally triumphantly found one that fitted."[24] Mantelshelves, needless to say, might well be of unbarked log.

Pine Knot was the most innovative of Durant's camps. In 1895 it was sold to Huntington, who added more buildings. Durant was already building Uncas (Plate 205), named after an Indian in James Fenimore Cooper's *The Last of the Mohicans*. It was larger than Pine Knot, and inspired fellow camp owner Dr. Arapad Gerster to note: "Mr. D's luxurious camp is as beautiful as ever."[25] But it seems that an architect was used, and this may have blunted Durant's creative edge. Within a year of completion it had been sold, with fifteen hundred acres, to the financier J. Pierpont Morgan. Soon Durant was building his most ambitious camp, Sagamore (Plate 206). "It has cost me a great deal more than any of the other camps I have built," he wrote to the photographer Seneca Ray Stoddard, "and is much more elaborate in the way of gas and water works, heating by furnace as well as by fireplaces, system of draining, roads and stocking the lake with fish, than anything I before attempted."[26] But, as a Sunday dinner guest observed, though it was more elaborate than Woodruff's Kamp Kill Kare, it was "not quite as unique and cozy."[27] It became rather more unique, if even less cozy, after its sale to Alfred G. Vanderbilt at the onset of Durant's financial troubles in 1901. He employed William L. Coulter, an architect who settled at Saranac Lake, to add several new buildings – notably the recreation room and a guest lodge called Wigwam – and enlarge some of the existing ones. When Vanderbilt went down on the *Lusitania* in 1915, he seemed, true to his code, "the personification of sportsman-like coolness."

By one estimate two thousand camps had been built by 1908.[28] Sometimes the themes introduced by Durant were taken further by others. For the preservation of natural forms in furniture it is impossible to exceed the weirdly beautiful bed at Kamp Kill Kare, its canopy made from a complete tree upon which a snowy owl (stuffed) has just alighted (Plate 207). The greatest of all fireplaces is surely that at Ne-Ha-Sa-Ne, built by

206. Sagamore Lodge, built by the Adirondacks entrepreneur William Durant in 1898–1900 and sold to Alfred G. Vanderbilt a year later. The outline suggests a Swiss chalet.

Durant's rival railroad owner, Dr. Seward Webb. It rises lopsidedly through two stories, a tour de force of crazy stone, looking as though it has been deposited by a glacier (Plate 208). The natural effect is completed by black bears and other creatures gamboling round the sides. In the course of time, particularly under the hand of Coulter's young partner, William Distin, the Adirondack style became sleeker and more stylized. Logs were used outside, perhaps concealing steel beams, but they were now stripped of bark. Inside there were fewer twigs, less bark, more polish. Earlier camps used small panes of glass which were easy to replace; by the 1930s large picture windows were thought essential for enjoyment of the view. In some ways, however, the natural forms that survived were even more powerful in their superficial gloss: the tortured shapes of the peeled spruce staircase newel at Distin's Eagle Nest – virtually an Expressionist sculpture – are an almost unsettling reminder of the forest. The woodwork of these later camps, built up to and beyond the Second World War, is as sensuous as that of the Japanese-inspired architects Greene and Greene in Pasadena.

Some values changed little. While turn-of-the-century camp owners disguised acetylene gas brackets as kerosene lamps, later authors suggested buying the real thing from antique shops. "Kerosene lamps are almost a luxury in this day of electricity," wrote Conrad E. Meinecke in 1945. "Log cabins are intimately associated with candles and kerosene."[29] Electric lighting was clearly a problem. In *Camps in the Woods* of 1931 Augustus Shepard suggested attaching the bulbs to rustic fittings made of peeled pole and wrought iron.

The note that did fade after the First World War was the obsession with dead animals (Plate 209). Their use as decoration symbolized the camp owner's supposed prowess as a hunter, at a time when, in *The Wilderness Hunter* and elsewhere, Theodore Roosevelt praised hunting as one of the noblest of American activities. There was nothing new in employing game, or parts of it, as an ornament, particularly in hunting lodges. Queen Victoria, for instance, had a whole room of antler furniture at Osborne, while

207. Bedroom at Kamp Kill Kare. Part of the skill of making Adirondack furniture was to retain the living form of the tree; in this case a stuffed owl watched over the sleeping occupant of the bed.

208. Living room at Ne-Ha-Sa-Ne. The use of massive boulders brought a taste of the wilderness indoors. Note the bears and other animals clambering over the chimneybreast.

209. Two views of the same room in the appropriately named Trophy Lodge. Big game trophies, including elephant and giraffe, complement those that might have been shot in the Adirondacks.

a Victorian shooting box in Scotland might contain any number of deer accessories, from panels of deerskin along the corridors to inkwells made of hoofs. No fewer than three thousand stags' heads bristled along the rafters of the Duke of Fife's ballroom at Mar Lodge. But few, if any, British country houses possessed a room for a resident taxidermist, as the Vanderbilts had at Sagamore. Some of his work, presumably, can be seen in the riot of stuffed creatures in the recreation room: buffalo, antelope, and moose heads over chimney and doors, a saddlebill stork by the billiard table, another large bird swooping overhead. The pièce de resistance is the stuffed alligator, upright, laughing, and holding a tray of ping-pong balls. Many of these big game trophies, including the alligator, were not shot in the Adirondacks, and presumably not stuffed there. This must also have been true of the hundred and ninety-three animal heads that adorned the great hall of Litchfield Park, including elephants, giraffes, dik-diks, and rhinoceroses. Nevertheless, it seemed appropriate to some people that taxidermy should become an art for ladies; certainly it would have given them something to do while their husbands were away on long hunting trips. In his *Practical Taxidermy and Home Decoration* of 1894 Joseph H. Batty describes the variety of natural effects that could be achieved, using birds' nests as well as antlers and feet. The taste did not entirely die out in later years. Stuffed animals seemed to scamper through the main lodge of Mrs. Merryweather Post's Topridge, built in the 1920s, and indeed the electric chandeliers were made of antlers (Plate 210). (Was this a conscious reference to the antler chandeliers seen in engravings by Dürer?) But the Topridge animals, unlike those at Sagamore, were small, furry, and hardly noticeable against the totem poles, Peruvian hangings, and tiger skins of this colorful interior.

It will have become evident from the decoration that in many ways the Adirondack camp was really a kind of glorified den, oriented almost entirely around male interests. No wonder, then, that the style reached its zenith in the masculine atmosphere of the recreation room. We have seen the one at Sagamore, with its alligator: significantly, perhaps, it was originally intended as a playhouse for the children, but converted to adult use. Cleveland Amory discovered some lines written in the visitors' book for 1937 which evoke the relentless pursuit of games and amusement of which the room is evidence:

> At the crack o' noon at Sagamore
> The battle's on for blood and gore

For everything's a contest there,
And while you test the bill-of-fare
Somebody says, "Guess who I am."
(Though nobody may give a damn.)
You venture, "Are you someone dead?"
Or maybe, "You're a mare who's bred."
Perhaps you are a kind of fly

210. Living room at Marjorie Merriweather Post's Camp Topridge. It was originally more crowded with American Indian artifacts, many of which have been removed to the Smithsonian Institution.

(The kind you do trout fishing by.)
When dinner's over rest your soul
But not your carcass – you must bowl.
Or play at ping or pong or pool
For Sport is King and Kings must rule.
And so to bed at Sagamore
To listen to young Alfred snore.

Most camps had a room like Sagamore's. Bowling alleys were also common (Plate 176); a lodge on Lake Wilbert had a curling rink.[30] Lieutenant Governor Woodruff concentrated all his amusements on an island five hundred yards from shore. There he erected a building called the Kabin:

This is a symposium of sport, equipped with all that the heart of man might crave for amusement. There are phonographs, ping-pong tables, an Aeolian piano, a buffet stocked with every "medicinal compound" known to "mixology"; a fishing corner, a trapper's corner, all sorts of nooks and corners made bewilderingly interesting with mounted specimens of fur, fin and feather. Great white bear rugs strew the polished floor; mountain lion, wolf, tiger and black bear skins lie about in profusion. Here is a birch canoe filled with pungent spruce boughs to form a divan where John Woodruff's chums from Yale may drift into the Land o' Nod after lunch. There near the huge fireplace are long Dutch oak settees contributed by Senator W.J. La Roche. Overhead are spears, assagai, guns, rods and a thousand emblems of the chase. It is a sportsman's dream "come true"![31]

"A sportsman's dream come true": what else were the Adirondacks? Against the overwhelming odds of nature, Durant and his contemporaries had succeeded in combining the great outdoors and the great indoors to provide both sport and comfort. It was a heroic achievement. If we need an epitaph, however, one is provided in the autobiography of Dr. Trudeau. In the early days he had gone shooting with E.H. Harriman, then a clerk, later a financier and organizer of railroads. Years later Harriman came back by his private railroad car to visit his old friend and inspect Seward Webb's Santanoni preserve:

A special engine was sent up by the New York Central at his order to take the car wherever he wanted to go, and Dr. Webb's guides and saddle-horses were to meet us when we arrived. As I remarked upon the beauty and comfort of his car some recollections of the old days must have crossed his mind, for he looked up at me with a keen smile and said,
    "This is not half as much fun, Ed, as the way we traveled about in the old days that summer at Paul Smith's." And he was right, for it certainly was not.[32]

211

SPECIAL
CONDITIONS

What Mizner sought was . . . that
everybody who came to Florida
should be able, day and night, to
fill his lungs with its marvelous
air, be always in the sun, if he
so desired.

Ida M. Tarbel
*Florida Architecture of Addison
Mizner*

Any house should be beautiful in
California in the way California
herself is beautiful.

Frank Lloyd Wright
Autobiography

211. Autochrome of Mr. and Mrs.
Joseph Choate in the gardens of
Naumkeag, Stockbridge, Massachu-
setts, about 1910.

— 13 —

Indoors-Outdoors

FLORIDA AND CALIFORNIA

HOWEVER ELABORATE the Adirondack camps became, there always remained one way in which their owners could keep close to nature – by sleeping in the open air. A number of provisions might be made for this in the architecture. Traditionally, the crudest of shelters in the woods was the lean-to, made of the boughs of a tree covered in moss and bark. It comprised no more than a slanting roof; the entrance side was open, and in front of it the trapper would build his fire. In this primitive state, lean-tos were expected to last no more than a night or two, but when they were adopted as a feature of the millionaire's camp, they were necessarily built more securely. "Their walls are like those of a log cabin, and the sloping roof is made rain-proof," wrote Lillie Hamilton French in 1899.

> An inclined floor is laid to protect the loungers inside from the damp earth. . . . On this wooden floor balsam boughs are laid. . . . Directly opposite the opening of this lean-to, which looks perhaps into the wood and perhaps down the lake, or again up a brook, wherever the view is fine and privacy best insured, a camp fire is laid on a high stone hearth – almost an altar. The comfort and charm of these lean-tos cannot easily be measured.[1]

A lean-to of this kind can still be seen at Sagamore. Miss French does not state that her lean-to was used for sleeping, though it probably was. Another arrangement is described by Alice M. Kellogg: "an open camp, a cabin with one open side, for those who desire the full benefit of the aromatic air and yet are thus sheltered from the inclemency of the weather." Less ambitious owners would still have themselves equipped with a sleeping porch or balcony – considered "very desirable in camps."[2]

Sleeping out of doors was part of the Adirondack mystique, but it was by no means confined to that region. Knowledge that fresh air helped in the treatment of tuberculosis encouraged house owners in all parts of the United States to experiment with the practice. The scale of the reversal that this represented can be judged from Clarence Cook, author of *The House Beautiful*. "The German horror of fresh air inside the house at any time, whether by night or day, is well known," he wrote in 1881; ". . . in France and Italy the prejudice is chiefly directed against fresh air at night."[3] England was thought to be more sympathetic to the opening of bedroom windows, and gradually it was realized that "night air" was not in itself noxious or malarial. "For my own part," wrote Cook, "I like as much sun and air as I can get." *Country Life in America* shared this

212. Detail of the King C. Gillette ranch in California.

213. This perspective of a country house by Wilson Eyre shows a generous provision for sleeping balconies in both the central block and wings. The client was P. W. Roberts of Villanova, Pennsylvania. Architectural Archives of the University of Pennsylvania

214. Three Connecticut children dressed for outdoor sleeping, from *Country Life in America*, May 1909.

opinion, and in the early years of the century ran a campaign for the sleeping porch. In November 1907 it illustrated the detached shed which the Coolidge family of Pasadena used as an all-the-year-round sleeping room. Two months later it published an article under the title "Outdoor Sleeping and Living: The Absurd Notion that There is Any Hardship About It." In May 1909 came "Sleeping Outdoors for Health: A Phase of Modern Life that Science Demands and that is Bound to Become Universal." It described the army of people who had taken to sleeping in the fresh air: "They are twentieth-century crusaders whose Peter the Hermit is 'oxygen'" (Plate 214). When *House and Garden* took up theme in 1914, it found that "the number of sleeping porches constantly increases."[4]

The assumption was that sleeping porches could be tacked on at will to an existing house or design. Not unnaturally, there was some resistance to this view in the architectural profession, and before long Aymar Embury had gone on the offensive against it:

The whole arrangement of the second story has recently been disturbed by the growing desire on the part of many people for sleeping porches, and it is in my mind something of a question as to whether we may not eventually find our second stories developing into a series of outdoor rooms with small dressing rooms opening from them. It hardly seems worth while to build large airy and comfortable bedrooms and then surround them with sleeping porches which make them warm, stuffy, and unpleasant, and if sleeping porches are to be used they should be so planned that they can be made comfortable in winter, and what are now bedrooms used for dressing rooms only. Very many people begin by sleeping on a second-story porch, roofed with an awning. Finding this unsatisfactory, they place a permanent roof above; then introduce glass screens to shut off wind; and matting, screens, or awnings to shut out light; finally they install radiators to warm them in winter, and in the end they have sacrificed the entire comfort of what was formerly a very excellent bedroom.[5]

Wilson Eyre liked sleeping porches in small numbers, but was equally concerned about proliferation.[6] Fresh air was highly desirable, but not at the expense of that other newly discovered health-giver, sunlight.

Health reformers began promoting the benefits of sunlight, like those of fresh air, in

216

the 1880s. J.H. Kellogg drew on his personal observations of Switzerland, where the inhabitants of deep valleys into which the sun penetrated for only a few hours a day suffered terrible ill health, the women deformed by huge goiters, a large proportion of the men being idiots; while those Swiss living on the higher slopes were much better physical specimens. Other theorists associated sunlight with magnetism, and when George William Sheldon praised the plan of Joseph T. Low's house, which opened the family rooms to the sun all the year round, he referred to the belief that "the iron in the rays of the sun is conveyed directly into the human blood through the pores of the skin."[7] Unscientific or not, these notions began to conquer the popular distrust of sunlight based on the Victorian lady's wish to preserve her milky complexion. By the turn of the century most country houses were built with a room known variously as a sun porch, sun room, solarium, or indoors-outdoors room (Plate 215). The theme of them all was to allow the admission of sunlight through a generous provision of "sunbath" windows; often it was possible to remove the windows altogether.

"With its wicker furniture, bright cushions, rugs, singing birds and plants, it metamorphosed January into June," wrote Joseph Dillaway Sawyer of his Sunshine Room on the bedroom floor. "The sun bathroom had a large south window and a roof skylight. A tiny fireplace hugged the wall and a mattress hammock swung in the sunlight."[8] Downstairs the solarium was "a veritable Sahara in July and August, as it faced south, but much used in early spring and late fall, being easily screened with glass, netting or awning. Loungingly furnished, it made life in the open possible for an even ten months." Not all sun rooms were as informal as these examples. While the lighter styles of furniture were preferred, in a grand house this was as likely to mean Louis Seize as wicker; such was the case at Edward Stotesbury's Whitemarsh Hall. Whitemarsh had sun rooms on both floors at either end of the building: one was published by *Town and Country* under the caption "A Garden Room Which Makes the Napoleonic Gesture."[9] For the sun room of Cherrywood on Long Island, Dr. John A. Vietor chose Queen Anne chairs (thought to possess "levity") upholstered in blue leather.[10]

To *le Sun Room* might be added *le Dining Porch* (Plate 216), or open dining room, according to Jacques Gréber in 1920.[11] It was now but a short step to the garden room that was completely unenclosed. This suited the fashion for old-fashioned formal gardens made up of compartments, divided by tall clipped hedges. Writers who favored

215. Enclosed sun porch at Shelburne Farms, Vermont. Wicker furniture was a popular choice for such rooms.

216. Outdoor dining room at Bellefontaine, in the Berkshires. Trellis and mirror provide a setting that is both architectural and gardenesque.

outdoor living looked to the English example. It was claimed, perhaps surprisingly, that conditions in England were specially propitious to it – not because of the climate, of course, but because of the extra hours of daylight in the summer, the absence of mosquitos, the hearty eating, and the devotion to all kinds of sport. Summer houses and arbors were even more necessary in America than in England because of the heat. Architecture and compartments could be overdone, according to the *Architectural Record*, which criticized the gardens of Bellefontaine, at Lenox, as being "outdoor rooms in which the occupant does not get a sufficient sense of being out of door."[12] Such was the power of the indoor-outdoor movement, however, that soon even town buildings were sprouting roof gardens, loggias, and terraces.

The pursuit of fresh air and sunlight did not stop with the sleeping porch and the solarium; the whole plan of the country house in northern states might reflect the desire to woo these sometimes fugitive elements. It was a progressive thing, like the wearing of loose clothes, and one would think that its fullest expression was to be found in the work of a self-consciously progressive architect like Frank Lloyd Wright. The long straggling limbs of his prairie houses (more often to be found on suburban streets than in open country) do open themselves freely to the outdoors, since each room may have two or even three external walls. At Fallingwater, built in the 1930s, much of the life of the house was clearly expected to take place on the spectacular terraces, hovering over the glen of Bear Run. But architects who were outwardly far stuffier worshipped with equal devotion at the open-air shrine. Take Alfred Hopkins, whom we have seen as a specialist in stables and farm groups. In 1925 he wrote an article "Building for Sunshine and Fresh Air," in which he took it "for granted that [the reader] is willing to admit that a room lighted on two sides is better than a room lighted on one side; and a room lighted on three better than a room lighted on two." To Hopkins the style that best adapted itself to sunlight and fresh air was Tudor. Bay windows, sheltered terraces, irregular plans, the deep U of an entrance courtyard – all either coaxed light and breezes into the rooms or enticed the owner outdoors (Plate 232).[13]

Hopkins was thinking principally of the northeastern seaboard, where for much of the year it is not possible to sit outside without shelter. The open-air question took another form in the more equable climates of Florida and California. Here life could flow from indoors to outdoors almost without a break: indeed the problem was not so much how to bring sunlight into the rooms as how to keep it out. Perhaps nowhere else in America were the natural conditions better suited to living in the country. They were so good that it was almost unnecessary to have a house at all – certainly not an elaborate one. Nevertheless, in both states there was a body of dedicated owners prepared to make the elysium complete by building a country house. Despite the apparent similarity of the challenge, particularly in the matter of sunshine and fresh air, the solutions found in Florida and California were rather different. The theme that unites them is what some writers were calling the Patio House.

The patio house, as the name suggests, was one built round an open courtyard or *patio* in the Spanish manner. Strictly speaking a patio is a hidden garden enclosed on all four sides by building (Plate 217), but it came to be used more loosely for a secluded terrace which might be open on one side. The form had been brought to America by the Conquistadores, but they had not been the ones to invent it: *House and Garden* asserted an unbroken line of descent from the ruined villas of Pompeii where the latest excavations had taken place as recently as 1893.[14] The patio house met with unbounded enthusiasm on the part of some architects. "I would engage to build a patio house under the North Pole, which should be the most comfortable dwelling an Eskimo ever

217. The cloistered patio of Edward Stotesbury's El Mirasol, in Palm Beach, Florida. It shows Addison Mizner at his most romantic

218. Internal patio or atrium at Mill Pond Plantation, Thomasville, Georgia, designed in a Mediterranean style by Hubbell and Benes of Cleveland, Ohio, in 1903.

dreamed of," rhapsodized the transplanted New England journalist and devoted advocate of California, Charles F. Lummis; "and in the tropics I need not play inventor." He was then constructing his own patio house, named El Alisal, out of rough boulders near Los Angeles. The chief benefit of the patio house, as might be expected, was that it introduced the maximum amount of ventilation:

> In a proper patio house, every room opens outdoors at least two ways. In the incomplete patio house which these, my fists, are building, there are already seven rooms which have three sides outdoors. It is probably needless to suggest what this means in the way of sun and air. It is impossible to ventilate the rooms of the average American home as any room should be ventilated which human beings are expected to dwell in; in a patio house it would be as difficult to avoid ventilation.[15]

According to Lummis, "The Greatest Patio House in California" was Phoebe A. Hearst's Hacienda de Pozo da Verona, named after a Renaissance wellhead brought back by her son, William Randolph Hearst, from Italy. The Hacienda had been designed for Hearst himself (though he never occupied it) by A.C. Schweinfurth in 1894, so it was also one of the earliest patio houses: a one-room-deep quandrangle with most of the rooms reached from an open corridor around the courtyard. The style was just as remarkable as the plan, its square shapes and bare walls and towers being an astonishingly bold exercise in unadorned geometry, wrapped up as Pueblo Revival. Only awnings over the slit-like windows and such foreign accents as pergolas recalling the Italian Riviera lighten the austerity of the exterior, though the interior would have been rich

219

with the colors of American Indian rugs. The idea, in this remote location, was to inspire a dreamy mood of "mañana, mañana," as the architect called it; or in Hearst's words something "totally different from the ordinary country home."[16] It was too different for his mother, who owned the cattle ranch on which it stood but had been away when work started. She stopped the work, finally agreeing to inhabit the Hacienda after it had been more comfortably remodeled by Julia Morgan.

219. Entrance façade of Carrère and Hastings's Whitehall, Palm Beach, Florida. A Spanish style was rejected by the owner, Henry Flagler.

220. Servants on the south lawn at Whitehall, about 1905. The house-keeper stands second from the right.

221. Henry Flagler being pedalled in an "Afromobile."

The Hacienda de Pozo da Verona was a brave attempt to create a country house in a Hispanic-cum-American-Indian style appropriate to California. But there were other cultural influences at work in the patio house. Before Bertram Grosvenor Goodhue began El Fureidis at Montecito in 1902, the client, James Waldron Gillespie, took him to Persia to visit the gardens. A decade later Delano and Aldrich's house for Mrs. Christian Herter at Santa Barbara combined hints of France, Spain, and Italy – "a combination which somehow seems at home under the southern California sky." Polyglot though it was, the patio house had soon made its way across America. By 1905 *Country Life in America*, a great supporter, could identify examples in Long Island and Wisconsin as well as California and Florida.[17] The patio was likely to form "the very heart and substance of the outdoor life of the household."[18] Such was its appeal that some houses possessed two, an outer patio and an inner one, the latter perhaps capable of being covered over.[19] At one hundred feet square, the most spectacular variant of the inner patio is that of Mill Pond at Thomasville, Georgia, built for Jeptha Homer Wade of Cleveland in 1903 (Plate 218). Unlike a true patio it is, rather surprisingly, permanently glazed in the manner of a conservatory, though there is an elaborate system of rods and ratchets to raise the panes for ventilation.

In Florida the pre-eminent country house, given its client, was Henry M. Flagler's Whitehall at Palm Beach (Plate 219), built around an inner court that was filled with palms and other exotic greenery. "It is classic in feeling and in detail [Plate 222], but bears unmistakably the character of a great American country house," wrote Barr Ferree.[20] The "but" indicates a hesitation as to whether this marble palace, a miniature version of the New York Public Library, was entirely appropriate to the setting (Plate 220). Both client and architect may have had similar misgivings, for they had originally intended to build something in a Spanish idiom – hence the patio, the last survivor of this scheme. In the end Flagler turned against it. "This afternoon I have noticed, for the first time, the elevation . . . of the gables of my house here," he wrote to his architects Carrère and Hastings on 12 February 1901. "I don't like them. I much prefer something more on the Colonial order, and less of the Spanish."[21]

221

Flagler had been John D. Rockefeller's secretary at Standard Oil (Plate 221). It was a powerful position, but his enthusiasm for the oil business ebbed after the death of his first wife in 1881. In 1883 he married again; his bride, at thirty-five, was eighteen years his junior, small, beautiful, blue-eyed, spendthrift, and violent-tempered. Their honeymoon was in Florida and this opened Flagler's eyes to the possibilities of the state. He began by building two enormous hotels, the Ponce de Leon and the Alcazar, in St. Augustine, then started thrusting a railroad down the swampy east coast to Miami (and ultimately the Keys), scattering more hotels and resort developments on the way. Ida Alice, it was said, found her position as wife of such a powerful man too much for her. Convinced that she belonged to a European royal family and would marry the Tzar of Russia, she was locked up. It caused some scandal when, in 1901, the court in Florida awarded Flagler a divorce because of his wife's incurable insanity – grounds that would have been inadmissible in New York and many other states. Within a fortnight he had married again, aged seventy-one. This time his wife, Mary Lily Kenan, was thirty-seven years younger. It was for her that Whitehall – "more wonderful than any palace in Europe, grander and more magnificent than any other private dwelling in the world," according to the *New York Herald*[22] – was begun the same year. Flagler expected the decorators, Pottier and Stymus, to make it "the greatest job of your life,"[23] and they responded by creating rooms in an archipelago of different styles, including art nouveau and Swiss. The house's greatest moment was the masquerade Bal Poudré with which it was opened in 1903.

Ferree contrasted Whitehall to the big country houses around New York and Boston:

Unlike a great country house in the North, this vast Southern palace has no outbuildings and subsidiary structures. One does not keep a stable of horses at Palm Beach, and one does not need elaborately planned and cultivated gardens to set off one's house. Plants and flowers, trees and shrubs, grow here unaided and with rare Southern profuseness and rapidity.[24]

It scarcely seems a country house at all, since it stands in only a few acres of grounds and is neatly lined up on the street. Henry James, both impressed and appalled, felt that it was the ne plus ultra of the villa, putting to "shame those remembered villas of the Lake of Como, of the Borromean Islands, the type, the climate, the horticultural elegance, the contained curiosities, luxuries, treasures, of which it invokes only to surpass them at every point."[25] (There was not much doubt as to which kind of villa James preferred; Whitehall, he concluded damningly, was "the apotheosis, the ideal form of the final home that may pretend to crown a career of sufficiently expensive boarding.") Yet country house it was – the center of Flagler's enormous Florida "domain." The settlers who came in the wake of the railroad were thought of as protectively as any paternalistic landlord's tenantry. "I am trying conscientiously to recognize the responsibilities of wealth," he wrote in response to a Philadelphia clergyman's appeal for funds.

Aside from my regular contributions through the various public channels (Christian and benevolent), I have a domain in Florida peculiarly my own.... My Land Commissioner, through my instructions, has exercised a great deal more care as to the character of the colonists who go in, than the numbers. Consequently we have a class of people whose first need is a school, next a church. Acting upon the principle that we appreciate that which costs us something, I have in all these cases required the colonists to raise all the money they could for such purposes, and then in some way they got the remainder, without exactly knowing how. I feel that these people are wards of mine and have a special claim on me.[26]

Flagler's organist, Arthur C. Spalding, saw a different side of the relationship. "Well, here I am on the threshold of high life!" he wrote to his family in 1907. "Just mention Salter's [Flagler's personal secretary] or Flagler's name down here and the servants will turn handsprings for you in the street."[27]

Flagler died in 1913. It was just too soon to see Palm Beach greet its most fashionable era, ushered in by the war in Europe, which denied the beaches of the Riviera to the American rich. For a moment what was ironically described as a "perfect spirit of

222. Urns at the head of the steps to Whitehall.

camaraderie and democracy" ruled on the sands of Palm Beach: "Anything may happen. A Vanderbilt may ask you what the time is."[28] This may have been appealing to the newly arrived middle classes, but the Vanderbilts themselves did not want to ask the time from anyone they did not know. Fashion threatened exclusivity, and the construction of Edward Stotesbury's spreading El Mirasol in 1919–22 inaugurated a decade of palacio building, so that owners could entertain each other behind closed doors.

With their color-washed walls, red pantiled roofs, Gothic windows and arcades, these large houses were like a bottled essence of the Mediterranean – infinitely evocative, blended, considerably more potent than the original. They were as often as not the work of Addison Mizner, a colorful figure who was himself described as artist, wanderer, wit, bon vivant, gay Bohemian, capitalist, and builder.[29] He established his own Mizner Industries Incorporated to satisfy the enormous Palm Beach demand for bumpy tiles, seemingly worm-eaten furniture and age-old electric light fittings made of wrought iron. Despite the considerable efforts spent in simulating the surface texture of crumbling Spanish buildings, the net effect of a Mizner house was almost diametrically opposite that of his models. The latter were essentially castles, with few outside windows, intended to deter both attackers and the rays of the sun. But to *Town and Country* in 1926 the very reason that the Spanish style "must obviously remain with us" was "the so agreeable habit" that had been formed "of sunning ourselves the year round."[30] Mizner himself was well aware of the difference between his architecture and that of old Spain.

> There was nothing to do but to turn the old Spanish house inside out, so to speak; put plenty of openings on the outside walls to let the sunshine and air into the house, and, in other ways, make people feel that they were living out-of-doors. The patio was retained so that people did not lose the openness inside of the Spanish plan.[31]

According to *Vogue* in 1925, all the Mizner houses were remarkable for the "feeling that one has of being out-of-doors even when within."[32]

Mizner was not the only architect to work at Palm Beach. For Mar-a-Lago, started in 1926 and now the most elaborate of the surviving palacios, Mrs. Edward F. Hutton (née Marjorie Merriweather Post) began by choosing Marion Sims Wyeth, a Princeton graduate trained at the Beaux-Arts. He had designed the Huttons' first Palm Beach house, which they had outgrown. Wyeth's taste, however, was too inhibited for this larger project, and Mrs. Hutton turned to the Viennese-born Joseph Urban, once architect to the Emperor Franz Joseph and the Khedive of Egypt and lately to the Ziegfeld Follies, to breathe life into the house. And soon the tall tower with its expressively handcrafted contours seemed to shimmer and wiggle like a chorus girl (Plate 223). The name Mar-a-Lago indicates that the Huttons' domain stretched from the Atlantic Ocean to Lake Worth – a distance that can be walked in a few minutes. While the seventeen acre estate is hardly large by country house standards, it ran to a golf course as well as a guest house and gatehouse and eventually a ballroom for square dancing and movie shows. Even more elaborate were the estate buildings at El Mirasol, which included a teahouse on the lake, greenhouses, ornamental, vegetable, and flower gardens, a zoo, and the inevitable hen house. Sometimes, as in the Gurnee and Charles Munn houses, two adjacent gardens would be landscaped as one to give the illusion of a spreading park.

By the 1930s, however, the palacios themselves had come to seem lacking in privacy and owners began looking further afield. The most conspicuous were Jacques Balsan and his wife, née Consuelo Vanderbilt and formerly the Duchess of Marlborough. In

223. Mar-a-Lago at Palm Beach, 1926, built for Edward F. Hutton by Joseph Urban, architect of the Ziegfeld Follies theater.

1934 they bought a house on a fifty acre estate fifteen miles south of Palm Beach. When it was built in 1925 it was called La Linda; renaming it Casa Alva, they employed Maurice Fatio to remodel it and install fourteen rooms of French paneling. Later Mrs. Balsan is supposed to have said that she only went to Palm Beach to have her hair washed and to go to the bank.

Palm Beach was not the only center of large houses in Florida. On Biscayne Bay the most compelling of all patio houses, Vizcaya (Plate 274) – a romantic combination of villa, fortress, and dream – was finished in 1917 for James Deering of the International Harvester Company; and nearby, Deering's half-brother Charles also had a jungle estate. At the tourist town of Sarasota, basking in Florida's land boom of the 1920s, the circus brothers John and Charles Ringling acquired adjacent small estates with farms and orange groves. Contrasting in personality and competitive in almost everything they did – buying yachts, building hotels, speculating in real estate, presiding over banks – they could hardly avoid becoming rivals when they both decided to build country houses in 1924. Charles, the less assertive brother, built a U-shaped, patio-hugging residence to the designs of Alfred Clas of Wisconsin. It would have been dull enough, except for the fact that it is entirely veneered in pink Georgia marble. Rather more charming is the house built for Ringling's daughter, Hester, connected to the main building by an arcade.

Next door John Ringling's house is anything but dull – the fatal consequence of a trip

225

224. "Biscuit-colored walls": an evocation of the circus king John Ringling's Ca'd'Zan at Sarasota, Florida, from *Country Life in America*, October 1927.

to Venice by Ringling's wife, Mabel, who returned with a portfolio full of specially commissioned sketches of architectural details. The original idea was to combine memories of those two cultural foci of the Western world: the Doge's Palace in Venice and the old Madison Square Garden in New York. The latter had been the scene of some of the Ringlings' greatest circus triumphs, and they were understandably fond of it. Local architect Thomas Martin produced a scheme that included a Madison Square Garden tower. When Martin, thought too expensive, was jettisoned and Dwight James Baum of New York called in as his replacement, the tower was dropped. Baum was not successful in persuading the Ringlings that they would prefer a "proper Georgian mansion" to a palazzo. Venetian it remained. Its name, Ca'd'Zan, translates from Venetian dialect as House of John.

"It was so riotously, exuberantly, gorgeously fantastic, so far out of the world of normality, that it surpassed the ordinary criteria for such things and emerged a thing of style and beauty by its magnificent indifference to all the so-called canons of good taste," wrote an admiring, embarrassed Henry Ringling North, John's nephew. "It was, in fact, the epitome of its owner."[33] Charles's pink marble is outshone by John's polychromy, rather too loud, like an overbright check suit (Plate 224). The building is redeemed by Ringling's collection of what were then unfashionable Baroque paintings, housed in a museum that itself incorporates antique columns and cartouches. Completed in 1929, the museum was designed by another New York architect, John Henry Phillips. Its enclosed Garden Court, ornamented with classical sculptures and geometrical flowerbeds, could be seen as an institutional development of the patio theme.

226

From the time that Flagler first developed St. Augustine, Florida had been thought of as a vacation land, and there were few country houses. This was not the case in California, where, despite the state's youth, surprising sophistication and expense were shown in the building of houses and landscaping of grounds in the period shortly after the Civil War. The Napa Valley near San Francisco, for example, "with its grand scenery; healing springs; magnificent vineyards; broad productive wheatfields; mild and healthful climate; wonderful and variously productive soil; excellent public and private schools; fine churches, and in fact every needed requisite for desirable residence," attracted several gentleman farmers who grew fruit, raised stock, and sometimes dabbled in viticulture.[34] A number came from old East Coast families, such as Major William Gouverneur Morris, the U.S. Marshal for California, who named his nine hundred acre farm Morrisiana of the Pacific, after the family seat, Morrisiana, outside New York. Serious wine-makers such as Charles Krug (Plate 225), J.C. Weinberger, Jacob Beringer, and Captain Niebaum of Inglenook lived in handsome houses, decorated with stained glass within and porticos or gables without.

The valley could also boast "many elegant country residences, where people residing in the city retire from the bustle of business to enjoy the quiet and beauty of the country."[35] The house that R.B. Woodward, proprietor of the famous Woodward's Gardens in San Francisco, built in the center of his large farm was described as "palatial." The valley was recorded in such folio volumes as the *Historical Atlas Map of Sonoma County* of 1877 and *Illustrations of Napa County, California, with Historical Sketch* of 1878. What is striking about the illustrations is the care expended on the grounds of the larger houses, with their fountains, shrubberies, neat fences, and perfect rows of trees. When in 1887 the actress Lillie Langtry, once the Prince of Wales's mistress but now escorted by an American man-about-town called Freddie Gebhardt, purchased a ranch in Coyote Valley while waiting for a California divorce, she cabled her attorney, General W.H.L. Barnes: "AM DELIGHTED. WORDS DON'T EXPRESS MY COMPLETE SATISFACTION. JOIN ME IN PARADISE."

By the turn of the century these early houses, luxurious by the standards of their day, had come to seem distinctly modest. Herbert Croly, writing "The California Country House" in 1906, dismissed them condescendingly:

> It so happened that the easiest and most economical way to build happened to make a tolerably pleasing building, and by the same happy chance, even the barns, thrown

225. The Krug residence, vineyard and cellars in Napa Valley, California. From *Illustrations of Napa Valley, California,* 1878.

226. The pool of Charles Templeton Crocker's Uplands, built by Willis Polk in 1912.

together as they were in the hastiest flimsiest way, frequently had a good curve or angle to their big roofs, and a certain symmetry in the arrangement of their fronts.[36]

Occasionally he saw people of taste converting these old ranch buildings into "eligible country houses," but this was not his view of how country houses in this state would develop. The landscape, considered more beautiful even than Italy, possessed something of the same Classic quality; and it required Classic, or Mediterranean, architecture to match it. Of the twelve houses shown in Porter Garnett's *Stately Homes of California* of 1915, the majority met Croly's requirement.[37]

Architecture, however, was only one ingredient of the Californian country house. Because the climate was so agreeable it became more than ever important to allow the owner an indoor-outdoor life. Gardens were a vital factor. The ease with which it was possible to make almost any kind of plant grow gave everyone the chance of being a gardener, and such was the *furor hortensis* that at times there seemed a danger of losing sight of the house altogether beneath rampant greenery. "Where gardens are so much used as part of the house, as they are in Southern California the year 'round," wrote an

228

227. Detail of Henry E. Huntington's house at San Marino, California, designed by Myron Hunt. Despite the Beaux-Arts style, Huntington persisted in calling it "the ranch" and had avocados and grapefruit shipped from there to New York.

228–29. The cactus garden and the palm garden at Henry Huntington's San Marino Ranch. In the same way that the rooms of the house often formed a sequence of contrasting styles, the garden was frequently divided into separate specialized sections.

authority on Santa Barbara, "the line between architecture and landscaping disappears and the houses tend more and more when properly designed to become actually a part of the garden."[38] This, however, was in the 1920s. Gardening had not reached such a point of luxuriance at the turn of the century, though in many cases the grounds were elaborately treated and viewed as of a piece with the house. Picturesquely the drive from the entrance gate would often twist and turn, perhaps making a relatively small estate seem larger. It was likely that the immediate surroundings of the house would be formally disposed with steps and terraces and balustrades, some statuary, perspectives formed by cypresses, shady olive trees, and that cousin to the Italian ilex, the ubiquitous live oak, echoing Renaissance Italy and seventeenth-century France. Within this larger scheme one would probably find a series of smaller, contrasting gardens, just as one might well find a number of rooms in different periods and styles throughout the house. This was a common goal of gardening around 1900. The difference was that California presented unrivalled opportunities to extend the range by the inclusion of such exotica as cactuses and palms (Plates 228 and 229).

Though Croly felt that the Californian country house had yet to fulfil its potential, he had the rosiest expectations:

The intention has not been as fully realized as it might, because wealth has not been accumulated in California so largely as it has in the East; but its completer realization is obviously only a question of time. Indeed one may safely prophesy that California, more than any other state in the Union, will little by little become the land of great country estates, because not only will the well-to-do Californians themselves seek more permanent and elaborate houses, but the New York and the Chicago millionaires will frequently covet a fitting residence in California – just as an English duke or a German prince has his villa on the Riviera.[39]

Certainly some "great country estates" were created: many of them were grouped south

230

230. Henry Huntington's San Marino Ranch. The north courtyard, seen here in the distance, was known as the patio.

232. Planting Fields on Long Island. The Tudor style, with its many courtyards, was thought particularly well suited to admitting sunlight and fresh air.

233. The Buffalo Bill mural at Planting Fields. The owner, W.R. Coe, was so much affected by the Western myth that he bought Bill Cody's Carter Ranch in Wyoming.

of San Francisco, around Woodside and Burlinghame. One of the few examples to survive intact is Filoli, a manor house originally built for William Bowers Bourn II, who had interests in gold and water; it was in English taste and equipped with formal gardens, breeding stable, and a seven hundred acre farm. Even the Tudor style found its way west, and, of course, there were no end of delectable Spanish and Italian villas built in the hills around Montecito (Plate 231) and Santa Barbara. But after the First World War the Californian country house followed a different route from that which Croly predicted. For houses that were genuinely of the country, a very popular form in California and other western states came to be the gentleman ranch.

An increasing number of people found they wanted to spend their retirement playing at the Western way of life, in close contact with horses and the great outdoors. They were following a vision, though in a slightly soft-focus version, that had been celebrated by Theodore Roosevelt, *The Virginian*, and Buffalo Bill. Later, Hollywood would ritualize the Western image, but its mystique was already being felt in the late nineteenth century. For the short time that she was in Coyote Valley, Lillie Langtry would, she claimed, be "up at daybreak and off immediately after breakfast, dressed in cowboy style, with shirt and breeches, and long moccasins as a protection from rattlesnakes and so forth, galloping about on a cowpony exploring every corner of the land."[40]

Mrs. Langtry, whether she knew it or not, was a dude. From as early as the 1870s dudes had been taking holidays on ranches in the western states, first principally to hunt, then simply to enjoy life as a genteeler form of cowboy. One of the earliest dudes was the Irish peer Lord Dunraven, whose first experience of the West was hunting elk in company with his private physician and William Frederick Cody, Buffalo Bill himself; he later established his own hunting lodge and cattle ranch in Wyoming and recorded some of his experiences in *The Great Divide*. Needless to say, buffalo hunting had an irresistible appeal for Theodore Roosevelt, whose acquisition of the Maltese Cross

231. Lotusland at Montecito, California. Originally built by Reginald Johnson in 1919, it was extended with a new wing and outbuildings only a few years later by George Washington Smith. The extensive planting of cacti and succulents enhances the regional style.

Ranch at Medora, North Dakota, in the early 1880s did much to boost the Eaton brothers' famous dude ranch on the so-called Custer Trail, to which Roosevelt was a frequent visitor.[41] Some of the unlikeliest Easterners came to identify with the Western myth. William Robertson Coe, for instance, had worked his way up from clerk to president of a marine insurance company in Philadelphia and married, as his second wife, a daughter of Henry Huttleston Rogers, one of the founders of Standard Oil. It is difficult to imagine from his thoroughly English, rather conventional country house, Planting Fields (Plate 232) on Long Island, known for its collection of camellias, that he should also have harbored romantic visions of frontier life. But after a trip to Wyoming in 1909 he, like Dunraven so many years before him, fell under the spell of Bill Cody (see Plate 233), and the next year he bought Cody's Carter Ranch. He went on to enlarge Cody's Irma Lake Lodge, amass a large acreage in Wyoming, and assemble a major collection of Western manuscripts and memorabilia now at Yale University.

Ranches – that is to say, architect-designed ones of the early twentieth century – share no one style. Despite its Beaux-Arts manner (Plate 227) and English portraits, Henry E. Huntington continued until his death to call his large and formal house at San Marino "the ranch" (Plate 230), and had avocados and grapefruit shipped from there to New York. (Officially the north courtyard was also called "the patio" – one of the less exact uses of the term.) One should not therefore be astonished that William Randolph Hearst thought of San Simeon as "the ranch," even after it had grown into a thing of Olympian elaboration (Plate 234). This, of course, explains the apparent incongruity of keeping ketchup bottles on the banquet table and using paper napkins with the silver service: whether the setting was propitious to it or not, the mood was one of relaxed informality, with everyone surrounded by animals and enjoying an outdoor life. When Hearst first visited the mountain as a boy, the family had slept in tents; as time went on these evolved into semi-permanent structures, before being replaced by permanent ones. Trail riding was so important that in 1932–36 he built a hacienda thirty miles away, as an object for his guests to ride to and spend the night.

Hearst thought deeply about the style of San Simeon. "It is quite a problem," he wrote in 1919. "I started out with the Baroc idea in mind, as nearly all Spanish architecture in America is of that character; and the plaster surfaces that we associate all Spanish architecture in California with are a modification of that style, as I understand it."[42] But he felt that even the Mission at Santa Barbara was too crude, and instead commissioned drawings of the buildings at the San Diego Exposition. "I understand that the San Diego Exposition stuff is largely reproductions from the best examples in Mexico and South America, and that we could not go to a better source to get the most agreeable specimens of that style."[43] He even offered to show Julia Morgan a motion picture called *Soldiers of Fortune*, which had been shot there.

Unfortunately something went wrong. The texture of the architecture at San Simeon, often from poured concrete, is far less sympathetic than that of the Mission buildings he deplored. Even Julia Morgan seemed to recognize that the house was best seen from a distance and that its strongest point was its color. But as a backdrop for the Hollywood folk who went there, it was in every sense ideal. It was not built around a patio: there was no need, for the place extended itself through several separate buildings grouped around highly architectural courtyards. This form may derive from that of the original tents; certainly the stationery continued to bear the legend "Hearst Camp." It was the apotheosis of the indoor-outdoor life.[44]

Most architect-designed ranches veered towards a Spanish idiom of some kind. The mighty King Ranch in Texas, presiding over a barony that was larger than the state of

234. The cloud-capped towers of William Randolph Hearst's "ranch" at San Simeon, California.

Rhode Island and two-thirds the size of Delaware, was rebuilt looking like a fort after a fire in 1912. Rather more romantic were Villa Philmonte in New Mexico and La Quinta at Bartlesville, Oklahoma, designed in the 1930s by Edward Buehler Delk; these princely buildings with their leisurely plans, their towers and turrets and arcades, resemble small villages more than individual farms. To help achieve this meandering effect guest rooms and servants' quarters were often placed, as at San Simeon, in separate buildings or straggling wings.

Virtually all ranches were patio houses, for nowhere did people feel closer to the great outdoors. "The social life of the ranch centers more or less in the patio, a delightful outdoor living room," *Country Life in America* observed of the King C. Gillette ranch (Plate 235) in the Malibu Canyon, California, designed for the inventor of the safety razor in 1929. "The gay Spanish tiles of the fountain, the turquoise blue stair risers, and the vivid hues of the Spanish flower pots combine to impress one with the joy of living."[45] It was possible to sit on the patio and enjoy the organ playing from the living room. The contemporary ranch for E.L. Doheny was arranged so that every room opened onto a terrace or patio in order "to have the maximum of cross ventilation in all rooms at all seasons."[46] Considering that Doheny was one of the richest men in Los Angeles, the style seems notably restrained – almost an abstraction of a Mexican hacienda. However, the plan has two points of interest: a chapel at the end of one of the wings of the forecourt and a sophisticated Art Deco bar off the living room, in which the emblem of a cock on walls, floor, and glasses personifies the cocktail hour.

The architect of both the Gillette and Doheny ranches was Wallace Neff, a man particularly well qualified to understand the ranching tastes of rich men. His father, son of the publisher Andrew McNally, founder of Rand McNally, had been a gentleman rancher who listed himself in the Pasadena City Directory once as "fruit grower," then "Secretary of the Southern California Horse Show Association." The Neff ranch, south of Los Angeles, had been intended as the center of a real estate development – or "country gentlemen's colony" – which never took off.[47]

The gentleman ranch became the Californian equivalent of the farm group in the East, but more so. With it went a whole way of life that could be enjoyed with open nostalgia. As one perceptive observer put it in 1935: "Ranching for pleasure is like farming in a flower garden. It is fun without a struggle, a pastime remodeled from an enterprise, as serious or as casual as you care to make it."[48] Like many builders of American country houses, gentleman ranchers did not, on the whole, wish to share the loneliness of the true frontiersman. They stuck together, able to help each other out in a cattle round-up, enjoying the camaraderie, however large their individual holdings. In the Santa Ynez Valley above Santa Barbara, John J. (Jack) Mitchell, originally from Chicago, owned six and a half thousand acres and a private airport, but he was within easy reach of three or four other gentlemen farmers in that valley alone. Mitchell called his ranch the Juan y Lolita, after his Christian name and that of his wife. On it he raised cattle, including some unusual breeds, but decidedly exotic species such as kangaroos and peacocks could

235. The King C. Gillette Ranch, California. The patio can be seen on the right.

236. Bar taken from a Santa Barbara saloon and installed in the Juan y Lolita Rancho, California. From *Country Life in America*, September 1935.

be spotted on the drive in. The tack room contained a collection of finely tooled saddles, ornamented in silver; from Santa Barbara came the complete bar of a Wild West saloon (Plate 236).

Each year the Juan y Lolita Rancho became the destination of a ritual that expressed the gentleman rancher's devotion to out-of-doors life. This was the Rancheros Visitadores, a revival of the early Californian custom of ranchers visiting, en masse, hacienda after hacienda. Everyone except the infirm rode horses; no women were allowed – indeed, women and children were expelled from Mitchell's ranch for a period of two days. During that time the men enjoyed an unbridled fiesta, doing whatever they chose. The party was described as "a whooping safety-valve for tired business men"; for the rest of the year the ranch formed "a sanctuary where John, Lolita, and their personal friends may find peace and pleasure, leaving the outside world beyond the mountains."[49] In other words the great outdoors provided, ironically, the vehicle for a flight of introspective nostalgia and escapism.

— 14 —

Resort Life and Country Life

NEWPORT, BAR HARBOR, AND JEKYLL ISLAND

By THE TURN of the century the country house in England was becoming less a fact than an idea: that is to say, a growing number of people were happy with the appearance of a life thoroughly tied into the country, without going through the tiresome, sometimes unprofitable business of owning great quantities of land. In the United States an attractive alternative to the country house had existed since before the Civil War – so attractive, indeed, that it has tended to obscure the fact that a country house movement existed at all. This was the resort, another manifestation of anti-city feeling which boomed after 1865. Nearly every successful resort – Cape May, Richfield Springs, Saratoga Springs, Long Branch, and so on – began its career of attracting summer visitors through the building of great hotels – hotels that strove constantly to be the biggest and most splendid in the world. Some offered their guests the convenience of separate cottages away from the main building, but serviced by it; this gave independence to a family who might be staying for several months and, it was said, privacy to gentlemen who were not there with their families. Visitors to the hotels came to like the place and eventually built their own private houses, perhaps within easy distance of the attractions of the town, almost certainly on a modest plot of land. One theory has it that they were called cottages because of the example of the hotels. Whatever the case, the hotel remained the dominant factor in social life; there was little point of contact with the country house.

Indeed, to the perceptive social critic Mrs. John King van Rensselaer, writing *Newport: Our Social Capital* in 1905, the significance of the resort was precisely the challenge that it offered to the country house.

> Up to that time the great American families has been scattered, as they had lived in their country-seats while the weather was warm, and only occupied their town houses in the cities during the winter. The men who were busy at their counting houses and the merchants made their homes in Boston, New York, Philadelphia, etc., and went with their families to some hotel during the hot months. It was a new departure to have these merchants establish themselves in cosey cottages, where they were sure of privacy and not burdened with the cares and responsibilities of a large country place.[1]

For those who could afford the choice, the great attraction of a resort over a country house was clear: in the words of another turn-of-the-century author, "we are a

239

237. Plum Orchard by Peabody and Stearns, one of several country houses built for the family of Thomas Carnegie, brother of Andrew, on Cumberland Island, Georgia.

238. Kingscote, Newport, Rhode Island, originally built by Richard Upjohn in 1839 and extended by Stanford White in 1880. White's work includes the tower on the left.

gregarious people – even a millionaire in America does not want to 'flock by himself.'"[2] The morning at Newport might be spent bathing on Bailey's Beach or playing tennis at the Casino; in the afternoon came the parade, the time for observing and being observed, when the elegantly dressed summer folk set out on horseback, or in a well-turned-out carriage, or perhaps in a glossy motorcar, delivering cards to people that they might already have seen two or three times that day. (The arrival of motorcars somewhat dimmed the glory of the parade, since they enabled the more advanced elements of Newport society to go further afield than Bellevue Avenue.) Then, on some evenings, a keen spirit of competition was abroad among the cottage owners to offer the most lavish entertainment of the season. There were high points, as when Mrs. Vanderbilt imported the entire cast of the Broadway musical comedy *The Wild Rose* to perform at Beaulieu, before a guest list that had been daringly pruned to two hundred. For the most part, however, wrote the disapproving Mrs. Busbey, the balls and fêtes were "of a magnificent monotony – electric lights in the shrubbery, tents built out from the villa for dancing, supper, and decorations, to give all newspapers and the 'Florist Gazette' adjectival orgies."[3]

It had not always been so. In earlier years, when Newport was still frequented largely

240

by Southerners and had not long grown out of being a whaling town, visitors affected a certain contact with nature; though they did not occupy country houses they sometimes managed to paint a picture of rusticity for themselves and their friends. Before the Civil War it had been the fashion to take a farmer's house for the summer rather than to live in town. The great arbiter of society Ward McAllister went so far as to buy a farm, Bayside, though after an initial period of disaster he wisely decided to have it managed by an experienced native rather than run it himself. He was enormously in demand as an organizer of farm picnics, holding that "grand elaborate entertainments are ofttimes not as enjoyable as country frolics."[4] Once when entertaining at his own place he hired an entire flock of sheep and other animals from a larger neighboring farm to enhance the rural effect. "Well, it is astonishing!" exclaimed his guests, some of whom were amateur farmers. "Mc has but fifty acres, and here he is, keeping a splendid flock of Southdowns, two yoke of cattle, to say nothing of his cows!" To which he smiled and replied: "My friend I am not a fancy farmer, like yourself; I farm for profit." When picnics began to pall, McAllister invented the cotillon dinner, in which refreshment alfresco was followed by strolling in the moonlight and dancing in a barn decorated with wheatsheafs, pumpkins, and ears of maize – remembered by Mrs. van Rensselaer as "making a capital background for the ultra-fashionable gowns of all the beautiful women of the place."[5] In a similar spirit barn dances were held at Oaklawn, a farm owned successively by Augustus Belmont and Alfred Vanderbilt. Another favorite amusement was the "aquatic picnic," which took place on yachts.

In the 1850s it was an adventure to build out of town. "So far off," exclaimed Mrs. Powell, when Edward King proposed that she and her husband should buy a field on Bowery Street next to his house. "Oh no it is too lonely."[6] But a glorious sunset persuaded them that the relative isolation would be bearable. When the house was built Mr. Powell pursued a country life, casting bullets from bits and pieces of metal around the house, tearing up old hats to use as wads and setting off to shoot waterfowl in Narragansett Bay. Like all the early cottagers, the Powells would have had their grass mown only once a year, thus fostering a rural look. In 1875 the local architect George T. Mason wrote of Newport's "beautiful country seats": the largest holding was Governor Lawrence's Ochre Point of sixty acres.[7] But this was exceptional. Few Newport houses stood on more than ten or twelve acres, and even Chateau-sur-Mer had only fifteen.

Chateau-sur-Mer offers a key to the development of Newport, from an informal, faintly artistic watering place, that had something of Venice in the light, to a kind of Fifth Avenue by the sea, whose excessively opulent villas were hung with rich tapestries that their owners brought with them, in the manner of a medieval progress, from New York. For both in its first manifestation, when it was built in 1851–52, and after Richard Morris Hunt's remodeling of the 1870s, Chateau-sur-Mer was the grandest dwelling in the resort (Plate 239). The original house was built by William Shepard Wetmore, Canton merchant and banker. Designed and constructed by a local builder, Seth Bradford, it was no more than a pleasant cottage, little different from other Italianate villas, except that it was constructed of stone. What gave a taste of the future was the elaboration of the offices and grounds, with lodges, stables, greenhouses, a palm house, and what looked like a detached stone hut, which was in fact the billiard room, for some reason built away from the house. The new scale of life that this represented is suggested by the princely fête champêtre Wetmore gave his old friend the London philanthropist George Peabody, when he came to Newport in 1857: "Nothing approaching it was ever before seen in this country," commented Walter Barrett in 1872.[8]

But already Wetmore's son and Peabody's namesake, George Peabody Wetmore, had begun the first of two campaigns of remodeling, which would set the pace for the other houses in Bellevue Avenue over the next thirty years. By 1877 it was "the most substantial and expensive residence in Newport."[9] Had the Wetmores wished to live a genuinely country life they could have done so. Wetmore senior owned ten thousand acres in Ohio and seven times that amount in Tennessee, where a town was named after him. On the other hand, Chateau-sur-Mer not only had all the accoutrements of a country house but was, from an early date, lived in all the year round, rather than just visited for the summer.

Friends of the painter Mary Cassatt, G.P. Wetmore's daughters were interested in art, to the extent of depositing a sample of every wallpaper used in the house with the newly founded Cooper-Hewitt Museum in New York. It recently proved an invaluable resource for the restoration of the house by the Preservation Society of Newport County. But the sheer bulk of the place was what their neighbors seemed to notice: soon Bellevue Avenue had become, in Henry James's words, a "breeding-ground for white elephants." "They look queer and conscious and lumpish – some of them, as with an air of the brandished proboscis, really grotesque – while their averted owners, roused from a witless dream, wonder what in the world is to be done with them."[10] It is hardly surprising that in the season The Breakers was finished, the daughter of the house, Gertrude, should have fantasized in her diary about a future married life: "A big establishment is the one thing I will not have.... Our house would be rather small, or very small would suit me better, homelike in the true sense of the word."[11]

By this time the world of Newport had diverged decisively from that of the country house – so much so that Edith Wharton and those like her regarded their country houses as a refuge from Newport's relentless urbanity. Other resorts, however, preserved their simplicity, or at least some of it. They continued to share the values of the country house: indeed the distinction between the two forms of away-from-town existence is sometimes blurred. The region that offered the most common ground was the coast of Maine. A view of life there, bracing, relaxed, close to Nature, seeking to create a specifically American version of the pastoral idyll, provides a necessary perspective to the country house, on which it touches.

* * *

"It is quite noticeable that parts of rough and pine-clad Maine bear a striking resemblance to some parts of Japan," wrote Charles Edward Hooper in 1905.[12] Nearly everyone who visited the state felt the need of a foreign comparison to evoke the scenery. The Norway of America was how one guidebook described Camden. Other visitors to the same spot recalled Lake Lucerne in Switzerland, Menton in France, and the Bay of Naples in Italy. "Mount Desert is not pure Norway," exclaimed the *Century Magazine*, "it is Norway and Italy combined."[13] More modestly, M.F. Sweetser, author of *Chisholm's Mount Desert Guide-Book*, claimed that the lonely offshore islets and blue hills around Mount Desert "present scenery not unlike that of Lake Winnipesaukee" in central New Hampshire, though he added that the "air is *tout à fait* different."[14] A drive near Bar Harbor was actually called the Cornice or Corniche Road, after the dramatic picturesque drives on the French and Italian Rivieras, and Sweetser spoke of the "*châteaux en Maine*" that you could reach from it.[15] The very name of Sorrento, across the water from Bar Harbor, was taken from the fashionable watering place on the Bay of Naples. From Beauchamp, summer home of Cyrus H.K. Curtis, the publisher of the *Ladies Home Journal* and the *Saturday Evening Post*, the view comprised "a miniature

239. The staircase made of white oak at Chateau-sur-Mer, Newport, decorated for Christmas.

Mt Desert
Time – two hours past dinner time —
Isabel — Oh Fred isn't it grand? I feel as
if I never wished to go away —
Fred — Teeth chattering — Yyye-e-ss
v-e-r-r-r-ry —

240. Frederick Edwin Church's view of
Mount Desert, in a cartoon showing himself and his wife. Olana, New York

241. "Sketches at Mount Desert" by A.W.
Brunner. From *Building*, December 1884.

Europe . . . with fishing and the charm of the islands and lakes."[16] It is with relief that
one turns from this babble of many tongues to Harvard president Charles W. Eliot's
confident American judgment: "The island [of Mount Desert] is by far the handsomest
piece of land on the Atlantic coast of the United States, its hills being the highest on the
whole coast, and its valleys being cut low between the hills."[17]

The plethora of foreign comparisons reflected some lack of confidence on the part of
Americans in their native scenery. This, however, was being overcome by the revela-
tions made by landscape painters such as Frederick Edwin Church (Plate 240). As one
guidebook observed: "Tourists flock annually to the Old World in search of natural
beauties, as if there were nothing in our own land to excite admiration. And yet we have
every variety of mountain and coast scenery, equal, if not superior, to that of foreign
countries, almost within sight of all our doors."[18] References to the famous sights of

Italy and elsewhere also struck a particular chord with the kind of people to whom Maine appealed, for these were sophisticated men and women who had probably traveled. They established themselves in various colonies along the coast. Generally the nucleus was a hotel, though the many islands offered the chance of greater privacy to those who sought it. The larger developments possessed a yacht club, a golf club, tennis courts, and some kind of social center – but this was just as likely to be a library as a casino. Bar Harbor had its Building of Arts, in which, commented one visitor approvingly, the audience seemed "far removed from the light mood of the usual watering-place."[19] There was an atmosphere of seriousness about Maine; at times it could seem austere. The twin stars that ruled it were the simple life and the out-of-doors.

Like many resorts, Bar Harbor, a rival to Newport itself, was first discovered by artists before being finally colonized by moneyed people who had seen their work. The painter Thomas Cole came in 1844 and he was followed in later years by many of his friends and pupils, including Church. Scientists arrived next, then yachtsmen, finally summer folk. But, unusually, even when Bar Harbor had been visited by fashion it managed to retain its artistic flavor. As Sherman's *Bar Harbor Guide, Business Directory and Reference Book* exclaimed in 1890: "Lake and ocean, mountain and forest, extend their arms lovingly toward those who seek happiness in the realms of Nature and Nature's God. No fashionable element can destroy their beauty or dim their charms." The artists stayed with local families, made friends with them, shared their meals and their hours, and rejoiced in the primitive character of their lodgings – at least they said they did. When the hotel era dawned, the accommodations became a byword for rusticity, and Sweetser is full of stories. One metropolitan guest is supposed to have said: "Mr. Landlord, I shall put my boots outside my door to-night." To which the reply came: "All right, sir, you'll find 'em there in the mornin'. We're all honest folks down here." The attitude is summed up in the supposed riposte to another complaining city visitor: "Wal, you came here for a change, didn't you? Now you've got it."[20] For many years guests were divided into boarders (who lived in), mealers (who walked from other lodgings to take their meals) and haul mealers (who had to be brought from elsewhere by cart).

Though a number of more luxurious hotels were built in the 1870s, the rich visitors who began coming in the next decade preferred to stay in their own summer homes. By 1889 the town of Bar Harbor itself, "with its irregular huddle of shanty-like shops and ungainly tenements, painted in inharmonious colors and dominated over by monstrous hotels of the same flagrant architecture, whose every line seems an affront to the canons of taste," had become positively offensive to the "lover of beauty."[21] It was typical of the rather arty tenor of the summer folk that they sought to improve the taste of the natives by encouraging Arts and Crafts industries such as lace-making, dying, hammering iron, and casting "beautiful garden decorations in cement."[22]

Bar Harbor stands on the eastern shore of Mount Desert Island – the "bar" is the little island that shelters what is a natural harbor. Originally the economy was based on the sea, but it was a hazardous life for the seafarer, because the area is notorious for its fogs. They tend to be particularly bad in the summer months. Naturally guidebooks sought to play down this disadvantage: "one must admit that fogs do occasionally visit this region," wrote a Boston publication, "but they are not the rule, by any means, and rather form a diversion for the guests of the island of Mt. Desert."[23] When *Harper's New Monthly* had visited, however, they were more forthright, quoting an old salt encountered during the voyage out: "Oh yes, Sir, I'm used to these fogs along this

242–47. Bar Harbor in postcards.

coast," he said. "I was born in one of 'em, and as boy and man I've been in and out of 'em all my life. You'll find fogs all the world over, but the Gulf Stream fog beats 'em all."[24] In the opinion of the day, it took "tolerable lungs" to find it "bracing and agreeable."[25]

As with visits to Scotland, a certain hardiness was required of those summering in Maine, and once there a greater degree of informality prevailed than, for instance, at Newport. This penetrated every level of activity. Ward McAllister recommended that an unknown young girl wishing to enter New York society should be tried at Bar Harbor the first summer and only exposed to Newport the second. "There's little heavy drinking or gambling here, and less of the Newport ostentation," commented a summer resident.[26]

It was claimed that Bar Harbor enjoyed "a peculiar freedom in dress, which is as natural as her surroundings."[27] Though people might change in the evenings, during the day they were likely to wear flannels, duck suits, and comfortable golfing clothes. Recreations retained something of the primal simplicity of the first visitors. Walking among the lakes and mountains came high on the list, followed closely by driving. Geological phenomena such as Balance Rock, "the largest and most interesting of Maine's boulders," must have formed a popular destination, to judge from the enormous numbers of stereoscope views. Frenchman's Bay, between Mount Desert and the

mainland, was described as "one of the finest sheets of water for boating on the eastern coast of the United States."[28] Certainly some people brought their own yachts – Cyrus Curtis virtually lived on his – but equally the Canoe Club had a membership of over three hundred. Lowly though canoeing may sound, the club had its own pretty boathouse on Bar Island, where it held weekly receptions in August. Paddling around among the Porcupines – three dome-like islands named for their bristling pine trees – was a popular activity, perhaps because it was difficult to chaperone, and Francis Marion Crawford's pot-boiling *Maidens Call it Love in Idleness* ends with a proposal of marriage being accepted in a canoe. Another young people's activity was "rocking," or scrambling over the cliffs.

For the fisherman Eagle Lake not only offered the native speckled trout but was stocked with salmon. From 1888 golf could be enjoyed at the Kebo Valley Club, and then there was the usual round of tennis tournaments, horse shows, and amateur theatricals. Typical of Maine, however, was the role played by the Mount Desert Reading Room, a meeting place as well as a library, not to mention the Village Improvement Association, which held an annual fête. But perhaps the most characteristic Bar Harbor institution was the Pot and Kettle Club. It was founded in 1888 by a group of Philadelphia men, the idea being that they would cook for each other. It was a little like playing at housekeeping, and early photographs show successful businessmen members equipped in uniform of apron and chef's hat. Informality did not, however, imply any loss of prestige – quite the reverse. The club was both exclusive and secretive, but it is known that guests included William Howard Taft, Theodore Roosevelt, Warren G. Harding, Franklin D. Roosevelt, and Harry S. Truman.

If life at Bar Harbor was less elaborate than at Newport, Northeast Harbor, around the cliffs from Bar Harbor, was at yet a further remove of simplicity. Dominated by the formidable personalities of President Eliot and Bishop Doane – the latter dressed English-style in shovel hat, apron, and gaiters – it inevitably had not only an intellectual and a religious caste, but a rigorous one; both were rigorous men. While the picnics could be delightful, it was Charles Eliot's invariable custom to set off on walks with no more than a sandwich in the pocket of his coat, and he expected those who accompanied him to do likewise. Through the Bishop's efforts to maintain the country values that he had experienced when he first came to Mount Desert, dinner was still, notionally at

248. Charles Dana Gibson's house on Seven Hundred Acre Island, built by Allen and Collens of Boston in 1903–04.

least, taken at midday and supper at night, long after the city practice of evening dining had become accepted at Bar Harbor. At least the evening meal continued to be called supper, out of respect to the Bishop, though, as one summer resident put it shrewdly: "Is the call of supper, but the food the food of dinner?"[29] Church services in the charming woodland chapel – many Maine resorts have one – were naturally important; the chief secular institution was the Library, a large private book club. After that came fresh air and exercise. "Active outdoor life – exercise both for brain and brawn; 'talk and walk' as the motto was – nobody asked for more," remembered another summer colonist. "Whether you saw Dr. Mitchell in tweeds on a mountain top or Bishop Doane acting coxswain to his grandchildren in a sort of arch-episcopal barge, you had the same effect of vivid enjoyment."[30]

Simpler even than at Northeast Harbor was the life of the many little islands. The cartoonist Charles Dana Gibson built his summer home (Plate 248) on Seven Hundred Acre Island, just off another island, Isleboro; the name itself denotes the size. One summer there was "worth a dozen summers abroad," he told reporters in 1907.[31] Gibson's house there was fairly large, and it has unusual outbuildings in the form of two follies – a playhouse and a ruined castle-cum-chapel – that Gibson erected himself for his children. Whatever the scale, though, island life always has complications. Letters to Gibson's caretaker reveal the difficulty of organizing things at a distance, since he constantly had to seek reports of what his workmen were up to. "I wonder if they have started to dig my well yet," he asked in December 1903. "Pendleton was to do it and the other Pendleton was going to build my dock. I wish you would find out some time what they are doing."[32] Needless to say, all goods and provisions had to be brought over from the mainland or Isleboro by boat. This was an inconvenience, but it ensured privacy and kept the developers at bay.

"Improvements" were the one danger that Olmsted saw when he reported on Cushing's Island, just outside Portland.

The Island is not a good place for a neighborhood of smart and fine suburban residences such as many prefer to pass their summers in.... Villas and cottages of the class in question would appear out of place, tawdry, and vulgar, upon it. Lawns and gardens appropriate to them are in large parts of the island out of the question. Notions of improving the island based on what has generally been attempted at many public favored places of summer resort should therefore be wholly abandoned.[33]

If improvement could be put out of mind, the place offered "attractions such as can be found, I believe, nowhere else on the Atlantic sea-board." This island came to be run, in theory, as a club of like-minded cottagers. In practice it was ruled with reasonably benign despotism by the Cushings, a Canadian family who had long before acquired the island to develop it in conjunction with their railroad interests. To this end they built the Ottawa House Hotel and eventually hit upon the club principle for developing the rest of the island. The architect for most of the cottages was John Calvin Stevens of Portland, and it would be charitable to think that, like the owners, he suffered some difficulty in attempting to direct operations from the mainland. Certainly he was given no quarter by James Dakers, a cottager from Montreal, who arrived in 1884 to find an unfinished house with a roof and chimney that he had to reconstruct – not to mention an escalated bill.[34]

In the center of the island was a farm, with cows that provided milk and regularly roamed into gardens and trampled across nascent lawns. Frank Cushing, "Grand Monarque," erected a house to block the view of a cottager who claimed damages after collective property rights were ignored through the sale of a third of the island to the army. In due course, Cushing's nephew Gordon took on his role: "For years it was run as his country estate."[35] Though this management style may not have been democratic, it ensured the island's preservation for, in Olmsted's words, "persons ... who have a taste for wildness of nature, and who value favorable conditions for sea bathing, boating and fishing."

The inspiration behind some of these Maine resorts was not very different from that which fired builders of the American country house. Generally, except at Bar Harbor, the houses themselves were simpler, smaller affairs. Though Mr. Dakers's cottage cost more than he expected, the bill was still only $1,485. Broad verandas were universal, and often interiors were paneled with boards that came virtually fresh from the mill, unpainted and unstained. Where they survive in their original state, they have now mellowed to an appealing tobacco color. Paths through the pine woods were also laid with boards and called boardwalks. So all-pervasive was the spirit of restraint that it infected public architecture, too. The main room of a golf club or yacht club, such as those at Camden, might be a large, unornamented space, open to the rafters, with little decadence in the way of soft furnishings.

The promoters of Sorrento believed that "Every year marks an increase in the luxury with which refined life seeks to surround itself during even its briefest flittings away from home."[36] Undoubtedly there were some houses at Bar Harbor in which this could be seen, but more summer residents would have identified with the austerer social judgment of Stevens and his partner Albert Winslow Cobb in 1889:

At a time when other sections of our country are developing an evidently demoralizing luxury, there is exhibited here throughout Maine a primitive simplicity and wholesome vigor of life which may serve as an object-lesson to the student of social problems. The path to social health which is being sought vaguely through abstract ideals, may perhaps be here fairly indicated by the concrete example of an existent

249

commonwealth. Already Maine is eagerly sought as a recreating-ground by people whose nerves need soothing. The natural scenery of this healthful region is an important factor in this recreative process; yet doubtless, too, another important factor is the prevalent wholesomeness of social conditions. One feels here no impending menace of some popular paroxysm; but feels rather the calm spirit of a contented people environed by the unperverted things of nature. Contrast the atmosphere of social security here with the social atmosphere of – well, say the northeast corner particularly of Illinois.[37]

While Sorrento never achieved the success that its directors had hoped for it, Stevens and Cobb (and Stevens on his own, after the dissolution of the partnership in 1891) went on to build numerous houses throughout the state – "good, wholesome, simple designs for the dwellings of simple people," as one critic called them; "houses and cottages that look and doubtless are homelike and comfortable."[38]

Nevertheless, there were some points at which resort houses became indistinguishable from country houses. Estates of thirty or fifty acres were uncommon, but not unknown. Some people felt sufficiently established in their Maine homes to wish to farm. Outside Camden, for example, the Hon. J.B. Stearns established Sagamore Farm as "an object lesson in dairy farming," and the guidebook *Glimpses of Camden on the Coast of Maine* proudly described the De Laval Separator, the Champion Milk Cooler, Aerator, and Deodorizer, and other up-to-date machinery with which it was equipped. Sometimes appearance was all. A rich Montana woman so missed the sheep when she came to Bar Harbor that she telegraphed to her agent to send a flock by train. It was widely said that, when she died, each sheep wore a black ribbon around its neck.

Baymeath, five miles from Bar Harbor, must be considered a full-blown country house. It was built in 1894–95 with, before later additions, six bedrooms, eight maid's rooms and ten bathrooms, and the owners, Mr. and Mrs. Joseph Tilton Bowen, came from just that northeast corner of Illinois that Stevens and Cobb deplored, Chicago. Their household staff comprised a butler, two footmen, eight gardeners, six stable hands, seven maids, and a cook. In the early years they had their horses transported from Chicago every summer by train. Stabling for twenty-two meant that this must have been quite a performance. When one year the hay in the freight car caught fire, the practice was discontinued and the horses were kept over the winter on a neighboring farm. In the carriage house they maintained about twenty different vehicles which were driven in some style. Mrs. Bowen remembered the grooms' colorful liveries.

The men wore black boots with tan colored tops, white broadcloth breeches, dark blue cloth coats, with silver buttons, white stocks, heavy white gloves, and high silk hats. They had morning suits of black and white cloth, cutaway coats and striped vests, wore black leather puttees and tall black straw hats. When it was very cold, they wore dark blue astrakan trimmed overcoats with much heavy braid across the front. Larson tells me these coats cost $300.00 each.[39]

All this may make it sound as though they intended to live in the country as they did in town. But equally they kept a feeling for the simple life that was typical of Maine. This was expressed in their first plans for their dwelling. "Our idea about the house," wrote Mrs. Bowen, "was that it should be a farm house, rather low, and, in order not to keep too many gardeners, its long grass was to come to the front door." It was their architect, Herbert Jacques of the Boston firm of Andrews, Jacques and Rantoul, who persuaded them that they would prefer something in the French Colonial style, and then the meadow no longer seemed appropriate. Even so, something of the original conception survived in the way the house was used. They declined all invitations, on the grounds that they had quite enough of that sort of thing during the winter; in addition to which Mr. Bowen would be tired "from working in the garden or being very athletic during the day." Consequently they did little formal entertaining, preferring picnics, clambakes, and cooking the lobsters caught off their pier in an open fireplace outside. The children were introduced to country ways, raising chickens and turkeys behind the garage. Mrs. Bowen's favorite occupation was gardening, and the garden became so well known in Bar Harbor that she held at-homes there on Sunday evenings. They were popular affairs. Mrs. Bowen received under the birch tree while her children and husband acted as guides. "When I asked him how he remembered the names of the flowers, he said he didn't remember any of them. He had learned the Latin names of two or three, and these he used indiscriminately, and very few people knew the difference, so he always enjoyed himself."

The greenhouse, very large and the idea of an incompetent gardener called Rose, proved a failure and it was turned into a swimming pool enclosure. Characteristically, the pool that they preferred was a naturalistic one on the beach. The sides were slatted with wood, the edge was covered with rocks and pebbles, and it was filled every day by the tide. The essence of Maine simplicity? Perhaps; but it would not have been practicable had not two men walked back and forth dragging a forty-foot mosquito net every morning, to remove spiders and bugs.

* * *

Resorts took many forms, as did country houses. In Maine the two worlds overlapped, elsewhere they ran in parallel. Nowhere was this more true than at Jekyll Island in Georgia. Privacy is, after all, the salient characteristic of the country house, but often it was the one thing lacking in a resort, where anyone with the money could buy a house. Keeping out the wrong sort was a particular obsession in America, where exclusive residential enclaves such as Tuxedo Park had a strong appeal. Country house owners were, and generally still are, more secretive than those in England, where not only is there a long tradition of visiting such places, even when they are not formally open to the public, but private property is often cut across by centuries-old rights-of-way and trespass of itself is not a punishable offence. For the resort one answer was to form a club that would be the ground landlord, allowing members the privilege of building houses on individual plots only when they had satisfied the committee. This was meant to have been the arrangement at Cushing's Island, but, even if it had been observed to the letter, the cottagers' territory was always liable to invasion from the guests of the Ottawa House Hotel. Jekyll Island, however, offers a more thoroughgoing example, since the whole island was owned by the club of rich New Yorkers who bought it in 1886. Originally the membership was limited to fifty, and included W.K. Vanderbilt, J. Pierpont Morgan, William Rockefeller, and Joseph Pulitzer. George M. Pullman of Chicago joined in 1888, George J. Gould in 1895 (by this time there was a waiting list of over a year). Later came scions of the Astors and the Fricks. When called upon to give their occupation in the membership book, most members simply put "capitalist." They were men who in many cases already owned country houses; not surprisingly their thoughts on Jekyll Island soon turned to architecture, and the opportunity was given for club members to build houses while adhering strictly to the principles of the club. Dedicated to the pursuit of sport, the club's ambitions were closely allied to those of the

249. A club experiment in "Transcontinental Radio Telephony," made at the Jekyll Island Clubhouse in 1914, Theodore Vail at the telephone.

country house. Since the history of the club is not well known, it is worth a digression to examine it in detail.

When the club was founded, the *New York Times* predicted that it would be "the 'swell' club, the *crème de la crème* of all." Half a dozen years later the newspaper returned and gave a whimsical account of the wildlife there, which it pictured as jostling for the privilege of being shot.

> One may readily imagine the thrill of excitement that ripples through the forests when some wise old squirrel, tired, perhaps, of awaiting his time to be bagged, skinned, and eaten, mounts a convenient fence and whispers to his companions of the wood, "Hist! W.K. Vanderbilt is out today . . . " Or the commotion under the branches when wild turkey tells the plover in strictest confidence that J. Pierpont Morgan is out with a gun and three footmen to carry the game.[40]

Despite the delicious early spring and late autumn climate, club members scarcely noticed the twelve and a half miles of hard white sand that formed the beach. This was used less for swimming than for racing bicycles (Plate 256), traps, and motorcars. Much more attractive were the wild hogs, mink, possum, crane, and even mockingbirds – the last specifically mentioned in the prospectus, though club rules banned the killing of singing birds. Dean Hoffman's bag for 1901 comprised twenty-one quail, ninety-three pheasants, eighty doves, a hundred and thirty ducks, ninety marsh hens, three wild turkeys, and an alligator.

Before the Civil War, Jekyll Island had been fertile cotton land – one of the famous "sea islands" off the Georgia coast. Its last private owners were a family called du Bignon, who had a herd of cattle roaming it, but otherwise found the place unprofitable.

252

In the second half of 1885, John E. du Bignon bought out the other members of the family for $13,100 and immediately began looking for someone to whom to sell. He found a buyer, but instead the club idea was suggested by his brother-in-law, a financier called Finney who had good New York connections. The club was run as a trust company with a hundred shares. Each original member had to buy two shares at $600 each.

With the first of the founding membership quickly subscribed, a visiting committee set out to inspect the island in May 1886. They took with them the early landscape architect Horace Cleveland, a follower of Olmsted who, according to the *Dictionary of American Biography*, "helped to spread the gospel of foresight and planning in the rapidly developing West." He had recently designed two hundred acres of park for Minneapolis and St. Paul in Minnesota. His report on Jekyll Island, which showed how the drives, clubhouse, and plots for cottages should be laid out on the landward side of the island, was delivered in August. Club members, he observed, wished not only to escape the cares of business but also "the conventionalism . . . of ordinary fashionable resorts." His scheme was consequently devised to require little upkeep. "The island may be made a natural Paradise, by the tasteful and judicious use of the materials which nature furnishes to our hand, and which will require little or no care, after being once established." At the time, however, it did not seem so idyllic. As he rode through forest, swamp, and savannah to make the survey, he "was bitten and stung from head to foot by red bugs, wood ticks and other benevolent machines, and thought myself fortunate in seeing only one rattlesnake."

Plans for the clubhouse were already under way when the executive committee first met in June 1886. The architect, Charles Alexander, is known for only two other works, both early: a church of 1854–55 and a hotel of 1868. He found that the Jekyll Island commission was fraught with difficulties: an ignorant contractor, an unskilled workforce, bad water, a boarding house of such low standard that it drove away the masons, an unsuitable landing pier, and the non-arrival of the promised tugboat, *Howland*. Altogether the anxieties of the commission seem to have told on him, for within a year he was dead.

Yet the clubhouse did rise slowly – four stories tall, with a corner tower and many balconies, brick-built, and painted brown (Plate 250). A piazza ran around three sides of the building. There were sixty sleeping rooms, but it was a club rule that they could not be reserved. While guests were allowed, they could not stay at the club for more than two weeks, and during that time they would have to give up their room to a member if the club was full. One of the special attractions of Jekyll Island was that the inner shore offered an ideal anchorage, and in the guestbook visitors frequently gave their address as their yacht. However, those members who wanted to be sure of adequate accommodation built cottages. In a cottage, member, family, and guests could stay for an unlimited period, without fear of losing rooms.

The cottages stand on several loops of drive, on a frontage to the sea of about a mile. Each plot was roughly an acre: larger plots would have meant that some cottages would have been too far from the clubhouse or the dock. First to build was the eccentric McEvers Bayard Brown, who never occupied his cottage. His example was soon followed by others, including the warehouse merchant Frederic Baker. He wanted a plot as near to the clubhouse as possible, and it was, as the minutes recorded in March 1889, "a matter of importance in the interest of the club, to have Mr. Baker build at once" (Plate 251). Gradually more plots were occupied in the 1890s. One was Indian Mound (Plate 255), built in 1892 by Gordon McKay, an engineer and inventor whose shoe-

250. The clubhouse of 1886 (left) with the annex of apartments built in 1901.

stocking machine had met the demand for army boots in the Civil War. It is in the Queen Anne style, and it may be significant that Stanford White stayed at the club in February that year. Later, Indian Mound was owned by William Rockefeller. Only half the cottages can be ascribed to known architects. Charles Gifford, a New Jersey man who also enlarged the clubhouse, built two: one for Pulitzer in 1897–98, the other for H.K. Porter, owner of a heavy engineering firm, in 1901. By far the most distinguished of the cottages is that built for the lumber merchant F.H. Goodyear, who joined the club in 1902. He went to Carrère and Hastings, who produced a house of Palladian proportions with an overhanging eave (Plate 257). It was not large: none of the early cottages was. Many members, including J.P. Morgan, did not build at all but remained content with rooms in the clubhouse or an apartment in a block known as Sans Souci. Moreover, the club remained a club. Members were expected to eat in the dining room, which had a French chef and a pastry cook, and as a consequence the cottages often had no kitchen.

The second phase of cottage building began in 1916. In that year the plumbing manufacturer Richard Teller Crane, Jr., of Chicago, caring nothing for the restraint of Old New York, employed David Adler to build a large Classical house with wings (Plate 252). It occupied the site of the burnt-out Solterra. The wings and the cloistered courtyard behind the main block could almost have been designed to make the building look bigger than it was – and worse, it had a dining room, kitchen, and butler's pantry. "There are two matters I would like to call attention to," wrote James W. Ellsworth to the club's chairman, George H. Macy, in 1917. "First, the building of pretentious houses on the Island by members, on account of the serious objection of architecturally overshadowing the Club building, which should be the principal feature. . . . Secondly, the practice of giving formal dinners in the Club by members." But the old, unpretentious ways were changing, and the club, which had been established to serve them, was coming to look old-fashioned.

Two further houses were built in 1928. For Walter Jennings, a Rockefeller associate

254

in Standard Oil, John Russell Pope built Villa Ospo, while George Gould's nephew Frank Miller Gould commissioned the Fifth Avenue architect and decorator Morgens Tvede to design Villa Marianna. Both were in Mediterranean styles; both had dining rooms. But dining rooms alone could not make up for the excitements of other holiday places as the fashionable world turned to the south of France and elsewhere. The great era of Jekyll Island was soon to pass.

In its day, however, the island provided an accurate index to changing tastes in sport. While sea bathing was not a primary attraction in the original prospectus, it slowly emerged as a priority: the minutes of the executive committee for 9 May 1906 note that "six more bath houses will be required on the beach." Although members had to wait until the 1920s for the club swimming pool to be constructed in front of the clubhouse, Edwin Gould, brother of George Gould, had a pool in the atrium of his cottage, Chicota, acquired in 1901.

Golf had a sufficient following by 1898 for a golf club to be laid out, using Bermuda grass. The club superintendent, Ernest Grob, went to inspect the adjacent one on Cumberland Island. On 11 May, during the war with Spain, he wrote patriotically to a member: "No, I don't think the 'Spaniards' will want to play 'golf' in our yard, they will have all they can do to play with Dewey and a few others." (When the Government sought permission to erect batteries on Jekyll Island to defend Brunswick, the negotiations were eased by the fact that Cornelius Bliss, Secretary of the Interior, was a member of the club.)

"For two years tennis has been the most popular outdoor sport," stated a letter read before the executive committee on 12 April 1905. There was already one tennis court, but another was needed and it was built the next year. In the 1920s Edwin Gould erected a "casino" which included an indoor tennis court; more indoor courts – in a long shingled building – were erected by J. Pierpont Morgan, Jr., in 1927.

It was not until 1907 that automobiles were officially permitted on the island, and then only with caution. They were confined to the beach and the back road from there to the clubhouse; and during the season, from 15 January to 1 April, they were banned completely between 10 a.m. and 12 noon, and 2 and 7 p.m. It was a rule that "Automobiles shall be brought to a full stop when meeting horses driven or ridden, and shall continue stopped until such horses have passed." The same year, William Rockefeller authorized the club to build, at his expense, a bicycle path – "with the condition that the same be used exclusively for bicycles." Like the principal drives, it was probably laid with oyster shells, left in huge middens by the Indians. However, there had been a "bicycle department" at the club for at least a decade before this (Plate 256).

Horse racing was a serious consideration for the founding fathers of the club. When

251. Solterra, one of the first Jekyll Island cottages, built for Frederic Baker in 1889. It burned in 1914.

252. The cottage built on the site of Solterra by the plumbing manufacturer Richard Crane in 1916 spelled the end of the era of restraint. It was designed by David Adler.

253. Members of the Jekyll Island Club on the beach, watching black shuffle dancers.

they submitted their petition of incorporation at Brunswick, Georgia, in 1886, their second object was "to maintain a race course," but there is no evidence that it was ever built. The committee found its attention fully engrossed by satisfying the club's prime object of rearing game. For Jekyll Island did not prove quite the sporting paradise that was hoped for; partly as a result of this, financial management was always a problem. The great shooting treat was wild turkey. There had been a few on the island when the club started but they had gradually disappeared. More were introduced from the mainland and did well; but after a few seasons' abstinence by the guns they were overshot and then died out completely. Pheasants were difficult and expensive, and, while at first it was possible to import several thousand quail each year, the tightening of the game laws in the states whence they came dried up the supply. Shooting restrictions were imposed – members being limited per share in the trust company of the club to sixty quail per week, and (in 1896–97) five pheasants, three wild turkeys, and three deer for the whole season. Guests could not shoot on more than one stay a year or when their host was off the island. Venison could be shipped from the island only with a payment

254. Cottage built by Walter Furness, himself an architect and nephew of the Philadelphia architect Frank Furness, in 1890. The cottage became the club's infirmary in 1930.

255. Indian Mound, built for the engineer Gordon McKay and later owned by William Rockefeller.

256. Members of the club's senior staff bicycling on the beach.

to the club. The restrictions were irksome to men used to shooting on a big scale. In 1913 Robert Goelet joined the club only on the understanding that he would have double shooting privileges, although, in a nice qualification, it was agreed that these would be canceled unless used in moderation.

Servants were another problem. "I do not think it will be possible for Mrs. Loomis to get a competent person for a maid here," Grob wrote to Colonel John Loomis of Chicago in 1898; "we have tried several of them, for a few weeks they seem to do right; but then seem to go off." The numbers employed were surprising. During the 1898 season, the club had a chef, a second cook, a baker, a fireman, a butcher, a pot washer, a kitchen girl, a head waiter, fourteen ordinary waiters, a pantry man, and a pantry woman. The laundry department comprised Miss A. Flanigan (head laundress), a shirt ironer, two family ironers, a starcher, two mangle women, three washers, a linen-room girl, and three chambermaids. They were sent down from New York with their fare paid one way.

Servant difficulties were hardly surprising, given that not enough thought had been

257. The lumber merchant F.H. Goodyear's cottage by Carrère and Hastings, built in 1902.

258. Moss Cottage, built by the stockbroker William Struthers in 1896; the banker and philanthropist E.W. Macy owned it from 1914.

259. The ruins of Dungeness, Thomas Carnegie's house on Cumberland Island, built in 1885.

paid to their accommodation when the clubhouse was built. "Our servants quarters are not fit for humans in cold weather," Grob wrote to the committee in 1914; "there is absolutely no heat in this house except the stove in Social Hall." Equally, conditions for the members themselves were less than ideal. One of them, Dr. W.H. Merrill, complained loudly of the short pipes discharging sewage into the creek. With a westerly wind, "the smell around the club grounds and piazza is very bad indeed" – and there had been cases of typhoid. A club physician was appointed with strict instructions not to leave the island without permission, and one of the members gave his cottage as an infirmary (Plate 254). The sewerage question festered on until the First World War.

260. Greyfield, built in 1891, for one of Thomas Carnegie's children.

It is sometimes said that the end of the club came in 1942 when a German U-boat was sighted off the Georgia coast: the President feared an attempt to kidnap the club members, who between them owned an immense proportion of the nation's wealth, and he had the island evacuated immediately. More plausible, though, is the story that when the civil servant came from Washington to see the order carried out, he found the island deserted.

Jekyll Island had been a remarkable phenomenon of American social life, encapsulating cherished ideas of privacy, community, informality, architecture, and sport. Did this have any direct connection with the country house? It did.

Next to Jekyll Island is the eighteen-mile-long sliver of Cumberland Island. James Oglethorpe, founder of Georgia, had named the island after the Duke of Cumberland, the third son of George II, who would gain notoriety as the Butcher of Culloden. Later, parts of it were run as a plantation, though the site of the future Plum Orchard seems to have fulfilled only one function with much success: that of a mass burial place for slaves. In 1881 four thousand acres were bought by Andrew Carnegie's brother Thomas, who replaced an old plantation house called Dungeness with a splendid new mansion, all

261. Spanish moss and the remains of a pergola at Greyfield.

piazzas, loggias, and belvedere. The new Dungeness was completed in 1885 (Plate 259). Next year Carnegie died, but his widow, Lucy, retained her fondness for the island, not only continuing to buy property until she owned virtually the whole of the island but building individual houses for each of her nine children as they grew up. The first of these dwellings, The Cottage, was built for Thomas Morrison Carnegie, Jr., shortly after Dungeness was finished. Like many so-called cottages, it was really quite a substantial dwelling, its thin white columns and double porches recalling the plantation houses of the lower Mississippi. However, the later houses were larger still. The grandest of all is Plum Orchard (Plate 237), designed by Peabody and Stearns in 1898 and enlarged with wings eight years later. Nine miles distant from Dungeness, it had its own swimming pool and squash court. It also possessed a generating plant, laundry, barn, water tower, and chicken house. The other two houses, Greyfield (Plate 260) and Stafford, were both built in 1901, the latter replacing a plantation house that had burned.

Servicing these houses was an elaborate operation. Every day the family's steam yacht, the *Missoe*, manned by a crew of seventeen, plied its way between Cumberland and the mainland bearing visitors and supplies. (Mrs. Carnegie achieved the distinction of becoming the first female member of the New York Yacht Club.) In other ways the island was remarkably self-sufficient. It supported some five hundred cattle, providing both fresh milk and meat. Quantities of chickens were to be found in the coops. A bakery at Dungeness supplied every establishment with bread. Before horse-drawn carriages were replaced by the battery-powered cars known as "electrics," large numbers of horses were kept in the various stables – up to fifty at Dungeness alone. Blistering summers and humid winters made constant maintenance of the houses a necessity; to meet it there was a large woodworking shop.

A paradise of wildlife, its houses shut comfortably off from the outside world by palmetto thickets and the sea, Cumberland Island is the family compound par excellence. Not surprisingly, frequent visits were exchanged between the Carnegies and the Jekyll Islanders. Cumberland could almost have seemed an extension of the club: in a sense it was its own club, organized for the benefit of the family. The values of the resort and of the country house had come almost to coincide.[41]

261

ENVOI

"The trouble with the rich American is that he feels uncouth and untraditional, and so he meekly trots to Europe to buy sun-dials and fifteenth-century mantelpieces and refectory tables – to try to buy aristocracy by buying the aristocrats' worn-out coats."

Sinclair Lewis
Dodsworth

"Houses of the best taste are like clothes of the best tailors – it takes their age to show us how good they are."

Henry James
The American Scene

262. Shady Paths, Vizcaya, by John Singer Sargent, 1917. Worcester Art Museum, Worcester, Massachusetts

— 15 —

Death in Venice
VIZCAYA

IF ONE HAD TO nominate a single building as expressing most thoroughly the attributes specific to the American country house, it would be James Deering's Vizcaya on Biscayne Bay, Florida. It is not just that Vizcaya possesses the full complement of organ, swimming pool, bowling alley, and den – features that we have seen to be particularly associated with this branch of architecture in the United States. It is also a patio house, it had its own farm, village, and dairy, and the technology was beyond compare: despite the tropical climate, the house could boast full central heating. Yet not even these outstanding characteristics would, of themselves, convince one of Vizcaya's supremely representative status. What seems truly American is the heroic determination to overcome all natural and manmade obstacles, including world war, to see the house built, and, when all the labors of building were over and forgotten, the particular poetry with which the result is invested. It is an autumnal poetry, sensuous and fleeting, rich and muted at the same time. "Is this a dream made real, or a reality greater than a dream?" mused Paul Chalfin, the man who gathered all the different threads together – "this house where no uniform style is worn by the sweet and human objects within, but where a garment of beauty is spread over the things of centuries by the understanding of a single mind."[1] Like Olana it became a work of art. The ingredients that make it so are peculiarly those of the American country house.

But product of a "single mind" it was not. Chalfin's first and essential collaborator was his client. One of the great mysteries of Vizcaya is why Deering built it. Formal in manner, always impeccably dressed, he was already fifty-five, unmarried, and suffering from pernicious anemia when he began. He knew that it was not a possession that would be maintained by his two nieces after his death. Having been tempted by Chalfin once again to spend more than he had expected – a regular occurrence – he spoke revealingly of "the huge investment that I already have here and which, I know, could not be given away by me or by my heirs."[2] His tastes were epicurean, but not extravagant. He was thought to be fastidious, dyspeptic – "an astringent little man," as he was remembered by his house guest, the actress Lilian Gish.[3] To business colleagues he was "the silent man of International Harvester" – too silent, perhaps, for his business life had not been an unqualified success. When the Deerings and the McCormicks had joined forces to form the International Harvester Company in 1902 he had been made a vice-president, but he was effectively put out of a job four years later when J.P. Morgan, the trust's supreme controller, examined its bad performance. Poor health was given as the reason

263. Looking towards the tea house at Vizcaya. Though this building is French in character, the striped poles for mooring ships – or gondolas – were clearly inspired by Venice.

for his retirement. Nevertheless, it must have been some consolation to read that his was "one of the cleanest fortunes in the country," according to *World*. The same source called Vizcaya "The Grandest House in America."

There were other ways in which James Deering stood out from the world of business in which he moved. His brother Charles, having once hoped to be a painter himself, had many artist friends, including John Singer Sargent and Anders Zorn. James claimed no personal talent, but he shared his brother's discrimination. The French journalist Jules Huret, writing for the aristocracy of the Old World, believed that he had "a mind as exquisitely cultured as one could imagine. I do not believe it is possible to find in all the aristocracies of Europe a nature more really distinguished than that of Mr. James Deering."[4] For Chicago, that was something.

On the face of it, Vizcaya would appear to be the story of how a rich client, cultivated, but somewhat vague as to his end in view, could be lead by the nose by a creative man who had, among other qualities, all the ruthlessness of genius. If so, it is also the story of the wiles and stratagems to which a creative man will be put to overcome the hesitancy of his client. In this, Chalfin showed a positively feline ingenuity, sometimes flattering, sometimes supple, sometimes invoking the sanctity of an artistic *crise*. He does not emerge as an agreeable man: his portrait at Vizcaya shows him dark-visaged, intense, scornful, and too highly strung for the comfort of others. But there can be no doubting his single-mindedness or vision. Like Charles Deering he had trained as a painter, though with more determination. Indeed he continued to study into his mid-thirties. Bad eyesight was blamed for his giving up; others were not slow to tender the more probable explanation that his pictures did not sell. But at Vizcaya his long tuition at last came into its own: color and texture, light and shade, all were controlled by Chalfin's painterly eye.

Having abandoned painting Chalfin wrote some art journalism, worked for a time as curator of Oriental art at the Boston Museum of Fine Arts, and dabbled in decoration. It was Elsie de Wolfe who recommended him to Deering – a decision she may have come to regret when she discovered the scale of the project. Deering also took soundings from Isabella Stewart Gardner, collector, patroness of Bernard Berenson, and builder of the Venetian palace of Fenway Court, Boston. Chalfin had been one of the minor figures at the court of "Mrs. Jack," as she was known, and it was at Fenway Court – rich in art and richer still in atmosphere – that his own decorative taste was formed. Nowhere were rare objects, sometimes of disparate dates and origins, more harmoniously displayed than at Fenway Court, where the most strident colors are those of Old Masters and old brocade.

James Deering had been preceded at Coconut Grove by his parents, who had built a house there, and his brother Charles, who had bought a jungle estate. It was a small but select winter community in 1910 when Deering first made his appearance: he later discovered that his nearest neighbor was the mighty political orator William Jennings Bryan. But land – the land that Deering wanted – was by no means as easy to come by as might have been expected in this underdeveloped region. It consisted of no more than black marsh and "hammock" (the Arawak Indian word for jungle) but the owner, Mary Brickell, perhaps out of a sense of civic responsibility, saw no reason for Deering's wishing to own so much. The difficulties of the purchase formed an all too appropriate overture to the building of Vizcaya. Only after many months of negotiation was she persuaded to part with a hundred and thirty acres for the exorbitant price of $1,000 an acre. It was later said that she did so only when she heard through Chalfin that Deering intended to build a new road for the community. Reaching terms with Mrs. Brickell

264. The centerpiece of the east façade, overlooking the sea. The decorator Paul Chalfin insisted that the seahorse should be the emblem of the house.

was not the end of the story: ownership of part of the property was disputed by other neighbors and a lawsuit followed.

The evolution of Vizcaya's design can be followed through an account that Chalfin gave to the *Miami Herald* in 1934. Naturally enough, given the region's history, Deering had first thought of a Spanish house, but many months were spent exploring various themes. Then, "with his characteristic abruptness in making decisions," he swept them

267

all away and "we came to the determination that the building should be of the Italian villa type." The "we" implies that Chalfin steered his client towards this decision, and, from what we know of their later relationship, this was almost certainly the case. When Deering's mind was made up the pair then left for a study tour of north Italy. The only memory of the proposed Spanish house was the name – itself to be the subject of a lengthy deliberation also involving Kirk Munroe, local resident and writer of adventure stories, and brother Charles. (It was taken from the supposed name of the master of one

265. The south façade from the parterre of the main garden.

266. The gardens as they appeared from the breakfast room on the second floor, in March 1916.

267. Avenue of newly planted royal palms, leading to the boathouse, 1914.

of Ponce de León's ships; subsequent research inconveniently revealed this to have been really Viscaino, but Vizcaya was felt to sound better.)

The weakness of Chalfin's account is that it omits all mention of the architect, F. Burrall Hoffman, Jr. This was no accident, for Chalfin also excluded Hoffman's name from the special issue of *Architectural Review*, written by himself, that celebrated the completion of the structure in 1917; nor did he ever allow credit to the brilliant young garden architect, Diego Suarez. Without Hoffman, however, the house certainly could not have been built, for Chalfin was not an architect. It is one thing to sketch out an idea, as Chalfin probably did; it is quite another to make it work in three dimensions, with every exigency of the plan accounted for and agreeable with the façades. Hoffman, a young graduate of Harvard and the École des Beaux-Arts, had already gained experience of planning and detailing large places, having worked in Carrère and Hastings's office on the design of E.H. Harriman's immense and soulless house, Arden, in New York State. Chalfin had met Hoffman when the latter stepped in at the last minute to give a lecture in a series organized by Chalfin at the Colony Club when William Delano fell ill.

Hoffman made his own trip to Italy. The inspiration for the basic shape of Vizcaya was found in the Villa Rezzonico at Bassano del Grappa, an austere stucco-faced building with a shallow pantile roof between corner towers. There were differences of proportion and detail. The most obvious is that Vizcaya has only two tall towers rather than four; when Chalfin proposed developing the four-towered idea in the manner of an Italian fortress, Deering said it would look like a shoe factory. Villa Rezzonico was altogether too spartan, and memories of other seventeenth-century buildings were called upon to enrich the façades. Facing the sea, the principal façade is crowned by a broken pediment supported by volutes, beneath which is an open Venetian window (Plate 264). On the ground floor is a three-bay arcade giving into a loggia, and this device is repeated on the entrance side. The effect of the loggias, felt Chalfin, was to form the gentlest of transitions between garden and interior, or as he wrote: "only the sense of the infinite outdoors, deftly shut away, brings one into the house."[5] On the entrance front the towers are shorter and broader, and the central section is only one story. The two side façades are unbalanced by the different heights of the towers, but each is given a full architectural treatment – something rarely attempted in the seventeenth century. On the garden front (Plate 265), facing south, the three-arch theme reappears, though glazed, giving onto the tea room. Beneath the eaves an open loggia of

269

268. Panoramic view showing the barge under construction, June 1915.

Ionic columns fronts the marble-floored breakfast room – a room in which to catch the breezes and the sound of fountains at the start of the day. On the north side, where the hammock reaches almost up to the house, the swimming pool flows into a grotto (Plate 271) at the base of the northeast tower.

Added to the problems of the design were those of where the house should be put. The obvious site lay on the cliffs, a fine commanding position that would have been seized upon by any nobleman of the Seicento. This was discussed; Chalfin backed it. But, on consideration, Deering decided against, and proved obdurate. His reasons were remarkably advanced for the time: he did not wish to see any of the great jungle trees cut down. It was a point on which he felt strongly and he intended his rule to be observed to the letter. "To me the charm of this part of the world is the jungle effect, and anything done to interfere with this must be against my wishes and without my knowledge."[6] To the despair of the engineer, it was decided to site the house on the uncertain subsoils by the sea. The escalation in cost was enormous.

Building in so untried an area required patience. Some of the coral-like local stone had a decorative appeal and could be used as steps, but the majority of the building stone came, irregularly and overpriced, from Cuba. Supplies of all kinds, making the long rail journey to Miami, arrived slowly, and after 1914 those from Europe were liable not to come at all. Finally even American manufacturers like General Electric had no spare capacity for domestic work. Mosquitos were a nuisance; at one point land crabs became a plague. Even the dredging operations, raising little islands of sludge and roots, caused anxiety when it was realized that these tiny, newly created territories could be claimed by the State of Florida (Plate 268). "If we do not get those islands," wrote Deering, "we shall curse the day we made them."[7]

As it turned out, these rubbish mounds caused one of the happiest inspirations from Chalfin's office. When Deering and Chalfin had toured Italy their cicerone in the gardens of Florence had been Diego Suarez. Born in Bogota, Suarez had imbibed the principles of Renaissance garden design from Arthur Acton, then restoring the gardens of La Pietra. In 1914 he found himself in New York, ran into Chalfin, and was inducted into his office; this was something for which he may have been grateful, since the outbreak of war had left him stranded. Suarez provided the theme for the gardens,

270

269. The barge, a masterly stroke of imagination, prompted by the desire to improve a small island formed after dredging. The boat-form derives from the gardens of Isola Bella, on Lake Maggiore.

rejecting the obvious idea of descending terraces, because sunlight hitting a sheet of water at the back would have been blinding, in favor of ones rising to a horizon planted with trees. Drawing on his deep knowledge of Italy he also conjured up the gardens of Isola Bella on Lake Maggiore as a solution to the largest rubbish mound. These gardens, covering the whole of an island, are in the form of a barque or barge. At Vizcaya the

271

conceit is translated into a stone barge with prows raised at either end, surrounded by a balustrade and decorated with statues and obelisks (Plate 269). A model was made and passed to Hoffman to detail. This led later to a bitter dispute between Hoffman and Chalfin about authorship; poor Suarez was forgotten.

The sculptor was Stirling Calder, acting chief of sculpture for the Panama—Pacific Exposition in San Francisco and father of the more famous Alexander. On 26 January 1915 a characteristic message crackled across the telegraph wires from Chicago: "YOU

270. Detail from the walled garden, inspired by the Villa Gamberaia near Florence.

271. Detail of one of the shell grottos, with volcanic stone carved in imitation of water.

TOLD ME WHEN PROPOSING ISLAND SCULPTURE WOULD BE COARSE AND CONSEQUENTLY CHEAP," stormed Deering. But he accepted the inevitable. "I CONSENT TO EIGHT THOUSAND DOLLARS SUGGESTED WITH REGRET." Chalfin replied silkily that he was "awfully gratified" to be allowed to proceed, and that he had never imagined that Deering would think coarse-textured sculpture "of a garden character" would be cheaper than fine. The steps opposite the barge, with chamfered corners, are of a Venetian type. The previous summer Chalfin had made them irresistible. "I send you a sketch made on my knees in a gondola at this famous landing before St. Giorgio Maggiore in Venice – Scannozzi [*sic*] or more probably Longhena."[8]

With the rough sculpture and the coral steps Chalfin was pursuing the devotion to texture learned at Fenway Court. One suspects that it was this rather than an Arts and Crafts respect for the artisan that made him insist on every aspect of Vizcaya being handwrought. He personally plastered part of the garden wall to show incredulous workmen the kind of finish he wished to see; they, of course, felt that they could do a much better job by machine. In the construction of the house Chalfin was proud that, despite an abundance of good, hard pine for building, little wood was used. The great Samuel Yellin was responsible for wrought-iron gates (see Plate 274) and bellpulls. When work was over, Chalfin, who was capable of generosity where his own reputation was not at risk, commended the plasterers for "the delicate modeling on the surfaces of the walls" and the color in the courtyard and the vestibules.

273

We have had a wonderful perforated and highly interesting stone to deal with for trim, but you have been able to marry to this the living surface in your stucco which embodies perfectly the live old hand methods of other centuries, just as your color often, where we needed it, brings one a positive conviction that ages of gentle tone work have been bestowed upon your walls by sun and rain.[9]

To achieve this ageworn effect there was nothing better than to use old materials. For the roof a hundred thousand "ancient Spanish tiles," some dated 1820, were imported from Cuba: a process fraught with customs delays. Chalfin was horrified when he discovered that on arrival they were being assiduously cleaned. What would now be called the distressed look was as evident inside the house as out. It was a point on which Deering, used to the pastel smartness of Elsie de Wolfe, needed particular coaxing. "It is hardly an exaggeration to say that wherever I go I find the upholstery of the chairs and other furniture going to pieces," he wrote to Chalfin. "I was a good deal annoyed, for example, a day or so ago to find that the chair that I was sitting in in the breakfast room is in rags."[10] Chalfin preferred to let the fabric, often original, wear out completely before it was replaced with something less deliciously faded. Deering had to be firm: "I think the time has now fully arrived when the chairs and lounge in Espagnolette must be reupholstered."[11]

Much of the architectural detail of the interior was similarly old. One of Hoffman's challenges had been to incorporate the chimneypieces, ceilings, and *boiseries* that Deering and Chalfin had bought in Europe. As Chalfin wrote exultantly: "hardly a modern door exists throughout [the house]; hardly a piece of contemporaneous furniture has found a place in any of its rooms; not a material has been purchased from a dealer's stock, not a fringe, not a tassel."[12] Shipping to the United States was severely disrupted by the war, though none of Vizcaya's consignments suffered the fate of one sent the other way: thirty-four cases of furniture destined for Deering's house at Neuilly near Paris went down with the Greek steamer *Parthenon* when it was sunk by a German submarine. Such were the delays, that one Venetian ceiling, of which all hope had been lost, turned up unexpectedly and was found to be too small for the reception room in which it was to be placed. Chalfin was only one of many clever decorators of the period who knew how such things could be "stretched."

Today such an unhistoric treatment may seem dubious, but in other ways Deering, his taste trained by Chalfin, valued authenticity at a time when it was not wholly usual to do so. Wisely, guarantees were invariably sought from the dealers from whom he bought. He and Chalfin had to have a keen eye for fakes. "There can be no doubt that the object has been constructed with a view to deception," Chalfin wrote in reprimand to Isaac M. Levy of New York about a supposedly old door he had been shown.[13] Because the Baroque was out of favor, some purchases could be made cheaply, or so Chalfin claimed. "There were even times," he said with a smile, "when other collectors accused me of attending bargain sales."[14] Perhaps he feared that a reputation for extravagance would frighten away other clients. Other objects were in the mainstream of Edwardian taste and priced accordingly: tens of thousands were paid for chimneypieces, French furniture, and tapestries.

Two tapestries that hang in the dining room had belonged to Robert Browning. Associations of this kind had great meaning to Chalfin and Deering, both of whom, in the manner of the time, viewed the past through a romantic mist and could almost see the people who moved in it. In the discussion over the name of the estate Deering had become wedded to a vivid picture of Vizcaya, later Viscaino, as a swashbuckling sea

272. Rusticated stonework flanks a stairway in the garden. The live oaks above are appropriate to the Italianate theme, being closely related to the ilex.

rover. "I see the old gentleman in a sugarloaf hat, a cloak, a sword, breeches . . . bold and swaggering." Later, sculptural representations of both Viscaino (or, puzzlingly, "Bel Viscaya" as the legend reads) and Ponce de León were put up in the Entrance Plaza (as Deering called the courtyard in front of the house); they were Italian statues, slightly modified, that had originally been Bernini and Palladio. Equally Chalfin hoped that ghosts of other centuries would populate his interiors. "Someone seems to lurk here, wearing old creamy satin, looking into dim mirrors at strings of pearls and corals upon a narrow and corseted bosom, ready with facile musical sighs."[15]

273. Cathay, a bedroom in the Chinese taste, as understood in the eighteenth century. Like other early-twentieth-century decorators, Chalfin loved the soft color harmonies that could be achieved with old textiles. He had a passion for fringes.

In coordinating the enormous number of suppliers and dealers from whom Deering bought, and finally arranging the rooms in a way that would make sense of every purchase, Chalfin's special genius came into its own. Furniture, *objets de luxe*, Spanish rugs, Empire beds, tablecloths by the score, edging for bellpulls, silk fringes, silver braid for curtains, old Chinese embroidery, an Italian altar frontal – they came not only from France and Italy but from New York. While French and Company would supply a

274. View from the tea room into the patio. The stairs lead from the north arcade to the second floor.

275. Looking across the barge, on to Biscayne Bay.

marble candelabra from ancient Rome, formerly owned by Stanford White, horn lanterns and silk tassels came from the Long Sang Ti Chinese Curio Co. Ltd. In the ledger, Elsie de Wolfe's name appears with that of the Japanese Fan Company (ceramics) and the Edison Shop (phonograph and attachment). On top of it all Deering had his own furniture and views of appropriateness. "NEITHER BEARSKIN NOR TIGER SKIN NEEDED IN MIAMI," Chalfin wired in 1918; but they still arrived.

As organized by Chalfin, Vizcaya offered a kind of menu of different rooms – each expertly blended from European ingredients, each possessing a distinctive flavor of its own, each recalling other meals enjoyed in other places. Deciding which room to occupy meant chosing which taste to sample. If the visitor was in the mood for substantial helpings he might go to the Renaissance Hall, with its fireplace from the Château de Regnéville and tapestry depicting Hercules. Something light and delicate? That could be found in the Marie Antoinette Salon, named from the wallcoverings of Lyons silk. Plainer fare was on offer next door, in the Library or Adam Room. The Rococo Room provided the cream for dessert.

Chalfin did not feel restricted to period accuracy: he worked by eye. Having persuaded Deering to buy some Renaissance shelves for the living room, he described the way in which he would fill them.

> I should like to have some books in part of them, some flowers in vases in others, and some objects of art of interest in others. The background would be dark, probably of the very poor and worn brocade, or perhaps there might be a simple brown wood paneling.... Then, I always hoped in the course of time, you would have a few Chinese porcelains, not the most expensive kind, but beautiful ones.[16]

Color, interest, and texture were the ruling principles. Deering replied typically: "I do not like the invitation that the structure will present for further expenditures, but will not object."[17]

The quality of the detail of Chalfin's interiors was legendary. *Town and Country* wrote of the "magnificent rumors" that had been rippling through the art world for months.

> Tales were told, and they were true, of weeks spent by expert fingers constructing a grandly proportioned tassel to hang over a bed suited to its arrogance; of ancient embroideries lifted from their tattered silken foundations and applied dexterously and with infinite patience to modern textures which the skill of woman had harmoniously aged to receive the dainty burden. An infinite number of such details there were which played a part in the building up of a palatial and imposing yet joyous whole.[18]

The use of rich fabrics was an essential element of Chalfin's style, as it was of firms such as Lenygon and Morant. They helped create an atmosphere that was both sensuous and subdued. Seventeenth-century altar cloths, Louis Seize appliqués and old Sicilian skirts could be bought at such shops as the Galleria di S. Gregorio in Venice.

There was never any supposition that Vizcaya would literally reproduce any one building from the past. The eclecticism of the approach would have forbidden it, and, as Chalfin admitted, "living conditions have changed." Evidence of this was the den: it was here that Chalfin managed to hide the tiger and bearskins, and he would not have it shown or described to reporters. Another change was the revolution below stairs. Deering was anxious, not only to incorporate the best modern technology, but to consult his trusted staff as far as possible. "Baylis is anxious to have a good sized lead sink and a marble topped table in the garde manger [still room]," he wrote of his butler, "and I think we had better gratify him." A new form of electric buffing machine for silver was also investigated. On another occasion Baylis "found a particularly satisfactory clothes hanger in California" and it was reproduced, with modifications. A standard kitchen range, kept burning throughout the day, would have added intolerably to the heat, so gas was used for cooking. The housekeeper requested cloth-covered hoses for the vacuum cleaner, which would avoid marking the furniture, though after long enquiries it was discovered that the only firm that made them had gone out of business. In pursuit of efficiency Deering regularly asked his acquaintance about their domestic arrangements. "PALM BEACH FRIEND USES FIRELESS COOKER AND THERMOS BOX TO KEEP PICNIC LUNCHEON WARM," he wired Chalfin in February 1917. "PLEASE SEND SAMPLES. ALSO BOTTLES IN IMITATION OF THERMOS BOTTLES MADE OF STEEL. CANNOT GIVE NAME."

The house was finally finished in 1921. In the decade that it was being created Deering had had a great deal to live through. Whenever he had not been there the participants had fought fiercely among themselves. The cost had mounted vertiginously. He had constantly seen his own express wishes diverted into other paths. He had tried to resist the building of the casino on the grounds that it would block the view; Chalfin countered by redesigning it with an open loggia in the middle. Even in the choice of the emblem of the house he was outmaneuvered by Chalfin. Deering insisted on having a caravel – a ship of the Columbus era – as suggestive of the sea rover Viscaino; Chalfin preferred a seahorse (see Plate 264). It was a point on which Deering for once became agitated. "HAVE COUNTED TODAY 13 SEAHORSES AT AND FOR HOUSE AND ONE CARAVEL," he cabled in March 1916. Supremely resourceful, Chalfin represented this protest as an attempt to fuss an artist who was already working at full stretch. "No less than a bit of thumb-screwing," he called it. As he generally did, Deering gave way. Before the end of the war, with all new work suspended, the estate was employing no fewer than a hundred and thirty-nine men.

But now Deering was free to enjoy Vizcaya, arriving in mid-December and leaving in mid-April for the remaining four years of his life. Much of his day would be spent in the patio (see Plate 274), where he received guests. Stiffening joints made it increasingly difficult to get around the gardens, and sometimes he was in bed by six. What pleasure did the house give him? He expressed a hint of it to his accountant, William J. Lauderback, when he asked for more of his money to be taken out of International Harvester: "When I started to build a house here, I did not expect to have anything so large and important or costly as it has turned out to be. Now that I have this large undertaking, I feel that it ought to be carried through properly.... I hope I may be forgiven on all sides."[19] He in turn forgave Chalfin for leading him further than he intended; the result, he told him, would be "a triumph – mostly your triumph." They really understood each other "pretty well."[20]

After Vizcaya, Hoffman developed a successful career in New York, remembered for his glamorous theaters as well as many houses; Diego Suarez married the former Mrs. Marshall Field III; but Chalfin's star was in decline. His talents required a client with Deering's resources, personal and financial, to give them outlet, but for him there would be only one Deering. Well may he have come to reflect that Vizcaya, evocation of the age of Tiepolo, was "Augustan," for to him at least it seemed that "such work never will be done again."[21] His vision had not seemed always so lofty. Years earlier he had written to Deering: "It is the little details like gold braid that make one's life miserable."[22] To some this will point to the inner triviality of a man preoccupied with soft furnishings. To others it will confirm his obsessive quest for perfection.

NOTES TO THE TEXT

References throughout this book are to *Country Life in America*, although this periodical was known by a number of titles through the years of its publication: *Country Life in America* (1901–17); *The New Country Life* (1917–18); *Country Life in the War* (1918); *Country Life* (1919–37); *Country Life and the Sportsman* (1937–38); *Country Life* (1939–42). References to *Country Life* indicate the British magazine.

Notes to Chapter 1

1. "The Richard Morris Hunt Papers," typescript comp. Catherine H. Hunt, ed. Alan Burnham, American Institute of Architects, Washington, D.C., vol. 1, pp. 244, 288.
2. Henry James, *Henry James Letters*, vol. 4, *1895–1916*, ed. Leon Edel (Cambridge, Mass., and London, 1984), p. 348.
3. "The Builders of Biltmore," *Architectural Record* 5 (October–December 1895), p. 200.
4. *Asheville Daily Citizen*, 15 December 1889, p. 1.
5. "Builders of Biltmore," p. 201.
6. Quoted in Laura Wood Roper, *F.L.O.: A Biography of Frederick Law Olmsted* (Baltimore, 1973), p. 416.
7. Olmsted to Vanderbilt, 29 January 1891, copy, Biltmore House Archival Collection, Asheville.
8. Roper, *Biography of Olmsted*, p. 417.
9. Gifford Pinchot, *Breaking New Ground* (New York, 1947), p. 49.
10. "Farmer Vanderbilt," *Asheville News and Hotel Reporter*, 20 February 1897.
11. Olmsted to Vanderbilt, 6 July 1891, p. 4, copy, Biltmore House Archival Collection.
12. *New York Times*, 27 December 1897.
13. Elizabeth Robins and Joseph Pennell, *The Whistler Journal* (Philadelphia, 1921), p. 237.
14. Newspaper clipping, n.d., Biltmore Archive.
15. Mrs. Sarah Whitman to Richard Morris Hunt, quoted in "Hunt Papers," p. 289.
16. Olmsted, Jr., to Miss Clergue, 17 February 1895, Frederick Law Olmsted, Jr., copybook no. 3, pp. 96–99, Frederick Law Olmsted Historic Site, Brookline, Massachusetts.

Notes to Chapter 2

1. William Herbert [pseud. of Herbert Croly], *Houses for Town and Country* (New York, 1907), p. 63.
2. Barr Ferree, *American Estates and Gardens* (New York, 1904). p. 1.
3. Harry W. Desmond and Herbert Croly, *Stately Homes in America* (New York, 1903), p. 383.
4. Henry van Brunt, quoted in "The Richard Morris Hunt Papers," typescript comp. Catherine H. Hunt, ed. Alan Burnham, American Institute of Architects, Washington, D.C., vol. 1, p. 291.
5. Ferree, *Estates*, p. 1.
6. "The Development of the Country Residence of Mrs. Arthur V. Meigs, Radnor, Pennsylvania," *Country Life in America* 41 (March 1922), p. 96; reprinted in Owen Wister et al., *A Monograph of the Work of Mellor, Meigs and Howe* (New York, 1923).
7. Herbert D. Croly, "The California Country House," *Sunset Magazine* (1906); reprinted in *Architect and Engineer of California* 7 (December 1906), p. 24.
8. Marianna Griswold van Rensselaer, "American Country Dwellings—I," *Century Magazine* (May 1886), p. 3.
9. "Idlehour," *Architectural Record* 13 (May 1903), p. 461.
10. Harvey S. Firestone in collaboration with Samuel Crowther, *Men and Rubber* (Garden City, N.Y., 1926), pp. 20–21.
11. Fiske Kimball, "The American Country House," *Architectural Record* 46 (October 1919), p. 298.
12. E.L. Godkin, "The Expenditure of Rich Men," *Scribner's Magazine* 20 (October 1896), p. 500.
13. Quoted in Jan Cohn, *The Palace and the Poorhouse: The American House as a Cultural Symbol* (East Lansing, 1979), p. 28.
14. Lewis F. Allen, *Rural Architecture* (New York, 1852), p. 21.
15. Quoted in Arthur W. Calhoun, *A Social History of the American Family from Colonial Times to the Present* (Cleveland, 1919), vol. 3, p. 164.
16. Edward Payson Powell, *The Country Home* (New York, 1905), p. 15.

17. Edwin LeFevre, "Interview with Henry Morrison Flagler," *Everybody's Magazine* (c. 1910); quoted in Curtis Channing Blake, "The Architecture of Carrère and Hastings," Ph.D. diss., Columbia University (1976).
18. See Cohn, *Palace and Poorhouse*, pp. 178ff.
19. Frederika Bremer, *Homes of the New World* (London, 1853), vol. 1, p. 47.
20. A.J. Downing, *The Architecture of Country Houses* (1850; reprint ed., New York: Dover Publications, 1969), pp. 257–58.
21. John Calvin Stevens and Albert Winslow Cobb, *American Domestic Architecture* (1889; reprint ed., Watkins Glen, N.Y., 1978), p. 26.
22. Isabel Bevier, *The House: Its Plan, Decoration and Care* (Chicago, 1907), p. 129.
23. "An Influence in the Architecture of Philadelphia," *Architectural Record* 15 (February 1904) p. 121.
24. Frank Miles Day, preface to *American Country Houses of Today* (New York, 1912), p. i. See also Herbert Croly (writing as William Herbert) in *Houses for Town & Country* (New York, 1907), pp. 78–79: "The most interesting contemporary American country houses are apt to be those which cost between twenty thousand and one hundred and fifty thousand dollars."
25. Augusta Owen Patterson, "A French Farmhouse in Connecticut," *Town and Country* (1 April 1931), p. 38.
26. According to Platt's friend Barry Faulkner, quoted in Keith N. Morgan, *Charles A. Platt: The Artist as Architect* (Cambridge, Mass., and London, 1985), p. 83.
27. Royal Cortissoz, intro. to *Domestic Architecture of H.T. Lindeberg* (New York, 1940), p. xiv.
28. Matlack Price, intro. to *The Work of Dwight James Baum* (New York, 1927), unpaginated.
29. For a discussion of Schutze's sources, see Marcus Binney, "Swan House, Georgia–I and II," *Country Life* 173 (5 and 12 May 1983), pp. 1168, 1240.
30. Richard J. Neutra, quoted in William H. Jordy and Christopher P. Monkhouse with contributors, *Buildings on Paper*, exh. cat. (Providence, 1982), p. 131.
31. Edgar Kaufmann, Jr., *Fallingwater* (New York, 1986), p. 104.

Notes to Chapter 3

1. For Sunnyside, see Joseph T. Butler, *Washington Irving's Sunnyside* (Tarrytown, 1974).
2. Church to W.H. Osborn, 25 October 1867, Olana Archive, Hudson-on-Hudson, N.Y. I would like to thank James Ryan for invaluable help in guiding me through Olana and its archive and in generously sharing his immense knowledge of the house with me. For the history of Olana, see Ryan's chapter "Frederick Church's *Olana*: Architecture as Landscape as Art," in Franklin Kelly, ed., *Frederick Edwin Church*, exh. cat. (Washington, D.C., 1989).
3. Reprinted in *The Elegant Homes of America 100 Years Ago*, vol. 1, compiled by Skip Whitson from *Art*

Journals of 1876–77 (Albuquerque, 1977).
4. Church to E.D. Palmer, 22 October 1867, Erastus Dow Palmer Collection, McKinney Library, Albany Institute of History and Art.
5. Church to Osborn, 29 July 1868, Olana Archive.
6. Frank J. Bonnelle, "In Summer Time on Olana," *Boston Sunday Herald*, 7 September 1890.
7. Church to Palmer, 27 July 1870, Erastus Dow Palmer Collection, McKinney Library.
8. Church to Goodman, 21 July 1871, Olana Archive.
9. Church to Martin Johnson Heade, 24 October 1870, Heade Papers, Archives of American Art.
10. Church to Palmer, 9 May 1867, Erastus Dow Palmer Collection, McKinney Library.
11. Church to Palmer, 18 October 1884, Erastus Dow Palmer Collection, McKinney Library.
12. Church to Osborn, 31 October 1870, Olana Archive.
13. Church to Martin Johnson Heade, 24 October 1870, Heade Papers, Archives of American Art, Washington, D.C.
14. Diary of Jervis McEntee, 22 June 1873, McEntee Papers, Archives of American Art.
15. Susan Hale, *Letters of Susan Hale*, ed. Caroline P. Atkinson (Boston, 1918), pp. 141–42.
16. Church to Osborn, 4 November 1868, Olana Archive.
17. Church to Clemens, 16 December 1887, source unknown; from copy in Olana Archive.
18. Church to Osborn, 4 November 1868, Olana Archive.
19. Church to Warner, 11 September 1889, Charles Dudley Warner Manuscript Collection, Watkinson Library, Trinity College, Hartford, Connecticut.

Notes to Chapter 4

1. *Tarrytown Argus*, 30 September 1893; quoted in Albert I. Berger, "'My Father's House at Pocantico Hills': Kykuit and the Business Education of John D. Rockefeller, Jr.," typescript, 1985. I am grateful to the staff of the Rockefeller Archive Center at Pocantico Hills, and in particular to Thomas Rosenbaum for help in the preparation of this chapter.
2. *Harper's Weekly* 34 (6 September 1890), pp. 82–84.
3. Louisine Havemeyer, *Sixteen to Sixty* (New York, 1961), pp. 28–29.
4. Peter Collier and David Horowitz, *The Rockefellers: An American Dynasty* (London, 1976), p. 78.
5. Rockefeller to Manning, 4 September 1896, letterbook 42, p. 459, Rockefeller Family Archives, RG2, Office of the Messrs. Rockefeller, Pocantico Hills, N.Y. (hereafter cited as OMR).
6. ibid.
7. Rockefeller, Jr., to Aldrich, 3 December 1903, letterbook 81, p. 36, OMR.
8. Ida Tarbell, "John D. Rockefeller: A Character Study – II, "*McClure's Magazine* 25, no. 4 (August 1905), p. 387.
9. "John D. Rockefeller's Pocantico Estate," *Country Calendar* 1, no. 7 (November 1905), p. 633.
10. Rockefeller to C.V. Hemenway, 26 February 1906,

letterbook 217, p. 185, OMR.

11. Rockefeller to Rockerfeller, Jr., 3 April 1907, letterbook 220, p. 224, OMR.

12. Quoted from the typescript in John D. Rockefeller, Jr., Homes, 161, Box 33, OMR.

13. Rockefeller to Rockefeller, Jr., 28 April 1908, letterbook III, p. 319, OMR.

14. Codman to Rockefeller, Jr., 21 October 1908, John D. Rockefeller, Jr., Homes, 162, Box 23, OMR.

15. Rockefeller, Jr., to Messrs. Koopman and Co., 17 April 1908, letterbook 111, p. 130, OMR.

16. Codman to Rockefeller, Jr., 26 September 1908, John D. Rockefeller, Jr., Homes, 162, Box 23, OMR.

17. Rockefeller to Rockefeller, Jr., 18 September 1908, letterbook 224, p. 386, OMR.

18. John D. Rockefeller, Jr., "My Father's House at Pocantico Hills," typescript memoir, January 1940, Box 21, "letterbook 3," unprocessed material, OMR.

Notes to Chapter 5

1. Arthur Meeker, *Chicago, with Love* (New York, 1955), p. 88.

2. Richard Pratt, *David Adler* (New York, 1970), p. 16.

3. Deering to Chalfin, 28 November 1914, Vizcaya Archive, Miami.

4. Huntington to Hunt and Grey, 24 February 1908, Huntington Library, San Marino.

5. Charles Edward Hooper, *The Country House* (New York, 1911), p. 14.

6. Porter Garnett, *Stately Homes of California* (Boston, 1915), p. 32.

7. Interview with Mrs. Alexandra McKay, 6 June 1977, quoted in the National Register Nomination for Chelsea, Muttontown, at the Society for the Preservation of Long Island Antiquities, Setauket.

8. Mrs. Mackay to White, 24 July 1899, New-York Historical Society.

9. W.J. Ghent, *Our Benevolent Feudalism* (New York, 1902), p. 41.

10. Quoted in Richard Guy Wilson, *McKim, Mead and White, Architects* (New York, 1983), p. 155.

11. Quoted in Charles W. Snell, *Vanderbilt Mansion*, National Park Service Historical Handbook Series no. 32 (Washington, D.C., 1960), p. 7.

12. Town Topics Publishing Company, *Fads and Fancies of Representative Americans at the Beginning of the Twentieth Century* (New York, 1905), p. 84.

13. Quoted in Alan Burman, "The Architecture of Wilson Eyre, Jr.," 1953, p. 32, Wilson Eyre Collection, Avery Library, Columbia University, New York.

14. Quoted in William Franklin Fleming, *America's Match King: Ohio Columbus Barber, 1841–1920* (Barberton, Ohio, 1981), pp. 265–66.

15. Matlack Price, "The English Type," in *The Work of Dwight James Baum* (New York, 1927), unpaginated. For the racial overtones of the Colonial Revival, see William B. Rhoads, "The Colonial Revival and the Americanization of Immigrants,"

in *The Colonial Revival in America*, ed. Alan Axelrod (Winterthur, Delaware, 1985).

16. Thorstein Veblen, *The Theory of the Leisure Class* (London, 1899), pp. 136–37.

17. See Edwin P. Hoyt, *The Whitneys: An Informal Portrait, 1635–1975* (New York, 1976), p. 200.

18. Doubleday Page and Company, *The Country Life Press* (Garden City, N.Y., 1919), pp. 36–37.

19. Geoffrey T. Hellman, "Full-Length Portrait of a Country Gentleman – I, Marshall Field," *Country Life in America* 65 (April 1934), p. 42. A fuller architectural description had already been given in *Country Life in America* 52 (August 1927), pp. 49–64. For Marshall Field III, see also John Tebbel, *The Marshall Fields: A Study in Wealth* (New York, 1947).

20. Hellman, "Marshall Field," p. 42.

21. ibid.

22. Quoted in Harry W. Desmond and Herbert Croly, *Stately Homes in America* (New York, 1903), pp. 200–03.

23. R. Clipston Sturgis, "Tudor Houses," in Henry H. Saylor, ed., *Architectural Styles for Country Houses* (New York, 1919), pp. 57–58.

24. Allen W. Jackson, "The Half-Timber House," in Saylor, *Architectural Styles*, p. 82.

25. "A Large House that Looks Small," *House Beautiful* 53 (February 1923), p. 113. The architects were Cross and Cross.

26. Elizabeth H. Russell, "One House from Many," *House Beautiful* 58 (July 1925), p. 21.

27. Elizabeth Bisland, "The Building of Applegarth," *Country Life in America* 18 (October 1910), p. 657.

28. Schneider to Seiberling, 25 July 1916, photocopy of correspondence in Stan Hywet Archive, Akron.

29. Bisland, "Applegarth," p. 659.

30. "Noteworthy Houses by Well-Known Architects – I, The Residence of Allan Lehman at Tarrytown-on-the-Hudson," *House Beautiful* 45 (June 1919), p. 337. The connection between old-seeming walls and "good breeding" was also made by Paul Cret, writing of the architect George Howe's High Hollow, Chestnut Hill, Owen Wister et al., *A Monograph of the Work of Mellor, Meigs and Howe* (New York, 1923).

31. Augusta Owen Patterson, "The Residence of Mr. Samuel A. Salvage," *Town and Country* (1 May 1929), p. 59.

32. "The Residence of Carll Tucker, Esq.," *House Beautiful*, p. 372. The architects were Walker and Gillette.

33. "Salisbury House," *Country Life in America* 54 (October 1928), p. 47.

34. Edward Wenham, "Interiors of Old Wood Panelling," *International Studio* 84 (May 1926), p. 79.

35. Hearst to Morgan, 12 September 1919, quoted in Nancy E. Loe, ed., *San Simeon Revisited* (San Luis Obispo, Cal., 1987).

36. See Augusta Owen Patterson, "Mr. David Dows' Long Island Residence," *Town and Country* (15 April 1931), pp. 52–56.

37. Augusta Owen Patterson, "Mr. Hutton's New Home at Palm Beach," *Town and Country* 83 (1 May 1928), pp. 55–70.

Notes to Chapter 6

1. George William Sheldon, *Artistic Country-Seats* (New York, 1886–87; reprint ed., New York: Da Capo Press, 1979), p. 155.
2. John Cordis Baker, ed., *American Country Homes and their Gardens* (New York, 1906), intro.
3. Harry W. Desmond and Herbert Croly, *Stately Homes in America* (New York, 1903), p. 7.
4. Frank Miles Day, Preface to *American Country Houses of Today* (New York, 1912), p. ii.
5. Matlack Price, intro. and commentary to *The Work of Dwight James Baum* (New York, 1927), unpaginated.
6. Thomas Colley Grattan, *Civilized America* (London, 1859), vol. 1, p. 109.
7. Desmond and Croly, *Stately Homes*, p. 393.
8. Bar Ferree, "'The Homestead': The Home of Nathaniel Thayer, Esq., Lancaster, Massachusetts," *American Homes and Gardens* (May 1906), p. 305. Compare "Conyers Manor" by Bar Ferree, *American Homes and Gardens* 5 (November 1908), p. 419. For another description of a family compound, see Keith N. Morgan, *Charles A. Platt: The Artist as Architect* (Cambridge, Mass., and London, 1985), p. 85.
9. "The Best House of the Year," *Country Life in America* 26 (October 1914), p. 35.
10. Information from the Dosoris Park survey, Division for Historic Preservation, New York State Parks and Recreation, Albany.
11. Marianna Griswold van Rensselaer, *Art Out of Doors: Hints on Good Taste in Gardening* (New York, 1903), p. 367.
12. William Winthrop Kent, "Outdoor Living-Rooms," *Country Life in America* 4 (October 1903), p. 425.
13. van Rensselaer, *Art Out of Doors*, p. 126.
14. Henry James, *The American Scene* (London, 1907), p. 153.
15. A.J. Downing, *The Architecture of Country Houses* (1850; reprint ed., New York: Dover Publications, 1969), p. 357.
16. Rexford Newcomb, *The Colonial and Federal House* (Philadelphia, 1933), p. 87.
17. Charles Edward Hooper, *Reclaiming the Old House* (New York, 1913), p. 13.
18. Baker, *American Country Homes*, intro.
19. Joseph Dillaway Sawyer, *How to Make a Country Place* (New York, 1914), pp. 212–13.
20. Spalding to his parents, 9 January 1907, Whitehall Archive, Palm Beach.
21. George Makepeace Towle, *American Society* (London, 1870), vol. 2, p. 268.
22. Grattan, *Civilized America*, p. 105.
23. See Jill Franklin, *The Gentleman's Country House and its Plan, 1835–1914* (London, 1981), p. 110.
24. Clarence Cook, *The House Beautiful* (New York, 1881), p. 269.
25. James, *American Scene*, p. 166.
26. Sheldon, *Artistic Country-Seats* (Edwin H. Benson's house, Chestnut Hill, Pa.).
27. Mabel Tuke Priestman, "Portières for the Country House," *Country Life in America* 9 (January 1906), p. 321.
28. Fiske Kimball, "The American Country House," *Architectural Record* 46 (October 1919), p. 350.
29. See Kathryn Chapman Harwood, *The Lives of Vizcaya* (Miami, 1985), p. 149.
30. The absence of the male preserve reflects a wider social difference between America and England. As Price Collier reflected in *England and the English*, "Society is so patently ... for the women in America, that to the American it is with some awe that he sees even social matters dominated by, and adjusted to, the convenience and even the whims of the men here." However, some American country houses made provision for crowds of visiting young men. C.W. Bergner's estate at Ambler, Pennsylvania, described in *American Homes and Gardens* 1 (August 1905), p. 83, had a "dormitory," as the family called it, on the third floor.
31. Lillie Hamilton French, *The House Dignified* (New York, 1908), p. 73.
32. Charles Edward Hooper, *The Country House*, 2nd ed. (New York, 1911; 1st ed. 1904), p. 155.
33. Flagler to Stymus, 7 December 1901, Whitehall Archive.
34. Augusta Owen Patterson, "A Palm Beach House in Native Stone," *Town and Country* 84 (15 December 1929), p. 59.
35. Jacques Gréber, *L'Architecture aux États-Unis* (Paris, 1920), vol. 1, pp. 70–72.
36. The Duke of Windsor, *A King's Story* (New York, 1951), p. 199.
37. Quoted in Harvey Green, *Fit for America* (New York, 1986), p. 108.
38. Desmond and Croly, *Stately Homes*, p. 522.
39. Harriet Martineau, *Society in America* (London, 1839), vol. 3, p. 151. Cornelius Vanderbilt, Jr., *The Vanderbilt Feud: The Fabulous Story of Grace Wilson Vanderbilt* (London, 1957), p. 151.
40. Orson S. Fowler, *A Home for All; or The Gravel Wall and Octagon Mode of Building* (New York, 1853), p. 137.
41. Quoted in Jan Cohn, *The Palace and the Poorhouse: The American Home as a Cultural Symbol* (East Lansing, 1979), p. 84.
42. Louis H. Gibson, *Convenient Houses* (New York, 1889), p. 24.
43. Gréber, *L'Architecture*, p. 44.
44. *House and Garden* 29 (January 1916), p. 39. For an account of the technology in contemporary English country houses, see Clive Aslet, *The Last Country Houses* (New Haven and London, 1982), pp. 100–17; this also contains a section on the servant problem (pp. 85–99).
45. Estelle H. Ries, "Closets – and More Closets," *Country Life in America* 42 (June 1922), p. 71.
46. Mary Elizabeth Carter, *Millionaire Households* (New York, 1903), pp. 28–29.
47. ibid., pp. 246–47.
48. William Cobbett, *A Year's Residence in the United States of America*, 3rd ed. (London, 1822), p. 192.
49. H.J. Habakkuk, *American and British Technology in the Nineteenth Century* (Cambridge, 1962), p. 196. See also S.B. Saul, ed., *Technological Change: The United States and Britain in the Nineteenth Century* (London, 1970).
50. Huto Munsterberg, *The Americans*, trans. Edwin B.

Holt (London, 1904), p. 540.

51. Grattan, *Civilized America*, vol. 2, p. 54.
52. Quoted in Arthur W. Calhoun, *A Social History of the American Family* (Cleveland, 1919), vol. 3, p. 185.
53. Carter, *Millionaire Households*, p. 181.
54. Lucy Maynard Salmon, *Domestic Service*, 2nd ed. (New York and London, 1901), p. 71.
55. Augustus D. Shepard, *Camps in the Woods* (New York, 1931), pp. 19–20.
56. "Servants and Sanitation," a note by Charles F. Wingate in "The Country House" section, *Country Life in America* 15 (January 1909).
57. Day, in *Houses of Today*, p. iv.
58. Cecil F. Baker, "What Every Kitchen Needs," *House and Garden* 28 (October 1915), p. 35.
59. Charles Schneider to Frank S. Seiberling, 7 December 1916, Stan Hywet Archive, Akron.
60. Cook, *House Beautiful*, p. 219.
61. A longer description of Nemours can be found in Clive Aslet, "Nemours, Delaware, USA," *Country Life* 183 (12 October 1989), pp. 92–97.

Notes to Chapter 7

1. Office of the General Passenger Agent, *Suburban Stations and Rural Homes on the Pennsylvania Railroad* (Philadelphia, 1874).
2. "The Paoli Local," verse by Christopher Morley from *Essays* (New York, 1918); quoted by Tello J. d'Apéry, *Overbrook Farms* (Overbrook Farms, 1936), p. 57.
3. Arthur Meeker, *Chicago, with Love* (New York, 1955), pp. 93–94.
4. The Rev. S.F. Hotchkin, *Rural Pennsylvania* (Philadelphia, 1897), p. 17.
5. ibid., p. 130.
6. Town Topics Publishing Company, *Fads and Fancies of Representative Americans at the Beginning of the Twentieth Century* (New York, 1905), p. 35.
7. Hotchkin, *Rural Pennsylvania*, p. 173.
8. Quoted in Suzanne G. Lindsay, *Mary Cassatt and Philadelphia*, exh. cat. (Philadelphia, 1985), p. 14.
9. Quoted in Frederick A. Sweet, *Miss Mary Cassatt* (Norman, Okla., 1966), p. 55.
10. Moses King, *Philadelphia and Notable Philadelphians* (New York, 1902), unpaginated.
11. John F. Harbeson, "Wilson Eyre, 1858–1944," *Journal of the American Institute of Architects* (March 1946), p. 133.
12. Joseph Hergesheimer, *From an Old House* (New York, 1925), pp. 45–46.
13. Joseph Hergesheimer, intro. to Philip B. Wallace, *Colonial Houses: Philadelphia, Pre-Revolutionary Period* (New York, 1931), unpaginated.

Notes to Chapter 8

1. E. McClung Fleming, "History of the Winterthur Estate," in *The Winterthur Story*, excerpts from *Winterthur Portfolio 1* (Winterthur, 1965), p. 20. I must repeat my thanks to John A.H. Sweeney for his hospitality at Winterthur and for guiding me so generously through its rooms and memories.

2. ibid., p. 21.
3. Jonathan L. Fairbanks, "The Architectural Development of Winterthur House," in *The Winterthur Story*, excerpts from *Winterthur Portfolio 1* (Winterthur, 1965), p. 86.
4. Fleming, "Winterthur Estate," p. 29.
5. Jay E. Cantor, *Winterthur* (New York, 1985), p. 92.
6. Fleming, "Winterthur Estate," p. 30.
7. Cantor, *Winterthur*, p. 92.
8. ibid., p. 77.
9. See John Cornforth, "Beauport, Gloucester, Massachusetts – I and II," *Country Life* 172 (28 October 1982), pp. 1318–21, and 172 (4 November 1982), pp. 1399–1403.
10. Theodore Sizer, "Our Golden Anniversary," *Walpole Society Note Book* (1960), p. 12.
11. Du Pont to Benkard, 22 July 1935, Winterthur Archive.
12. Du Pont to Thomas T. Waterman, 24 February 1935, Winterthur Archive.
13. Du Pont to Lloyd Hyde, 6 October 1927, Winterthur Archive.
14. Augusta Owen Patterson, "Colonel H.H. Rogers' 'Port of Missing Men'," *Town and Country* (15 September 1926), p. 54.
15. Sleeper to Du Pont, 2 September 1924, Winterthur Archive.
16. Cantor, *Winterthur*, p. 39.
17. ibid., pp. 32–35.
18. Waterman to du Pont, 31 July 1936, Winterthur Archive.
19. Waterman to du Pont, 3 September 1935, Winterthur Archive.
20. Du Pont to Waterman, 4 September 1935, Winterthur Archive.
21. John A.H. Sweeney, "The Evolution of Winterthur Rooms," in *The Winterthur Story*, excerpts from *Winterthur Portfolio 1* (Winterthur, 1965), p. 109.
22. ibid., pp. 117–120.
23. Cantor, *Winterthur*, p. 152.

Notes to Chapter 9

1. Barr Ferree, *American Estates and Gardens* (New York, 1904), pp. 1–2.
2. "The Lighting of Dreamwold Hall," *House and Garden* 7 (April 1905), p. 204. The buildings at Dreamwold were described at length in the *Architectural Review* and I am grateful to Robert McKay for showing me the specially bound copy of this article which exists at the Society for the Preservation of Long Island Antiquities, Setauket.
3. See Adam Hochschild, *Half the Way Home* (New York, 1986), pp. 43–44.
4. Brendan Gill, *Many Masks: A Life of Frank Lloyd Wright* (London, 1987), p. 48.
5. Edward Payson Powell, *The Country Home* (New York, 1905), p. 328.
6. Henry Hudson Holly, *Holly's Country Seats* (New York, 1866), p. 22.
7. John Burroughs, "Picturesque Aspects of Farm Life in New York," *Scribner's Magazine* (November 1878), p. 54.
8. Joseph Dillaway Sawyer, *How to Make a Country*

Place (New York, 1914), pp. 31–33.

9. See Tom Pyle, told to Beth day, *Pocantico: Fifty Years on the Rockefeller Domain* (New York, 1964), p. 9.

10. Several of the buildings of Beauty Ranch, including the ruins of Wolf House, survive in what is now the Jack London State Historic Park. The development of the ranch is described in Homer L. Haughey and Connie Kale Johnson, *Jack London Ranch Album* (Stockton, Cal., 1985).

11. See L.H. Bailey, "The Making of Clean Milk" (a description of Brookside Dairy Farm), *Country Life in America* 6 (June 1904), pp. 170–72; and Edgar Mayhew Bacon, "The Inspiration of a Great Farm," *Country Life in America* 2 (May 1902), pp. 12–15.

12. "Stormfield: Mark Twain's New Country Home," *Country Life in America* 15 (April 1909), p. 608.

13. W.B. Cleveland, "Using the Porch All Winter," *Country Life in America* 13 (December 1907), p. 211.

14. Gervase Wheeler, *Rural Homes* (New York, 1851), p. 14.

15. Town Topics Publishing Company, *Fads and Fancies of Representative Americans at the Beginning of the Twentieth Century* (New York, 1905), p. 105.

16. ibid., p. 41.

17. Robert V. Hoffman, "The Country Gentleman of To-day," *Country Life in America* 61 (January 1932), p. 65.

18. Barr Ferree, "Notable American Homes: 'Woodcrest,' the Estate of James W. Paul, Jr., Esq., Radnor, Pennsylvania," *American Homes and Gardens* 1 (September 1905), p. 163.

19. The Rev. S.F. Hotchkin, *Rural Pennsylvania* (Philadelphia, 1897), p. 201.

20. Arthur Meeker, *Chicago, with Love* (New York, 1955), p. 91.

21. For a description of George Washington Vanderbilt's farming activities, see George F. Weston, "Biltmore," *Country Life in America* 2 (September 1902), p. 180.

22. Henry I. Hazleton, "Shelburne Farms," *New England Magazine* 25 (November 1901), p. 274. See also Edwin C. Powell, "Shelburne Farms: An Ideal Country Place", *Country Life in America* 3 (February 1903), pp. 152–56.

23. Newspaper cutting, probably from the *Troy Times*, in one of the scrapbooks at Shelburne Farms. I am grateful to Megan Camp for her assistance in consulting this resource.

24. "Reynolda Farm, Splendid Country Estate of Mrs. R.J. Reynolds: Its Origins and Development, and the Aims of its Owner," *Twin-City Sentinel*, 7 July 1917, quoted in Margaret Supplee Smith, "Reynolda: A Rural Vision in an Industrializing South." I am most grateful to Professor Smith of Wake Forest University for showing me this unpublished manuscript.

25. Reynolds to Keen, 5 July 1912, quoted in Smith, "Reynolda," n. 69.

26. Ohio C. Barber, *Anna Dean Farm, Barberton, Ohio* (n.d.), p. 14.

27. Alfred Hopkins, "The Farm Group of Mr. James Speyer, Scarboro, New York," *Country Life in America* 25 (March 1914), p. 73.

28. T.C. Turner, "A Group of Farm Cottages," *American Homes and Gardens* 11 (May 1914), p. 160.

29. Alfred Hopkins, "Farm Barns," *Architectural Review* (September 1902), p. 243.

30. Radclyffe Dugmore, "The Oaks: A Long Island Seaside Estate," *Country Life in America* 4 (July 1903), pp. 202–03.

31. Arthur J. Meigs, *An American House* (New York, 1925), p. xiii.

Notes to Chapter 10

1. Part of an "impression" from the Lenox correspondent of a Chicago newspaper, quoted in Clark W. Bryan, *The Book of Berkshire* (Great Barrington, Mass., n.d.), p. 51. For a survey of the past and present history of the country houses here, see Carole Owens, *The Berkshire Cottages: A Vanishing Era* (Englewood Cliffs, N.J. 1984).

2. N.H. Eggleston, "A New England Village," *Harper's New Monthly Magazine* 43 (November 1871), p. 816.

3. Catherine M. Sedgwick, *A New England Tale* (New York, 1852), p. 59.

4. Various Writers, *Houses of American Authors* (New York, 1854).

5. Mallary DeWitt, Lenox and the Berkshire Highlands (1902), p. 204.

6. Charles Dudley Warner, *A Little Journey in the World* (New York and London, 1889), p. 270.

7. See Lila S. Parrish, *A History of Searles Castle in Great Barrington, Massachusetts* (Great Barrington, 1985). The alterations made after Searles had married Mrs. Hopkins were almost certainly designed by Henry Vaughan; see William Morgan, *The Almighty Wall* (Cambridge, Mass., and London, 1983), pp. 139–41.

8. Quoted from the manuscript "The History of Blantyre" by Mark Farrington, based in part on material gathered in a report by Carolanne Gervasi, 1984. Consulted at Blantyre, which is now a hotel.

9. For this and the history of the Stokes family, see Phyllis B. Dodge, *Tales of the Phelps-Dodge Family* (New York, 1987).

10. Edith Wharton, *The Writing of Fiction* (New York, 1925), p. 10. For a brilliant discussion of Wharton's response to buildings, see Judith Fryer, *Felicitous Space* (Chapel Hill, N.C., and London, 1986), pp. 65–94.

11. Edith Wharton, *A Backward Glance* (New York, 1934), p. 124.

12. According to *Berkshire Resort Topics*, 10 September 1904.

13. Wharton, *Backward Glance*, p. 125.

14. *Berkshire Resort Topics*, 10 September 1904.

15. Codman to Mrs. Codman, 8 October 1902, Codman Family Papers, Society for the Preservation of New England Antiquities, Boston.

16. R.W.B. Lewis, *Edith Wharton: A Biography* (London, 1975), p. 143.

17. Frederick Vanderbilt Field, *From Right to Left: An Autobiography* (Westport, Conn., 1983), p. 24.

18. ibid., p. 21.

19. Beatrice Bishop Berle, *A Life in Two Worlds* (New

York, 1983), p. 12.

20. Quoted in Morgan Bulkeley, *The Choats at Naumkeag*, published by the Trustees of Reservations Concerning the Massachusetts Landscape, who now own Naumkeag.

21. E.L.D. Seymour, "How the Lenox Folk are Helping to Win," *Country Life in America* 35 (November 1918), pp. 54–57.

Notes to Chapter 11

1. The Duke of Windsor, *A King's Story* (New York, 1951), p. 200.
2. Barr Ferree, *American Estates and Gardens* (New York, 1904), p. 35.
3. Quoted in Harvey Green, *Fit for America* (New York, 1986), p. 183.
4. Taylor Scott Hardin, "A 'Pleasure Dome' at Southampton," *Town and Country* (1 July 1931), pp. 32–35.
5. Emily Kimbrough, "Mansions on the Hudson," *Country Life in America* 74 (August 1938), p. 51.
6. Edith Wharton, *The Fruit of the Tree* (New York, 1907), p. 342.
7. "New Sports Building for Mrs. Vincent Astor at Rhinecliffe, N.Y.," *Country Life in America* 28 (November 1915), p. 38.
8. John D. Rockefeller, Jr., Homes, 161, Box 36, folder: Playhouse Group, Rockefeller Family Archives, OMR III.
9. Augusta Owen Patterson, "The Decorative Arts," *Town and Country* (1 August 1931), p. 38.
10. Ethel McCall Head, "Sports Plaza in the Ojai Valley," *Country Life in America* 75 (January 1939), p. 76.
11. Robert H. van Court, "The Bathing Pool and the Country House," *House and Garden* 26 (August 1914), p. 79.
12. "Mr. Payne Whitney's Home at Manhasset," *Town and Country* 70 (1 February 1915), p. 30.
13. Augusta Owen Patterson, "Important Sculpture in a Modern Garden," *Town and Country* 81 (1 October 1926), p. 63.
14. Augusta Owen Patterson, "A Private Beach House and Swimming Pool," *Town and Country* 84 (15 November 1929), pp. 64–69.
15. *Leslie's Popular Monthly* (January 1895), p. 15.
16. "How to Buy a Country House on Long Island," *Country life in America* 8 (May 1905), p. 124.
17. For Thomasville, see William R. Mitchell, Jr., *Landmarks: The Architecture of Thomasville and Thomas County, Georgia, 1920–1980* (Thomasville, 1980). I am grateful to Nancy Tinker for her help in discovering this fascinating community.
18. "The Richard Morris Hunt Papers," typescript comp. Catherine H. Hunt, ed. Alan Burnham, American Institute of Architects, Washington, D.C., vol. 1, p. 244.
19. James Fullarton Muirhead, *The Land of Contrasts* (London, 1900), p. 119.
20. The Rev. S.F. Hotchkin, *Rural Pennsylvania* (Philadelphia, 1897), p. 141.
21. Theodore Roosevelt, "Cross-Country Riding in America," *Century Magazine* 32 (July 1886), p. 335.

22. Published in "Hunting Letters of Theodore Roosevelt," *Country Life in America* 41 (December 1921), pp. 54–55.
23. See Harry T. Peters, *Just Hunting* (New York, 1935), pp. 2, 36; see also Roosevelt, "Cross-Country Riding," p. 335.
24. Quoted in M. Christina Geis, *Georgian Court: An Estate of the Gilded Age* (Philadelphia, 1982), p. 74.
25. Duke of Windsor, *King's Story*, p. 198.
26. Robert McClure, *The Gentleman's Stable Guide* (Philadelphia, 1870), p. 17.
27. Henry William Herbert, *Hints to Horse-keepers* (New York, 1863), pp. 139–40.
28. Francis M. Ware, "Stables and their Essentials," *Architectural Review* (September 1902), p. 236.
29. James Fullarton Muirhead, *The Land of Contrasts* (London, 1900), p. 120.
30. Richard V.N. Gambrill and James C. Mackenzie, *Sporting Stables and Kennels* (New York, 1935), pp. 12ff.
31. ibid., p. 12.
32. The description of Gould is from *Munsey's Magazine* 23 (June 1900), pp. 305–07, quoted in Geis, *Georgian Court*. Geis also describes in detail the stabling and other horse arrangments. The casino at Georgian Court can be compared to the riding academies of Alfred G. and Reginald C. Vanderbilt: see "Two Riding Academies," *Architectural Record* 21 (March 1907), pp. 229ff.
33. Gambrill and Mackenzie, *Sporting Stables*, p. 5.
34. *South Side Signal*, 22 July 1871, quoted in *The Old Oakdale History*, vol. 1, published by the William K. Vanderbilt Historical Society of Dowling College (Oakdale, Long Island, 1983).
35. Robert V. Hoffman, "Racing on a Private Estate," *Country Life in America* 66 (August 1934), p. 69.
36. Edith Wharton, *The Reef* (London, 1912), p. 137.
37. Quoted in Zachary Studenroth, project coordinator, *Eagle's Nest, Historic Structures Report*, Society for the Preservation of Long Island Antiquities, Setauket (September 1982), p. 37.
38. ibid., p. 35.
39. Augusta Owen Patterson, "A Rambling Spanish House on Long Island," *Town and Country* 83 (15 October 1928), p. 45.
40. William Phillips Comstock, comp. *Garages and Motor Boat House* (New York, 1911), p. 91.
41. "Commuting by Water", *Country Life in America* 52 (October 1927), p. 69.
42. H. Hamilton Gay, "Ladies of the Air," *Country Life in America* 60 (September 1931), p. 42.
43. "Margrove: An Aviator's Home at Mill Neck, Long Island," *Country Life in America* 60 (April 1932), pp. 57–60.
44. Mackay to White, 3 November 1902, New-York Historical Society.

Notes to Chapter 12

1. Journals and diaries of Litchfield Park, Tupper Lake, New York, preserved at Adirondack Museum, Blue Mountain Lake.
2. *The Aristocrats, Being the Impressions of the Lady Helen Pole during her sojourn in the Great North Woods*

as spontaneously recorded in her letters to her friend it. North Britain, the Countess of Edge and Ross, 6th ed. (London and New York, 1901), p. 10.

3. William James, *The Letters of William James*, ed. Kisson Henry James (Boston, 1926), vol. 2, pp. 75–76.

4. Quoted in Harvey H. Kaiser, *Great Camps of the Adirondacks* (Boston, 1982), p. 31.

5. Quoted in Frank Graham, Jr., *The Adirondack Park: A Political History* (New York, 1978), p. 43.

6. Alice M. Kellogg, "Luxurious Adirondack Camps," *Broadway Magazine* 21 (August 1908), p. 208.

7. William Dix, editor of *Town and Country*, quoted in Kaiser, *Great Camps*, p. 58.

8. Henry Wellington Wack, "Kamp Kill Kare," *Field and Stream* 7 (February 1903), p. 653.

9. Harvey Ellis, "An Adirondack Camp," *The Craftsman* 4 (July 1903), p. 281.

10. Kellogg, "Adirondack Camps," p. 209.

11. Emily Post, *Etiquette* (New York, 1922), p. 445.

12. Quoted in Craig A. Gilborn, "Oh for a Lodge in Some Vast Wilderness," *Nineteenth Century* 2 (Summer 1976), p. 26.

13. Quoted in Marcus Binney, "Luxury in the Wilds," *Country Life* 169 (2 April 1981), p. 868.

14. *Aristocrats*, p. 88.

15. Martin V.B. Ives, *Through the Adirondacks in Eighteen Days* (New York, 1899), p. 91.

16. Kellogg, "Adirondack Camps," p. 208.

17. Marc Cook, *The Wilderness Cure* (New York, 1881), pp. 30–31.

18. Robert H. van Court, "Vacation Homes in the Woods," *Independent*, n.d., p. 1240, cutting in the library of Adirondack Museum.

19. Mildred Phelps Stokes Hooker, *Camp Chronicles* (Blue Mountain Lake, N.Y., 1964), p. 36.

20. Chilson D. Aldrich, *The Real Log Cabin* (New York, 1928).

21. Cutting in the library of Adirondack Museum.

22. Kathrin S. Hochschild, *The Walter Hochschild Camp at Eagle Nest* (Blue Mountain Lake, N.Y. 1975), unpaginated.

23. Ellis, "Adirondack Camp," p. 283.

24. Hochschild, *Hochschild Camp*.

25. Craig Gilborn, *Durant* (Blue Mountain Lake, N.Y., 1981), p. 100.

26. ibid., p. 105.

27. ibid.

28. Kellogg, "Adirondack Camp," p. 208.

29. Conrad E. Meinecke, *Your Cabin in the Woods* (Buffalo, 1945).

30. Davis, McGrath and Shepard, Architects, "An Adirondack Lodge on Lake Wilbert, Franklin County, New York," *House and Garden* 12 (December 1907), p. 206.

31. Wack, "Kill Kare," pp. 656–58.

32. Edward Livingston Trudeau, *An Autobiography* (New York, 1916), p. 91.

Notes to Chapter 13

1. Lillie Hamilton French, "Adirondack Camps," *Harper's Bazaar* 32 (16 September 1899), p. 775.

2. Alice M. Kellogg, "Luxurious Adirondack Camps," *Broadway Magazine* 21 (August 1908), p. 209. August D. Shepard, *Camps in the Woods* (New York, 1931), p. 12.

3. Clarence Cook, *The House Beautiful* (New York, 1881), p. 267.

4. Frederick N. Reed, "The Problem of the Sleeping Porch," *House and Garden* 25 (June 1914), p. 462.

5. Aymar Embury II, *The Livable House* (New York, 1917), p. 126.

6. Wilson Eyre, "The Planning of Country Houses," intro. to *Detached Dwellings, Country and Suburban* (New York, 1909), unpaginated.

7. George William Sheldon, ed., *Artistic Country-Seats* (New York, 1886–87; reprint ed., New York, 1979), p. 110.

8. Joseph Dillaway Sawyer, *How to Make a Country Place* (New York, 1914), p. 227.

9. *Town and Country* 82 (15 February 1928), pp. 48–49.

10. "Eighteenth Century Furniture in a modern House," *International Studio* 95 (April 1930), p. 45.

11. Jacques Gréber, *L'Architecture aux Etats-Unis* (Paris, 1920), pp. 37–39.

12. *Architectural Record* 27 (June 1910), p. 64.

13. Alfred Hopkins, "Building for Sunshine and Fresh Air," *Country Life in America* 51 (November 1926), pp. 62–64.

14. "'El Fueidis' at Monetecito, California," *House and Garden* 4 (September 1903), p. 101. See also "A House Built Around a Garden," *Country Life in America* 8 (October 1905), p. 617.

15. Charles F. Lummis, "The Greatest California Patio House," *Country Life in America* 6 (1904), p. 537.

16. For a longer description of the Hacienda de Pozo da Verona, see Richard Longstreth, *On the Edge of the World* (Cambridge, Mass., 1983), pp. 279–86.

17. "House Built Around a Garden," p. 617.

18. Augusta Owen Patterson, "An Important Palm Beach Residence," *Town and Country* (1 December 1926), p. 69.

19. See Augusta Owen Patterson, "A Portfolio of California Homes and Gardens," *Town and Country* 81 (15 January 1927), p. 49.

20. Barr Ferree, *American Estates and Gardens* (New York, 1904), p. 105.

21. Flagler to Carrère and Hastings, 12 February 1901, Whitehall Archive, Miami.

22. *New York Herald*, 30 March 1902.

23. Flagler to W.P. Stymus, 10 December 1901, Whitehall Archive.

24. Ferree, *American Estates*, p. 115.

25. Henry James, *The American Scene* (London, 1907), p. 447.

26. Flagler to the Rev. Charles S. Stevens, n.d., Whitehall Archive.

27. Spalding to Flagler, 9 January 1907, Whitehall Archive.

28. Kenneth L. Roberts, *Sun Hunting* (Indianapolis, 1922), p. 30.

29. See Donald W. Curl, *Mizner's Florida* (Cambridge, Mass., and London, 1985).

30. Augusta Owen Patterson, "An Important Palm Beach Residence," *Town and Country* (1 December 1926), p. 68.

31. Quoted in Curl, *Mizner's Florida*, p. 131.
32. *Vogue* (April 1925), reprinted in *Palm Beach Times*, 31 May 1925, p. 1.
33. Henry Ringling North and Alden Hatch, *The Circus Kings* (New York, 1960), p. 202.
34. Smith and Elliott, *Illustrations of Napa County California with Historical Sketch* (Oakland, 1878; reprint ed., Fresno: Valley Publications, n.d.), intro.
35. Mrs. Tillie Kanaga and Capt. W.F. Wallace, *History of Napa County, California* (Oakland, 1901), p. 17.
36. Herbert D. Croly, "The California Country House," reprinted in *The Architect and Engineer of California* 7 (December 1906), p. 26.
37. Porter Garnett, *Stately Homes of California* (Boston, 1915).
38. Charles H. Cheney, preface to H. Philip Staats, ed., *California Architecture in Santa Barbara* (New York, 1929), p. vii.
39. Croly, "California Country House," p. 32.
40. Lillie Langtry (Lady de Bathe), *The Days I Knew* (London, 1925), quoted in Joan Parry Dutton, *They Left Their Mark* (St. Helena, Cal., 1983), p. 67.
41. See Laurence R. Bourne, *Dude Ranching: A Complete History* (Albuquerque, 1983).
42. Hearst to Julia Morgan, 21 December 1919, quoted in Nancy E. Loe, ed., *San Simeon Revisited* (San Luis Obispo, Cal., 1987), unpaginated.
43. ibid.
44. A vivid contemporary description of life at San Simeon can be found in "Hearst at Home," *Fortune* (May 1931). See also Thomas R. Aidala, *Hearst Castle: San Simeon* (New York, 1981), and Sara Holmes Boutelle, *Julia Morgan, Architect* (New York, 1988).
45. "A Ranch in the Hills of California, belonging to King C. Gillette, Esq.," *Country Life in America* 59 (December 1930), p. 45.
46. "A Ranch in the Hills: The Estate of E.L. Doheny, Esq., in California," *Country Life in America* 61 (March 1932), p. 50.
47. Wallace Neff, Jr., comp. and ed., *Wallace Neff* (Santa Barbara, 1986), p. 15.
48. Martha B. Darbyshire, "Ranching it in Santa Ynez." *Country Life in America* 68 (September 1935), p. 14.
49. ibid., p. 84.

Notes to Chapter 14

1. Mrs. John King van Rensselaer, *Newport: Our Social Capital* (Philadelphia and London, 1905), p. 22.
2. Katherine G. Busbey, *Home Life in America* (London, 1910), p. 329.
3. ibid., p. 335.
4. Ward McAllister, *Society as I Have Found It* (New York, 1890), p. 363.
5. van Rensselaer, *Newport*, p. 33.
6. Memoirs of Mary Edith Powell, Historical Society of Newport Country, Newport.
7. George C. Mason, *Newport Illustrated* (Newport, 1875).
8. Walter Barrett, *The Old Merchants of New York City* (New York, 1872), vol. 2, p. 299.
9. William P. Clark, *Newport, and the Resorts of Narragansett Bay* (1877), quoted in old Chateau-sur-Mer guidebook.
10. Henry James, *The American Scene* (London, 1907), p. 224.
11. B.H. Friedman, *Gertrude Vanderbilt Whitney* (Garden City, N.Y., 1978), p. 93.
12. Charles Edward Hooper, *The Country House* (New York, 1911), p. 15. I would like to take this opportunity of repeating my thanks to Earle G. Shettleworth, Jr., without whose generous help in (at times) literally ferrying me and my wife around the coast of Maine this section could not have been written.
13. Robert Haven Schauffler, "Unique Mount Desert," *Century Magazine* 82, no. 4 (August 1911), p. 490.
14. M.F. Sweetser, *Chisholm's Mount-Desert Guide-Book* (Portland, n.d.), p. 13.
15. ibid., p. 47.
16. Joe M. Chapple, "Golden-Rod Days in Maine," *National Magazine* 24 (September 1904), unpaginated.
17. Charles W. Eliot, *The Right Development of Mount Desert* (privately printed, 1904), p. 1.
18. B.F. DeCosta, *Rambles in Mount Desert* (New York, 1871), p. 11.
19. Schauffler, "Mount Desert," p. 478.
20. Sweetser, *Chisholm's Mount-Desert*, p. 18.
21. *The Coast of Maine: Campobello to the Isle of Shoals* (Boston: Henry G. Peabody, 1889), unpaginated.
22. Schauffler, "Mount Desert," p. 482.
23. *The Front Door-Yard of Our Country, and What it Contains* (Boston, 1888), p. 28.
24. "Mount Desert," *Harper's New Monthly Magazine* 45 (August 1872), p. 322.
25. DeCosta, *Mount Desert*, p. 152.
26. Schauffler, "Mount Desert," p. 482.
27. *Bar Harbor Record*, souvenir ed. (July 1896), p. 25. For the history of Bar Harbor, see Richard Walden Hale, Jr., *The Story of Bar Harbor* (New York, 1949).
28. W.H. Sherman, *Sherman's Bar Harbor Guide* (Bar Harbor, 1890), p. 47.
29. An old summer resident, *Northeast Harbor Reminiscences* (White and Horne Company, 1930), p. 37.
30. ibid., p. 82.
31. Earle G. Shettleworth, *The Summer Cottages of Isleboro, 1890–1930* (Isleboro, Maine, 1989), pp. 61–64.
32. Gibson to Arthur P. Webster, 10 December 1903, Gibson Collection, Maine Historic Preservation Commission.
33. Frederick Law Olmsted, *Report and Advice of Frederick Law Olmsted, for the Development and Improvement of Cushing's Island, Maine* (Brookline, Mass., 1883), unpaginated.
34. Dakers to Stevens, letters in the Maine Historic Preservation Commission.
35. Robert and Agnes Hale, *Cushing's Island: Two Memoirs* (privately printed, c. 1971), p. 14.
36. Frenchman's Bay and Mount Desert Land and Water Company, Directors' Annual Report, 1889, p. 8.
37. John Calvin Stevens and Albert Winslow Cobb, *American Domestic Architecture* (New York, 1889; reprint ed. with new introd. by Earle G. Shettleworth, Jr., and William David Barry, Watkins

Glen, N.Y., 1979), pp. 26–27.

38. ibid., intro.

39. Louise de Koven Bowen, *Baymeath* (privately printed, 1944), p. 50.

40. *New York Times*, 19 April 1892, p. 10. I have given a longer account of Jekyll Island in "America's 'Winter Newport'." *Country Life* 176 (27 September 1984), pp. 834–37, and "Changing Enthusiasms," *Country Life* 176 (4 October 1984), pp. 947–50. Since this book went to press my attention has been drawn to *The Jekyll Island Club* by Bart and June McCash (Athens, Ga., 1989). I have used the modern spelling of Jekyll Island, which had only one *l* in the early days of the club.

41. Louis Torres, *Cumberland Island National Seashore, Georgia, and Historic Structure Report: Historical Data Section of the Dungeness Area,* National Park Service's Historic Resource Study (Denver, November 1977).

Notes to Chapter 15

1. Paul Chalfin, "The Interiors at 'Vizcaya': A Description of their Color and Style," *Architectural Review* (July 1917), p. 143. This issue of the *Architectural Review* is entirely devoted to Vizcaya. I am grateful to Doris Littlefield for reading the draft of this chapter.

2. Kathryn Chapman Harwood, *The Lives of Vizcaya* (Miami, 1985), p. 222.

3. James T. Maher, *The Twilight of Splendor* (Boston, 1975), p. 208.

4. ibid., p. 163.

5. Chalfin, "Interiors at 'Vizcaya'," p. 141.

6. Harwood, *Lives of Vizcaya*, p. 21.

7. ibid., p. 26.

8. Chalfin to Hoffman, 10 June 1914, Vizcaya Archive, Miami.

9. Chalfin to John B. Orr, 10 May 1917, reproduced in an advertisement in *Architectural Review* (July 1917), p. ix.

10. Deering to Chalfin, Vizcaya Archive.

11. Deering to Chalfin, 16 December 1919, Vizcaya Archive.

12. Paul Chalfin, "Vizcaya,' the Villa and the Grounds: A House at Miami, Florida," *Architectural Review* (July 1917), p. 123.

13. Chalfin to Levy, 23 February 1915, Vizcaya Archive.

14. "Architect Tells How Deering Planned Vizcaya Estate," *Miami Herald*, 9 December 1934.

15. Chalfin, "Interiors at 'Vizcaya'," p. 141.

16. Chalfin to Deering, 14 August 1919, Vizcaya Archive.

17. Deering to Chalfin, 26 August 1919, Vizcaya Archive.

18. William Paterson, "A Florida Echo of the Glory of Old Venice," *Town and Country* (20 July 1917), p. 23.

19. Harwood, *Lives of Vizcaya*, pp. 80–81.

20. ibid., p. 9.

21. Paul Chalfin, "Vizcaya Represents Inimitable Augustan Era of Rome ...," *Miami Herald*, 30 December 1934.

22. Harwood, *Lives of Vizcaya*, p. 220.

INDEX

293

296

297

298

PHOTOGRAPHIC ACKNOWLEDGMENTS

Adirondack Museum, Blue Mountain Lake, New York, 197, 198, 199, 201, 202, 207, 208, 209

The Athenaeum of Philadelphia, 21, 107, 110

Avery Library, New York, 158, 164, 165

Barberton Library, Ohio, 131

H.K. Barnett, 178

Biltmore House, Asheville, North Carolina, 3, 4, 10, 11, 12, 13, 14, 15, 16, 96

Michael Boys, 77, 86, 98, 99, 103, 104, 105, 106, 108, 109, 111, 112, 140, 163, 167, 186

State of California Department of Parks and Recreation, 234

Richard Cheek, 27, 64, 68, 118, 179, 191, 238, 239

Courtesy, Henry Francis du Pont Winterthur Museum Library, Winterthur, Delaware:
    Collection of Printed Books, 114, 115, 116, 117, 119, 120, 121, 122, 123
    Winterthur Archives, 135, 136, 137, 138

Mark Fiennes, half-title, 5, 6, 7, 8, 9, 26, 29, 31, 37, 38, 39, 42, 43, 44, 45, 58, 59, 61, 62, 63, 67,
    69, 78, 79, 80, 94, 125, 133, 141, 146, 151, 153, 154, 155, 166, 175, 176, 184, 196, 200, 203, 204,
    206, 210, 212, 218, 219, 222, 223, 227, 228, 229, 230, 231, 232, 233, 235, 237, 259, 260, 261,
    263, 264, 265, 269, 270, 271, 273, 274, 275

The Henry Morrison Flagler Museum, Palm Beach, Florida, 24, 220, 221

Hicks Nurseries Inc., New York, 23

Henry E. Huntington Library and Art Gallery, San Marino, California, 225

Jekyll Island Museum, Georgia, 249, 250, 251, 253, 256

Lenox Library, Massachusetts, 152, 156, 216

Maine Historic Preservation Commission, Augusta, 241, 242, 243, 244, 245, 246, 247, 248

Van Martin, 252, 254, 255, 257, 258

Moss Archives, Seabright, New Jersey, title-page, 169, 180; 181, 189, 190

Gabriel Moulin Studios, San Francisco, 226

National Trust for Historic Preservation, Washington, D.C., 19, 20, 161, 173, 211

The Metropolitan Museum of Art, New York. Gift of Estate of Ogden Codman, Jr., 1951, 92
    (51.644.80.9), 93 (51.644.80.8)

Museum of the City of New York, 142, 143, 192

New York Public Library, 25, 47, 177

New York State Office of Parks, Recreation and Historic Preservation, Bureau of Historic Sites.
    Olana State Historic Site, Taconic State Park Region, 32, 33, 34, 35, 40, 41, 240

The New York Times, 53, 170

Historical Society, Palm Beach County, Florida, 217

Architectural Archives of the University of Pennsylvania, Philadelphia, 83, 84, 172, 213

Library Company of Philadelphia, 195

Museum of Art, Rhode Island School of Design, Providence. Gift of the Richard Neutra Office,
    30

Courtesy of the Rockefeller Archive Center, 46, 48, 49, 50, 51, 52, 54, 55
Shelburne Farms, Vermont, 85, 127, 128, 185, 215
Stan Hywet, Akron, Ohio, 22, 71, 72, 73, 126, 174
Vizcaya Museum and Gardens, Miami, Florida, 91, 266, 267, 268
Worcester Art Museum, Worcester, Massachusetts. Museum Purchase, Sustaining Membership Fund, 262
Yale University Library, New Haven, Connecticut, 18, 28, 36, 57, 65, 66, 70, 82, 89, 100, 101, 102, 129, 130, 132, 147, 148, 149, 150, 168, 171, 193, 194, 214, 224, 236

ACKNOWLEDGMENT
The Cole Porter lyric quoted on pages 132–33: Copyright 1957 Warner Bros. Inc. (Renewed). All rights reserved. Used by permission.